THE CALIFORNIA TRAIL

For the Lord thy God bringeth thee
into a good land, a land of brooks
of water, of fountains and depths
that spring out of valleys and hills;
a land of wheat, and barley and
vines and fig trees, and pomegranates;
a land of oil olive; and honey;
a land wherein thou shalt eat bread
without scarceness; thou shalt not
lack anything in it. *Deuteronomy* 8, 7-9,

read at services held
Sunday, August 19, 1849,
on the trail

THE CALIFORNIA TRAIL

AN EPIC WITH MANY HEROES

BY GEORGE R. STEWART

University of Nebraska Press
Lincoln and London

First Bison Book printing: August 1983
Most recent printing indicated by the first digit below:
  2   3   4   5   6   7   8   9   10

Library of Congress Cataloging in Publication Data

Stewart, George Rippey, 1895–
  The California trail.

  Reprint. Originally published: 1st ed. New York :
McGraw-Hill, 1962.
  Bibliography: p.
  Includes index.
  1. Overland journeys to the Pacific. 2. West (U.S.)
—Description and travel—To 1848. 3. California—
History—To 1846. I. Title.
F592.S797 1983   978'.02   83-5758
ISBN 0-8032-9143-4 (pbk.)

Published by arrangement with Mrs. George R. Stewart

CONTENTS

MAPS

MILEAGE CHARTS

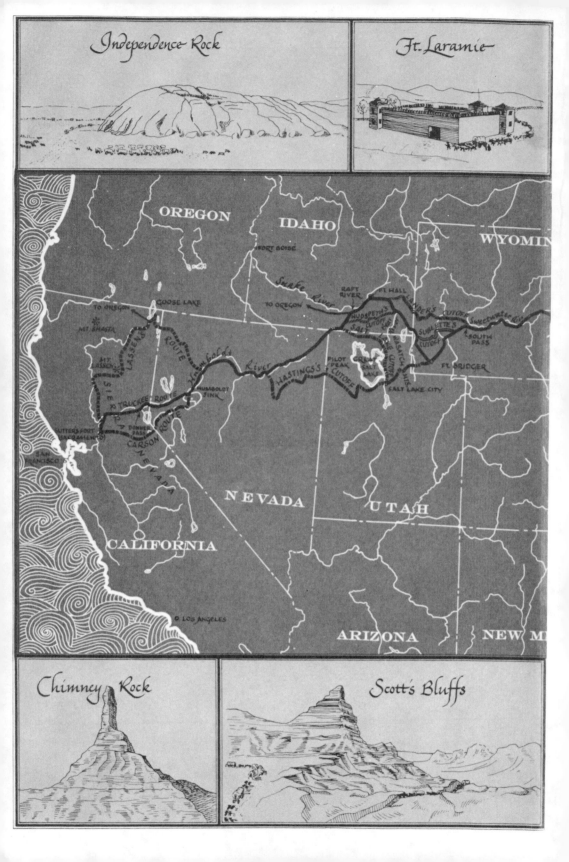

Independence Rock

Ft. Laramie

OREGON

IDAHO

WYOMIN

FORT BOISE

Snake River

RAFT RIVER

FT HALL

LANDER'S CUTOFF

TO OREGON

TO OREGON

HUDSPETH'S CUTOFF

Sweetwater R

SUBLETTE'S CUTOFF

SALT

SOUTH PASS

GOOSE LAKE

MT. SHASTA

LASSEN'S ROUTE

Humboldt River

GREAT SALT LAKE

SALT LAKE

WASATCH MTS.

FT BRIDGER

MT. LASSEN

SIERRA

TRUCKEE ROUTE

HUMBOLDT SINK

HASTING'S CUTOFF

PILOT PEAK CUTOFF

SALT LAKE CITY

SUTTER'S FORT SACRAMENTO

DONNER PASS

CARSON ROUTE

NEVADA

SAN FRANCISCO

NEVADA

UTAH

CALIFORNIA

○ LOS ANGELES

ARIZONA

NEW M

Chimney Rock

Scott's Bluffs

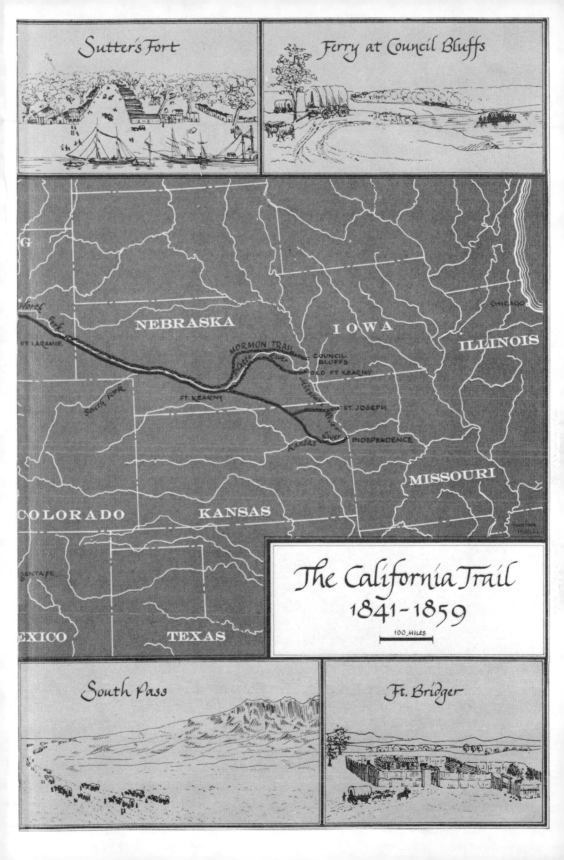

Sutter's Fort

Ferry at Council Bluffs

The California Trail
1841-1859
100 MILES

South Pass

Ft. Bridger

THE CALIFORNIA TRAIL

PROEM

First of all, let us remember a far-off land with the strange name California. The great Cortés heard of it—a rumor of gold and griffins and black Amazons. Two centuries later, so distant was it and so unknown still, that Jonathan Swift, wishing to put his giant Brobdingnagians in the most unknown parts, wrote that their country lay northwest of California. But a few years later the Spaniards came up from Mexico, and peopled the land thinly.

By that time the English had come ashore on the other side of the continent and were slowly advancing inland. Decade by decade they (and the Americans whom they became) went toward the sunset, seen through the trees of the great forest. Most often they moved by little companies and by families, carrying their goods on pack horses or in carts or wagons. But the heroic tales of those centuries—and they are many—are told of the explorations and the wars and the Indian fights and the hunting of wild beasts, and scarcely one tale is of the journeyings. This is because they were not of the stuff for a storyteller—lasting not more than a few weeks, extending over only a few hundred miles, made mostly on known roads, and passing chiefly through friendly country, without deserts or high mountains. If an ox died, or an axle-tree broke, or a child fell ill, there was always the chance to get aid.

At last, if we may so write, the westward-moving Americans saw the forest grow thin ahead, and soon they looked at the setting sun across treeless country. Then they paused—hesitating, during the time of a generation—having come in two centuries about a thousand miles, only a third of the way across the continent.

At this same time, in Washington, someone decided that this curious country without trees could never offer a good home to the Americans, and must always belong to the Indians. So, for this reason also, the people stayed there at the edge of the trees, and grew restless at waiting, since it was, as they said, "in their blood" to move west.

So it stood—and the year came to be 1840. That fall the people shouted and paraded for log cabins and hard cider, and elected "Tippecanoe" Harrison to be President. The census showed all of seventeen million people in the United States, although they were by no means as prosperous as they had been before the panic of '37, and for that reason, too, were the readier to think of moving somewhere else. By this year everyone had decided that steamboats were here to stay, but they were not so sure about railroads. People were still reading *The Waverley Novels* and were just getting interested in the works of a talented young man called Charles Dickens. More important in connection with going west, they were also reading *The Prairie* by Fenimore Cooper and some of the recent works of Washington Irving.

But, more than from books, people were learning by word of mouth about what lay beyond the broad and treeless plains of the Indian country—about Oregon and California. Both, the stories went, were good places. Oregon was more like what the people knew already, and was part of their own country, or so claimed. California was stranger, but more attractive to some, being thus more romantic. It was a part of Mexico, but the foreignness did not bother the people much, for they remembered that Texas also had been Mexican when the Americans settled there. California, it was good to learn, was not reserved for the Indians. But, it was bad to learn, there was no place to stop on the way. The next move, then, must be for all or nothing—a greater distance to be covered in one season than their ancestors had accomplished in more than two centuries.

4

In Missouri, most of all, men heard these stories, and chafed as they heard them, for now, as they said, the country was filling up, and it was a long time since they had been able to move west.

As for the storytellers, they were most often those known as "mountain-men," the trappers for beaver, or else the traders who already for twenty years had been taking their goods to Santa Fe in caravans of big wagons.

But if you asked, "How do you get to California from Missouri?" any answer was vague. You could go by Santa Fe, but that trail was roundabout and hard. Any direct route was little known but undoubtedly difficult, and only two parties of Americans had so traveled. One had been led by Jedediah Smith, but that was far back in '27, and Smith was long since killed by the Indians, and nearly all his men too. But there was also Joe Walker, and his was a great name among the mountain-men. In '33 and '34 he had led a party to California and had returned. Walker was still alive, and many of his men. They could tell—but of a hard journeying.

It was a tale to keep most men from setting out, particularly with their families—the distance unmeasured but certainly great; the country inhospitable, with deserts and mountains, inhabited only by savage Indians; the way, for much of the distance, untraversed by a single wagon. If an ox died, or an axle-tree broke, or a child fell ill . . . ! This journey, then, would be different from those earlier ones, and there might be something to tell.

In one special way this story would be unique among American heroic tales. For in the wars and explorations and sea voyages and in all the colorful bickerings of mining camps and cow towns, there were no women or children, or else they held some minor place. But the western journey was to be one of families, and so to come closer home.

Thus, for these several reasons, that story—with its chief symbol the covered wagon—has become one of the epic tales of that much-storied people, the Americans. . . .

This book is of that journeying—of how the chief trail to California was established and traveled by families with wagons. It was called a trail, because "road" meant to those people something that was regularly constructed, but "trail," which is a word first thus used by the Americans themselves, meant a trackway that merely developed from the passage of people and animals along it.

It is here called the California Trail, as it was generally called by the people who used it, though parts of it, at different times, were also known as the Oregon Trail, the Mormon Trail, and by other names. The focus must be upon the people, not upon the thing. If, then, people were going to California, they are here considered to be on the California Trail.

But if anyone asks, "What man did it?" there can be no sure answer. Some might pick Joseph Walker; others, Elisha Stevens or Joseph Chiles. There are women also to be remembered, such as Nancy Kelsey and Tamsen Donner and Lydia Waters. Essentially, then, it was a great work accomplished by the labors and courage of many people together. Thus, though it may be termed an epic, it fails to center—as those older aristocratic epics always did—about a single hero. This might be thought a democratic epic. And so the book is called *The California Trail: An Epic with Many Heroes.*

CHAPTER ONE

But young John Bidwell, when he arrived at the appointed place, found only one wagon already there. Oh, it had been brave and glorious, that preceding winter, to plan going to California! In Missouri alone, five hundred had enrolled in the Western Emigration Society, and many letters had come in from Kentucky, Illinois, and Arkansas. Each man pledged himself to be ready to start, with a suitable outfit, on May 9, 1841. They would meet at Sapling Grove, about twenty miles west on the Santa Fe Trail from the Missouri frontier town of Independence.

Although a certain amount of interest in California had been in the air for some years, the immediate incitement sprang chiefly from two informants. One of these was an old trapper named Robidoux who had been in California and had returned to Missouri. He talked freely, and pictured that far-off Mexican province as being little short of an earthly paradise. The other informant was John Marsh, an American who had lived in California since '36 and so should know something about it. He wrote letters in which he extolled his adopted country and its possibilities. Thus, toward the end of '40, there had arisen a considerable interest in this new project.

Then an adverse report on California had appeared in the newspapers. Besides, the long months of winter provided time for sobering second thought. Doubtless some men could not persuade the womenfolks. The longer the thought, the longer the odds must have seemed. So, after Bidwell had arrived, there were only two wagons.

During the next few days, more came in, one or two at a time until some fifty people had assembled. About thirty-five were men. Five were women—three wives accompanying their husbands, a widow (sister of one of the wives), and a marriageable girl. There were about ten children.

At this point the men considered that the party had grown to be strong enough, and they made the decision to start. Thus these people became the first band of emigrants to set out upon what was later, by an accident of nomenclature, to be more commonly called the Oregon Trail. Their goal, however, was California.

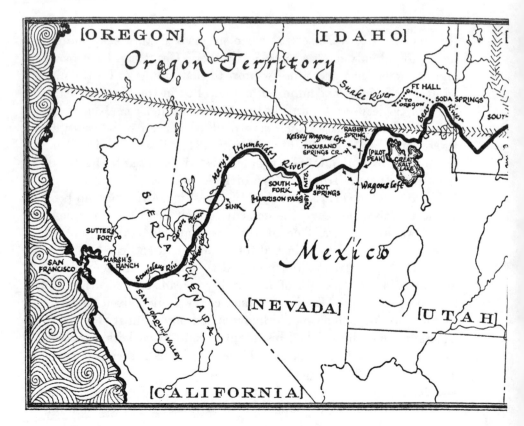

What motives can we ascribe to these people thus to embark upon such a rash and even desperate venture?

As for the young, unmarried men, several of them have left record of their reasons, and these were simple enough. As one of them put it: "to see something of Indian life, and indulge in hunting on the plains, and all that sort of thing." Another of them mentioned that he had read Cooper's novels and Irving's books of western adventure. What more could you wish than fun, excitement, an extended camping trip, new scenes, and the bright face of danger?

Many of them were not even interested in settling in California. They were foot-loose. If they did not like it there, they could return. Some of them, apparently, even when they set out, had no intention of settling, and were planning a two-way trip.

Similar motives of adventure were undoubtedly important

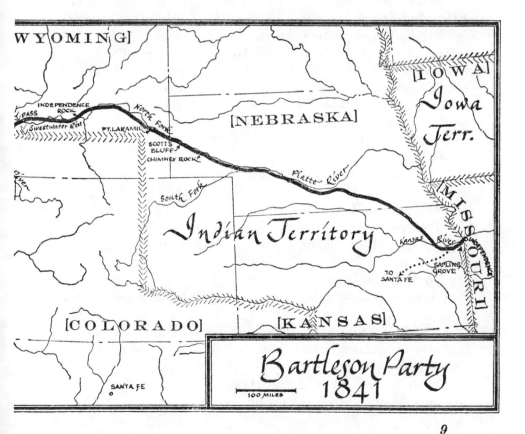

with the three married men. But they could also give other reasons. Hard times and prevalent malaria were making people discontented in the Mississippi Valley, and at the other end was the lure of a healthy climate and a new country to be settled. On such a basis they could give a kind of reasonable explanation of their action.

We may suspect, however, some unconscious motivation. Moving was an established folk custom. Most of these people had already moved once, or oftener, and to do so again was only natural. Moreover, we may suspect that many of them were driven on by mere boredom. To exist for a few years on a backwoods farm with almost no means of amusement or stimulation meant the build-up of an overwhelming desire to see new places and people.

Even so, the party was very short on family men. The gamble was more than they wished to take.

Indeed, the problem that these people faced, though not one of them knew much about it, was almost overwhelming. The country that they were to traverse was unmapped and very imperfectly explored. Beyond the Rocky Mountains, over a distance of a thousand miles, there was no road and not even an established trail. The emigrants must expose themselves to attack by powerful Indian tribes. They must cross broad deserts beneath a scorching sun. They must scale high and rough mountains—particularly, near the end of the journey, the lofty Sierra Nevada, seamed by often-impassable canyons.

But worst of all, as a foe, was distance itself—or, rather, distance set against time. They must travel two thousand miles, and they must do this within the limits of a single summer and fall. They could not carry sufficient supplies of food to last over till spring, and they would have little chance of surviving through the winter on any local supplies of game.

To meet this seemingly impossible task, the emigrants had certain equipment and resources—partly physical and partly psychic.

The most important physical item was the covered wagon itself—so important, indeed, that it has come to stand as the symbol of the whole migration. The tradition of the wagon was already so firmly implanted that these emigrants of '41 seem to have considered no other method of travel.

As for favorable psychic qualities, we may say first, paradoxically, that these people were fortunate in having a great ignorance. This ignorance and the optimism that went with it were essential. Before the bout was to be finished, one man would be heard exclaiming, in words reminiscent of the Prodigal Son, that if he could ever get back to Missouri, he would gladly eat out of the trough with his hogs. How many, with such foreknowledge, would have started?

Yet, perhaps, some would have. Most of them were young, and had the zest, vigor, and resiliency that goes with youth. Individually they were highly endowed with courage. Indeed, we might even think this courage to be rashness. Also, they were tough and inured to hardship, as people of the backwoods farms must necessarily be, expecting nothing better.

Moreover, they shared in the long American tradition of victory. Their people had always gone west, and had always been successful. They themselves would expect to do the same. They were the sons and grandsons of the pioneers who had pushed through the forest into Kentucky, Tennessee, and the old Northwest. Were they any less men than their fathers and grandfathers?

Also advantageous was their native acceptance of that rather curious mode of organization which we may call frontier democracy. Every man was as good as his neighbor, and insisted upon his final right to the decision. He asked no backing from his government or from a big company. Here was free enterprise in a degree which has now become only a dream. At the same time, these people recognized the necessity of cooperation. In their own way and on their own terms they were willing to organize, to submit to the will of the majority, to work for a common good. This mingling of individualism and cooperation was flexible, and therefore efficient. It did not always work, but it could bend without breaking.

These qualities are listed here because they were important not only in '41, but also in the whole history of the trail. In fact, this first company offers a preview of much that was to happen later. . . .

So they were ready to start, and they then arrived at a curious frustration. How did you *get* to California? It lay to the west, they agreed on that. One man remembered the latitude of San Francisco Bay. If they worked west along that latitude, he thought, they would get there all right. (No one had an instrument to take the height of the sun; perhaps they just thought they could judge by looking at it.) One man told of having seen a map showing a large lake with two rivers running out of it, clear to the Pacific Ocean. Obviously, the thing to do was to make for the lake and then follow a river. There was even an idea of building boats and floating down.

Actually, this state of ignorance involved chiefly the country beyond the Rocky Mountains, the second half of the journey. Some of the people must have known about the Santa Fe Trail and about the fur-traders' route that extended to Fort Laramie and on toward Oregon. In fact, much of the uncertainty at the start must have involved the question of which of these two trails they should take, in order to reach California eventually.

Then came a stroke of luck. A party of three priests, Jesuit missionaries under the leadership of Father Pierre Jean De Smet, arrived at the camp. They were starting for Fort Hall, in the eastern part of what was then considered to be Oregon. They were going to travel over the Fort Laramie Trail, and would be going in the general direction of California for about a thousand miles. Moreover, they had with them as guide one of the half-dozen people in the world best qualified for that work. He was no less a one than Thomas "Broken Hand" Fitzpatrick, among the most notable of the mountain-men.

The emigrants joyfully attached themselves to this party, thus gaining a guide and giving additional strength to the missionaries against Indian trouble.

By this decision the emigrants committed themselves to the route by way of Fort Laramie. The choice of the Santa Fe Trail might have changed a good deal of history by focusing American attention upon the Los Angeles area. As it was, the chief overland contact was made with the Sacramento Valley. In particular, the goal became Sutter's Fort, on the site of present Sacramento. . . .

On May 12 they got started. They followed the well-beaten Santa Fe Trail for about two days' journey, and then turned off on a faint line of wheel-tracks, showing where fur-traders and

missionaries had already taken carts and a few wagons to Fort
Laramie and even beyond it. On May 17 they came to the Kansas
River, and on the next day they got themselves ferried across to
the north bank by the local half-civilized Indians, who used primitive "bull boats," made by stretching raw buffalo hides over
wooden frames.

On this day, also, the emigrants held a meeting for organization. A much-liked young man called Talbot Green presided, and
John Bidwell was secretary. They elected John Bartleson to be
captain. "He was not," as Bidwell wrote later, "the best man for
the position, but we were given to understand that if he was not
elected captain, he would not go; and he had seven or eight men
with him, and we did not want the party diminished." Perhaps
Bidwell was here being wise in retrospect, but in any case democracy does not always choose the best man, and here we have a
good example of "practical" politics. Besides, why worry? They
would be the Bartleson Party, but the captain himself had little
power.

The meeting took another action. In Bidwell's words, "it was
understood that everyone should have not less than a barrel of
flour, with sugar and so forth." A barrel of flour to each person
would have been sufficient, but actual supplies were much less
than this. Perhaps the sense of the resolution was only that each
wagon should have a barrel. By this time there was little use of
passing resolutions; the emigrants were already a hundred miles
west of any town. But no one seems to have worried. They optimistically underestimated the time it would take them to get
through; besides, they believed that they could live on game—
especially, buffalo.

From the Kansas River crossing the emigrants bore off on
the long sweep to the northwest, over which thousands of wagons
were to follow in the years to come.

They moved slowly for a few days, since they had had word
that three men with another wagon were hurrying to overtake
them. On May 23 this group came up. One of the three was
Joseph B. Chiles, a redheaded Missourian thirty-one years of age,
who was to be notable in the history of the trail.

After this, they settled into a routine. Day after day, across
the open prairie, under Fitzpatrick's skillful direction, the train

moved in regular order. First went the missionaries' four carts, each drawn by two mules, hitched in tandem. The missionaries also had a small wagon. In a second division came eight wagons of the emigrants, some drawn by mules, some by horses. Finally came the slowest-moving vehicles, six wagons pulled by oxen.

Thus constituted, the train provided almost a laboratory experiment in prairie travel. Anyone could compare the relative advantages and disadvantages of carts as against wagons, and of horses, mules, and oxen. Even the wagons were of various types.

Fitzpatrick gave them lessons by example. A little before nightfall he galloped ahead, and selected a camping spot. Then he had the wagons put into a hollow square, with a space between each two for tents and campfires. Horses, most prized by Indian thieves, were allowed to graze outside until night, and were then picketed inside. A guard was kept all night upon the grazing oxen. Thus, rapidly and surely, the hard-won and now dying tradition of the mountain-men was transferred to the emigrants.

The chronicle of the trip is well preserved. In its incidents, those details thought worthy of mention in the diaries, the journey was like many later ones. . . . On May 20, and again two days later, oxen strayed in the night and had to be hunted up. On May 26 two wagons broke down and had to be repaired. On May 28 the first antelope was killed; two days later, a deer. Next day, they met some trappers returning from the mountains. On June 1 they reached the Platte River, and had the inevitable hailstorm. Preacher Williams officiated at a marriage, though doubtful about his right to do so, considering it to be "without law or license, for we were a long way from the United States."

Williams, an oldster of sixty-four, had overtaken the party on May 26, traveling by himself on horseback. He left a vivid narrative of his experiences with the company, though we must make allowance for his strait-laced piety. "There are," he wrote in troubled spirit, "some as wicked people among them as I ever saw in all my life." Perhaps the reference was to the Kelsey brothers, but he also described Fitzpatrick as "a wicked, worldly man" and "deistical in his principles," and he declared the whole company to be "mostly composed of Universalists and deists." He lamented their profanity: "That night, dreadful oaths were heard all over the camp ground. O, the wickedness of the wicked." Their Sabbath breaking also disturbed him: "We have nothing but swearing, fishing, etc." He sometimes talked theology with the Jesuits, who found him wholly naïve.

Yet there is a touch of saintliness about Williams, which is not equaled even in Father De Smet. No youngster in his twenties showed more courage than did the old man, as he rode into the West, trusting: "All is right that the Lord doeth; why then should we fear?"

On June 4 young Nicholas Dawson, out hunting, was caught by a band of Indians, robbed of mule, pistol, and rifle, and stripped of most of his clothes. Fitzpatrick rode out, discovered the Indians to be only high-spirited and friendly Cheyennes, and got back everything except the pistol. (Dawson bore the nickname "Cheyenne" to the day of his death.)

On June 7 they killed three buffalo. On June 9 they successfully forded the South Fork of the Platte, a ticklish business. On June 11 they had an Indian scare. On June 13 a young man, portentously named Shotwell, accidentally shot and killed himself.

Five days later they passed the notable landmark called Chimney Rock, and the next day they killed two mountain sheep near Scott's Bluff. Then, on June 22, they ended the first leg of the journey by rolling into Fort Laramie. The fort, indeed, was only a small and poorly equipped fur-trading post, but still it was a landmark.

So far, remarkably successful! They had made Fort Laramie on the forty-second day, and even in the heyday of the trail that would be good going. The distance was about 635 miles; so the daily average was fifteen miles. This was, indeed, *too* much, and must have worn the teams down excessively, even though the company was liberally supplied with animals. Since the rate of an ox team was two miles an hour, such a daily average would mean, with allowances for stream crossings and other difficult places, that the oxen were in the yokes nine or ten hours a day. Obviously Fitzpatrick considered it his duty to go ahead as rapidly as his light mule-drawn carts could go, and to let the wagons keep up or not, as they might. On one occasion the emigrants had held a meeting to consider whether they should drop behind. They

15

decided that they could take the risk of ruining their teams rather than of leaving their guide.

The men had often been forced to make road, digging down stream banks, filling gulches, and removing stones. Even so, the fast rate of progress suggests that the almost natural prairie provided a better road than the more-traveled trail of later years, which must have developed mudholes and gullies. Undoubtedly, however, the rapidity was made possible only because of very lightly loaded wagons.

Fitzpatrick gave them one day's rest at the fort. Westward, only a few wheeled vehicles had ever gone. In fact, on the third day out, even Fitzpatrick missed what trail there was and went another way, and when "Broken Hand" missed a trail, you can be sure that there was not much there to see. Nevertheless, he still drove them like the devil himself, and in a week of continuous travel they maintained the same rate.

All of July 1 they spent at getting the wagons across the North Fork of the Platte—swift, difficult, dangerous water. One wagon was upset, and one mule was swept away and drowned.

Another ten days of hard travel took them past Independence Rock, into the valley of the Sweetwater. Then they halted from necessity; they had to "make meat." The limited supplies of flour and provisions with which in their ignorance they had optimistically started were now almost exhausted. The only solution was to kill buffalo and dry the meat.

But they had waited too long and had come into a region where buffalo were scarce that season. Their biggest kill, twenty, had been on July 8, but they were traveling then, and probably none of this meat was saved. So it was also on the next day, when they killed ten. But on July 11 when they settled down to hunting, they got only two buffalo, and only four on the next day, and a single one on the day after. July 14 was a better one, and they got eight or nine. All this added up to a good many pounds of meat. Still, counting both companies, there were about eighty people to be fed, for a period which might run into many weeks.

On July 18 they crossed South Pass, and came to water flowing toward the Pacific!

They made twenty miles this day, and continued to travel hard. On this leg of the journey they went southward over the line of the 40th parallel, and dipped into Mexican territory. But the boundary line had never been surveyed or marked, and in the mountains people paid no attention to it, if they even knew where it was theoretically supposed to be.

On July 23, making only a short journey, they arrived at Green River, and thankfully found that it was low enough to ford easily. But this was the only good news that they got there.

They made camp and stayed through the next day, having encountered a party of sixty trappers. This meeting on Green River, in the very heart of the mountain country, may be viewed as symbolic. In '40 the trappers had held the last of the great *rendezvous*. Now, in '41, came the emigrants. As one era ended, another was beginning.

Emigrants and trappers did a little trading. Some of the emigrants had been carrying stores of alcohol in their wagons, for such an occasion. Alcohol passed for whisky in the mountains, and could be traded for dressed skins, buckskin clothes, and moccasins. With a good supply of alcohol in circulation, there must have been a considerable celebration.

These trappers, who could be expected to know if anyone did, said flatly that it was impossible for wagons to get through. You could take them down along the Snake River toward Oregon, but not to California! All this must only have been what Fitzpatrick had already been telling them.

That same day seven men started back to Missouri. They had had an interesting summer's holiday, and that was that!

The others went on, making shorter daily journeys now, since the country was rough and the trail almost nonexistent. "We were compelled," wrote Father De Smet, "to clear a passage, sometimes in the middle of a ravine, sometimes on the slope of a rock, and often through bushes." Many of the emigrants, not unreasonably, were talking now of going toward Oregon, not California.

On July 30 it was Father De Smet's turn to perform a marriage ceremony, the Widow Gray having decided to try again. Secure in the universality of Rome, he did so without expressing doubt as to his authority, as Preacher Williams had done.

On August 2 Fitzpatrick missed the way, got trapped in a defile, and had to backtrack two miles and start again. The next

17

day he managed to guide the wagons across a high divide and down to Bear River. Then they rested a day. They followed the river down for six days, leaving Mexican territory. On August 3 they came to the bubbling spring which they knew by the jolly name of the Soda Fountain, more commonly known as Soda Springs.

They had finished a second and harder leg of the journey, having averaged less than twelve miles a day; in forty-eight days they had traveled about 560 miles from Fort Laramie. They had reached the parting of the ways. From here the missionaries went north for Fort Hall. About a third of the emigrants also chose the more prudent course, and kept on to the north, to arrive in Oregon late in the year. Naturally, most of the men with families were included in this group.

Resolute for California remained thirty-one men—with them one woman and her baby girl. Thus, as with Gideon's band, only the most stouthearted remained—or, we might consider, the rashest. Father De Smet, a Belgian, paid them the parting tribute, that they "were pursuing their enterprise with the constancy which is characteristic of Americans."

Since these thirty-three made the first attempt to open the emigrant trail to California, we may fittingly pause to consider them. . . . They were predominantly Americans of the western states. Most of them had grown up on farms, had handled firearms since childhood, and knew something about hunting, but they cannot be called real frontiersmen, except in so far as they had picked up some knowledge under Fitzpatrick's tutelage. They were young—most of them under thirty. Charles Hopper, the oldest whose age is known, was forty-one.

Bartleson remained titular captain, but was apparently held in scant respect. Benjamin Kelsey, according to Bidwell, really assumed the leadership because he showed himself "expert in finding the way." He and his brother Andrew, Kentuckians, have been mentioned by a historian as "rough men, often in trouble with the authorities." But such native backwoodsmen were very comforting to have along on a trip such as this. Of similar type was Grove Cook, another young Kentuckian; he was brother-in-law to the famed fur-trading brothers, the Sublettes, but he had left his wife at home.

18

Hopper, Bidwell noted, was the "best and most experienced hunter." As an older man of strong character, he exercised much influence.

The four keepers of diaries may be considered as a group— with the general comment that the presence of so many diarists in a small company shows a high degree of literacy and of historical responsibility. Little is known of James Springer, whose diary has not come to light. He took well to western travel, and he later became a guide for other parties. Bidwell, Dawson, and James John had much in common. The first two were twenty years of age; John, thirty-two. Bidwell and Dawson had both been teachers, shifting from school to school on the frontier, as was the custom. Dawson had decided to take five years off and see the world. On the journey Bidwell and John shared some adventures together. Of him Bidwell could write, when he himself was old and had known many men: "Of all men I have ever known I think he was the most fearless." John might well have written the same of Bidwell. Because the diaries were kept by such devil-may-care characters, the story of the journey, even in its blackest days, remains zestful and even lighthearted.

To judge from success in later life, several of the men were unusually able—Bidwell, Chiles, Josiah Belden, Robert Thomes, "Talbot Green," and Charles Weber. The last was a young German, and two or three others of the company were German, too.

Special attention should be given to that pleasant and well-liked young man "Talbot Green." He had some medical supplies with him, and acted as doctor. One curious thing about him was that he was carrying to California a good-sized chunk of lead. No one knew why he was doing this, but the asking of too many questions was not considered good form in the early West.

Nancy Kelsey, wife of Benjamin, is certainly not to be passed over. Let us not too readily grow sentimental about her. Let us be slow to write that she stands as the type of the pioneer mother. She seems to have been well matched to her husband, and he was, you must remember, a rough man, often in trouble with the authorities. But granting all this, we find something in Nancy Kelsey that makes the blood throb more strongly. Married at fifteen, she had now reached the maturity of eighteen years. When questioned about going to California, she had replied roundly,

"Where my husband goes, I go." She added, "I can better endure the hardships of the journey, than the anxieties for an absent husband." Years later, Chiles wrote of her with sentiment, remembering her "cheerful nature and kind heart." He added: "She bore the fatigues of the journey with so much heroism, patience, and kindness that there still exists a warmth in every heart for the mother and her child."

She carried with her the baby Ann, probably about a year old.

Thus composed, the Bartleson Party differed from a group of mountain-men in that it included no individuals who were experienced in the West. It differed, on the other hand, from the typical emigrant party in that it was composed almost wholly of young men. But, lacking as it was in experience, the party was in many essential ways outstanding. In its concentration of vigor, toughness, and ability, we can believe that no later company—indeed, few chance-gathered groups of Americans ever assembled —could surpass it. . . .

The men had arms and ammunition. Many of them had saddle horses. There were nine wagons, about half of them ox-drawn and half mule-drawn. Because of the hard journey already accomplished, the animals were somewhat worn down.

An immediate problem was food. The original provisions were now almost exhausted. The supplies of jerked buffalo meat were dwindling fast. . . .

On August 12 the party proceeded down the valley of Bear River toward Great Salt Lake. They had no guide and so little information that they were forced, as one of them put it, to "smell" their way. In an attempt to obtain more information they sent two of their men to Fort Hall.

Though they were breaking trail for wagons, they had no serious difficulty in getting through, and found plenty of the two essentials, water and grass. After a few days they again crossed the imaginary and unregarded line into Mexican territory, in which they were to remain during the rest of their journey.

On August 20, after getting involved with the mud flats near the Great Salt Lake and turning back eastward, they camped for the last time on Bear River. The next morning they struck out north of west, intending to pass just to the north of the lake, thus acting upon the basis of whatever information they may have had. That night, having made about fifteen miles, they camped by a large spring, which (a bad omen) was brackish and barely drinkable. The grass around the spring was scarcely fit for the animals to eat.

During the night the oxen strayed off looking for better fare. So, in the morning, there was nothing to do but to stay camped and send riders out on the trail of the oxen. During this day the men who had gone to Fort Hall rejoined.

Their report was brief and discouraging. They had not even been able to obtain any extra supplies, since the post had nothing to spare. They had hoped to find Joseph Walker there, the one man who might have been able to serve as a guide, or at least to give sure advice, on the basis of his trip to California in '33 and '34. (Fitzpatrick could have told them to look for Walker.) But he had not been there, and the men at the fort had said to strike west from the lake.

People trying to get to California, the advice continued, should not get too far north, for then they would get into a broken country of steep canyons, where they might wander about and eventually die, as parties of trappers were said to have done. But, then, they should not get too far south either, because there they would enter a desert where the animals would die for lack of grass. But just what was "too far" in either direction? There were not two rivers flowing westward from the lake, as the map had shown. There was not even *one* such river. Farther west, indeed, they could—somewhere—strike a river flowing to the southwest, known as Mary's or Ogden's. They could follow this river, if they found it, a long way toward California. As to what they should do after this river came to an end, there seemed to be no advice at all.

As they waited in camp that day, August 22, they must have sensed a crisis. Undoubtedly many of them were discouraged, though the youthful keepers of diaries recorded no sense of accumulating disaster.

But there was trouble in the air. The animals were tired and half-starved. Food was low, and there was little game. The country had suddenly become desert and savagely inhospitable —strange and therefore terrifying. So far they had generally kept close to streams—the Platte, the Sweetwater, the tributaries of the Green, the Bear. Following a stream meant that you were never far from water, that the chances for grass were excellent, and that you did not lose the way. Now, over an indefinitely long stretch, there was no river. And the country, at best, was covered with a growth of scattered sagebrush; at worst, it was bare salt-flats.

So they waited that day, scorched by the desert sun, digesting the grim news, waiting for the oxen to be driven in, looking out over the desolate country, even more desolate toward the west, where they must go. No one turned back, though many must have thought of doing so. (Perhaps they felt that they had already, in the phrase of a later age, passed the point of no return.)

Next morning they set out, westward. From some barren hills they looked ahead toward the northern arm of the lake. After a long day's pull they camped near the lake at a spring with water having a bad smell of sulfur. (By experience they found that such water could be made more palatable by making it into strong coffee. On one occasion a man found that his horse refused to drink the water but would accept the coffee.)

That night the oxen strayed again, and the march could not be resumed until noon. They made only ten miles northwestward, and camped, near the northern tip of the lake, again at brackish springs. Moreover—another trick of this treacherous country—these springs were deep holes where an animal might fall in and drown. Fortunately the men recognized the danger in time, and kept the stock away.

Next day they remained in camp, to rest the oxen. Most likely, also, they sent scouts ahead. The more experienced among them—Hopper, Chiles, the Kelsey brothers—must have been realizing that by blindly blundering ahead in such country they were only inviting disaster.

By the following day, August 26, all of them realized it. . . . They made an early start and pushed on steadily, leaving the lake behind. Fifteen miles—a full day's stint for the teams! Still there was no water, or sign of it ahead. Twenty miles, and the oxen and mules were jaded! But there was no water. Off to the north, ten miles or more, they could see mountains. Sunset now, and darkness! Perhaps a touch of panic! Surely they sent riders ahead, but these must have come back without finding water. Twenty-five miles, and the teams were about done in! So they turned north toward the mountains they had seen. Already, doubtless, they were grasping the great fact that in desert country their best chance for water was close to mountains. They pushed on for a few miles through the darkness, and then the teams could go no farther. The camp that night, without grass or water, was a dismal place. Probably they made it merely a halt in the darkness, not even loosing the animals, which could have found no grazing in any case.

At daybreak, with teams a little rested, they plugged ahead, and after five miles reached good grass and water at the foot of the mountains.

There was nothing for it except more rest, and several days of it, even though many must now have begun to realize that time was running out. But the teams had been overdriven since the very beginning, and now to the cumulative weariness had been added the strain of a forced march after several days of insufficient grazing.

The horses and mules and oxen ate at the grass in the little oasis. Some friendly Indians were camped nearby, and the emigrants traded with them—powder and bullets for berries. There must have been plenty of fretting at the delay. By now, at the end of August, the days were getting shorter. Yet to force the march with exhausted animals would be suicidal. Besides, no one knew for certain what route to follow.

On the third day they took a compromise action by sending Bartleson and Hopper off on horseback to look for Mary's River. Undoubtedly many of them expected, with their usual optimism, that these scouts would find the river very close by, perhaps just beyond the next rise. The two horsemen disappeared to the west, and the animals kept on eating. In fact, they began to exhaust the grass in a few more days, and still the scouts did not return.

So, on September 5, the emigrants again took action by deciding to move westward by easy stages. At this camp one wagon may have been abandoned, since the next mention is of eight, instead of nine.

In three days they made an estimated twenty-two miles, moving along the southern base of the range. Near the mountains the country was not too bad. They found grass and water, and even some trees—desert birches and junipers. They killed some rabbits and a few antelope. They also slaughtered some oxen for food, further evidence that they had abandoned a wagon.

On September 7 they came again to the necessity of decision. The range that they had been following curved sharply to the south, blocking direct progress to the west with wagons. Probably, however, the trail of the two scouts went straight ahead up a canyon that was easy enough for horsemen. There were then three possibilities, or even four: to encamp again and wait for the scouts to return, to move to the south with the wagons, and to attempt to go west across the mountains, either taking the wagons along or abandoning them. By this time most of the emigrants considered that the two scouts had been killed by Indians. The uncertainties of the situation were great, and the company fell into dissension.

Indians were camped nearby, and some of the emigrants opened negotiations for a guide, presumably using sign language. Among many tribes such language was highly developed, but none of these emigrants had ever been in the West before. One may doubt that they made it plain just what they wanted, though some of them thought that they did.

In the morning there was a split. Two wagons—their "owners being contrary," as Bidwell wrote—went to the south, being "guided" by two Indians. Six wagons remained in camp. That night was very cold, and ice formed in the water-buckets, a disturbing reminder of the lateness of the season and the rigors of the desert country. In the Middle West you did not expect frost early in September, when corn was standing high and the nights were thick with humid heat.

The next day, by luck, Bartleson and Hopper came riding into the camp where the six wagons still remained. The two had been gone eleven days, and should have been able in that time to ride a hundred and fifty miles to the west and return. They had discovered a small stream that they believed to be a branch of Mary's River, as it doubtless was. But they did not think that wagons could be got through the mountains in that direction, and thus they added their opinion to the action of the Indians that the party should go south in the hope of circling around to reach the river.

24

The six wagons followed the trail of the other two, and by evening the party was reunited.

On September 10 the "guides" were dismissed, with their pay. Probably the Indians were anxious to be gone, having accomplished what we can consider to have been their object, that is, to get the game-destroying whites into some other territory. The emigrants then took the eight wagons a long day's journey to the south, and camped without water. But a dry camp was probably no longer so terrifying as it had once been, since the men were learning that their animals could go without drinking overnight and not suffer too greatly.

Early the next morning they started southwestward across desert country. Possibly they followed one of the Indian trails, which in that region always led eventually to water, or else they could see from a distance the evidences of vegetation around a spring. After an estimated fifteen miles they came to what they called Rabbit Spring. (By coincidence it still bears that common name, though it must at some time have been renamed by later comers.)

At this point, though no one knew it, the Bartleson Party was within striking distance of success. A bold push to the west, a single hard day's journey, would have brought the wagons to the headwaters of Thousand Spring Creek, and along its course (hospitable, as the name indicates) the party could have gone easily, in three days intersecting what was later to become the main trail, and in two more days reaching the head of Mary's River. Such procedure would have changed the history of the migration. But apparently their scouts had missed the narrow opening of the creek.

So, in the morning, they moved southward again, toward a high mountain which offered immediate hope of water. After making a moderate distance they found what they called Mountain Spring, and camped there. (They had now arrived at that great landmark which Frémont, four years later, was to name Pilot Peak.)

The team-animals were failing again. The Kelsey brothers faced the situation, and decided to abandon their two wagons. Probably there was little left in them anyway. Nearly all of the food was gone, and what was left could be carried on pack ani-

25

mals. Nancy, with the baby, either rode horseback or found a place in one of the other wagons.

With the line of white-tops shortened to six, the train moved southward—mountains to the west and a far-reaching salt-plain to the east. They made a march of seventeen miles, and camped at a fine spring, large enough to form a little lake.

Through the three days following, they blundered on desperately—south around the end of the mountains, westward over a pass in another range, north-of-west across a desert plain to a fine spring at the eastern base of mountains. There, on September 15, they unyoked the oxen and unharnessed the mules—for the last time.

The necessity was clear. The almost empty wagons were a useless encumbrance. Without them the people could travel faster, and could cross mountains and rough country. They could also begin to slaughter and eat the oxen. So, during the next day, the camp was not moved. The men worked at making pack saddles, and the Kelseys doubtless said, "We told you so!"

Throughout most of the following day they were busy packing up. Unused to loads, the oxen objected by bucking the packs off—as one of the irrepressible and high-spirited diarists commented: "which caused some sport and a little trouble."

Some Indians appeared, and with one of them, an old man, the emigrants became friendly, giving him presents of things they would have to abandon anyway. He seemed highly thankful for this enforced charity. Anything that he received he held up between himself and the sun, at the same time uttering some long rigmarole. The emigrants took this to be a prayer, and were much amused.

Toward evening the pack train started on. The site of the camp of abandonment is the present Johnson Ranch at the base of the Pequops, a few miles south of where U.S. 40 crosses Pequop Summit.

With the leaving of the wagons, the journey of the Bartleson Party lost much of its historical significance. Its people ceased to be an emigrant party establishing a trail, and became merely some badly lost men with a woman and her baby, making their way to California as best they could. They failed to discover a good route, and no one afterward followed them. Even where they went is difficult to determine, in spite of the help of three diaries. One sure point is marked by the hot springs which they passed on September 21 and which Bidwell described in some detail. These beautiful springs still bubble out near the base of the Ruby Mountains, just as they did when Bidwell saw them.

Going south from the springs, the emigrants crossed the mountains, apparently by Harrison Pass, and eventually reached Mary's River (now called the Humboldt) by following its South Fork northward. They went along the river clear to its sink.

Gradually their journey became one of those starvation marches so common in the history of the West. They killed the oxen, one by one, for food. Very rarely the hunters got an antelope, and they did not despise a wild duck, a jack-rabbit, or a coyote. Jimmy John, an ardent fisherman, occasionally got a few trout. Now and then they traded with the Indians for a little food of uncertain origin.

They split for a while into two groups, but eventually and by accident the two were reunited. They went much farther to the south than was advantageous, and approached the Sierra Nevada by way of the West Fork of the Walker River. On October 18 they crossed the summit at Sonora Pass, or near it, without great difficulty. West of the pass, they were ensnared in the almost impassable canyon country of the Stanislaus River. On October 22 they killed the last ox. "Let this speak," wrote Bidwell, at last sensing tragedy, "for our situation and future prospects."

Some horses and mules remained, but they were more a potential food-supply than anything else, most of the country being too rough and precipitous for riding. Much of the time Nancy Kelsey walked barefoot, carrying the baby.

Mule meat became a delicacy. One day someone shot a coyote, and Bidwell, arriving late, was happy to eat the windpipe and lights. They tried boiling acorns, but even the hardy Benjamin Kelsey suffered the gripes at such fare. Finally, on October 30, they came out into the San Joaquin Valley, reached the wooded banks of the Stanislaus River, killed twenty-six deer, and feasted.

A few days later they arrived at Marsh's ranch. Some

horses and mules still remained. The men had rifles and ammunition. Doubtless a little money was stored away here and there in a pocket. Everything else was gone. The young man called Talbot Green had even, a few days previously, cached his long-treasured chunk of lead. In doing so, he had formed an alliance with Grove Cook, perhaps because Cook, being a more experienced woodsman, would be able to find the cache again. . . .

The Bartleson Party was thus the first company of American emigrants to enter California overland.

Of the thirty-three who arrived, about a dozen went east on horseback in '42, though at least four of these returned later to California. A dozen others drop out of the record.

A remarkably high proportion of the men attained wealth and prominence in their new home. Robert Thomes held the large Tehama Ranch, the nucleus of Tehama County. Charles Weber grew very wealthy, and founded the city of Stockton. Josiah Belden became the first mayor of San Jose, and through various business ventures acquired a great fortune. John Bidwell also became wealthy; among other properties he held the Arroyo Chico Ranch, where the city of Chico now stands, and he is honored as the founder. Politically prominent, Bidwell was a delegate to the convention which nominated Lincoln, and served in Congress. In 1892 he ran for President as the Prohibition Party candidate. He lived until 1900.

Chiles and Hopper, though not attaining riches or great prominence, lived long and prosperously, and died in California as highly respected citizens.

A few members of the Bartleson Party lived more dubious lives. One of these was that well-liked young man "Talbot Green." He and Cook soon returned to where they had made their cache of "lead," and afterward it was noted that they enjoyed some affluence. "Talbot Green" became one of San Francisco's most liked and trusted businessmen. In '51, wealthy and respected, married, a popular candidate for mayor, he was publicly and dramatically denounced as being really Paul Geddes, a defaulting bank clerk, who had deserted wife and children. He left the city by ship for the East, with the avowed purpose of clearing his reputation. A large number of prominent citizens escorted him to the pier to show their confidence. He never returned. The curious story of his chunk of "lead" is told by "Cheyenne" Dawson, who obviously considered it to be the bullion with which Green had absconded.

Cook made money in '49 and then lost it. He died in '52, and a historian has given him the obituary: "A man whose wit and generosity went far to counterbalance some less desirable qualities."

Andrew Kelsey obtained grazing rights near Clear Lake, and there, being the dominant character that he was, he subjected the local Indians to what amounted to slavery. In '49 the Indians, becoming tired of this, killed him. They were then, as the custom was, slaughtered by a punitive expedition. Benjamin Kelsey, though his methods with Indians were much the same as his brother's, escaped such an ending. A thorough itchy-footed frontiersman, he kept on the move through the years, turning up in Oregon, Texas, and southern California.

One would like to know more of his baby daughter, Ann. But, having established herself as the first American child to cross the Sierra Nevada and enter California by the central route, she disappears from history. Infant mortality was excessive in those days. In '61 a Kelsey daughter, after the family had "drifted" into Texas, was scalped by Comanches, but this girl must have been younger than Ann.

Nancy followed her husband in a career that remained full of adventure for eighteen years after '41. Then the family settled down a bit, but as she said, up to that time "enough incidents happened to me to make a book." (One book? Mrs. Kelsey, you are modest!) Summarizing her life for a newspaper interviewer, she said, two years before her death: "I have enjoyed great riches and suffered the pangs of poverty. I have seen U. S. Grant when he was little known. I have baked bread for General Frémont and talked to Kit Carson. I have run from bear and killed most all other kinds of small game." Her husband died in '88; she, in '95.

"Cheyenne" Dawson, dying in 1903 in his eighty-third year, is supposed to have been the last survivor.

The map of California surprisingly commemorates the members of the party—Kelsey Creek and Kelseyville, Thomes Creek, Weber Creek, Chiles Valley, and Bidwell Bar, Creek, Butte, Lake, Peak, Point, and Fort Bidwell. There is also Green Street in San Francisco, which has not been changed to Geddes Street.

CHAPTER TWO

LIKE THAT RENOWNED CHAPTER on the snakes of Ireland, this one might consist of the mere statement: "In '42 no wagons started for California."

In this year, however, there was indirect progress at establishing a trail. Some wagons were taken to Oregon, following the route of those people who had left the Bartleson Party at Soda Springs, and thus leaving a little more clearly marked a trail that could also be used, over much of the distance, by wagons bound for California. In fact, you could even go to Oregon first and then to California southward over trails used by the Hudson's Bay fur-traders. In the next few years a number of people reached California by that route. But to make the push clear to Oregon and then go seven hundred miles more was too long a journey for a single season, even if a trail for wagons should be established. So the regular plan for reaching California depended upon following the trail to Oregon for some distance, and then branching off. Just where the point of separation should be was a basic question, which was to involve a great deal of experimentation.

Moreover, the story of any human endeavor includes not only what people are doing, but also what they are thinking. Thus considered, also, '42 saw progress. Most important of all was what was happening in the mind of Joseph B. Chiles, who had been a member of the Bartleson Party.

Chiles was born in Kentucky, in 1810. As he grew up, he conformed to the great early American archetype—like Jefferson, Houston, Jackson, and Lincoln, being tall and gangly, finally measuring six feet four. He shared an additional likeness with Jefferson in being redheaded. He had a notable sense of humor, and was a great joker.

Reaching the age of twenty, Chiles married, and then followed the due course of western life by "moving." He went to Missouri, and became a prosperous farmer, the father of four children. His wife's death in '37 allowed his restless instincts to take control. As the custom was for a widower, he established his children in the homes of his friends. He then enlisted for the Seminole War, and fought at the battle of Lake Okeechobee. He found that a life of adventure suited him, and so he was a natural one to set out for California in '41. Because of his military experience and the respect in which he was held, Chiles was known as "Colonel."

The members of the Bartleson Party, having arrived in California, scattered for the winter, working at various jobs. Some of them agreed to meet at Sutter's Fort in the early spring, and then to return east together. Chiles visited for a while with George Yount, a friend and former neighbor, one of the few Americans holding land in California. Yount had left his family in Missouri, and still had two daughters and two grandchildren there. He arranged with Chiles to have them brought to California. The incident shows that Chiles, scarcely arrived from his arduous trip, was already planning not only to return to Missouri but also to make a second trip to California. It shows, too, that he was willing to bring women and children with him. He must therefore have considered the experiences of the Bartleson Party to have been not too discouraging.

That expedition—even Chiles must have admitted—had been a failure. The frightful experiences in the Sierra Nevada suggested that wagons could never be taken across those mountains. The journey, in fact, had ended in a rout that was close to demoralization. A little more, and they would all have left their bones to lie in the wilderness!

Yet—Chiles could also maintain—there were results on the positive side too, a measure of success. The people had, after all, got through alive. Moreover, though they were essentially a band of young men, adventurers more than emigrants, they had brought with them a woman and a baby. While they had not got the wagons through, they had taken wagons farther toward California, by several hundred miles, than anyone had done before.

They had gained some valuable geographical knowledge—for instance, the desert country was passable, even with wagons, because there was never a stretch of more than thirty-five or forty miles without water and grass. Such dry drives—"*jornadas*," as people were beginning to call them, using the Spanish term—though hard on teams, were not impossible. But, Chiles and his comrades had learned, merely to attempt to go across that desert country without a definitely known route was a bad

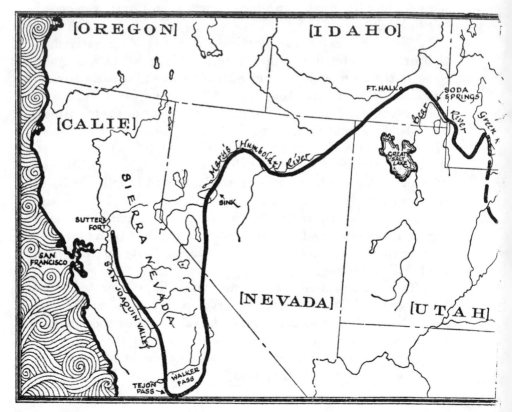

idea, largely because the mountain ranges all ran north and south, so that you either had to cross them, which was difficult, or to go around them, which increased the distance greatly. The essential thing was to get to Mary's River as soon as possible and follow it for as far as possible.

These men of the Bartleson Party, the first ever to try taking wagons across the Great Basin, had learned the hard way, but such knowledge was to be essential in the development of the trail.

Moreover, these men had probably picked up additional geographic information from Marsh, Yount, Sutter, and others. The great Sierra Nevada might shut off California from the east like a Chinese Wall, but there was an easy pass far to the south, that one used by Joe Walker on his return in '34. And the wall did not extend indefinitely north, either—as the trail from Oregon now demonstrated.

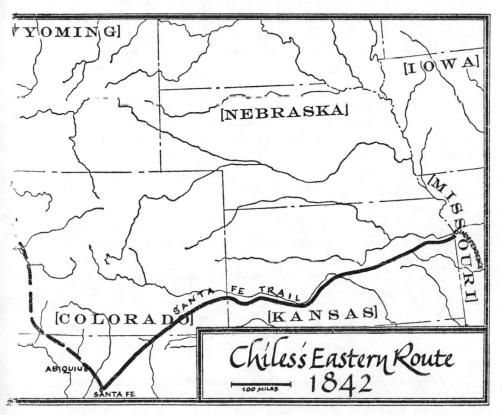

[WYOMING] [IOWA] [NEBRASKA] [MISSOURI] SANTA FE TRAIL [COLORADO] [KANSAS] ABIQUIU SANTA FE

Chiles's Eastern Route
100 MILES
1842

Finally, another positive result of '41, Chiles and the others had amassed a great deal of valuable experience. They had learned much about teams and equipment. They had learned essential techniques—how to take wagons across rough country and difficult fords, how to arrange a camp at night, how to set a guard so that the animals could graze and yet not stray off or be stolen by Indians, how to locate water in the desert. They had learned something of how much time the journey would require. They had learned that the local Indians were not of much use as guides, and that someone who really knew, like Fitzpatrick, was invaluable.

So, all in all, the men who assembled at Sutter's Fort for the return were a much more experienced lot than those who had set out from Sapling Grove. Among them were Bartleson, Chiles, Hopper, and Springer.

Little record has been preserved of the return journey. Thirteen men left the fort in April. The rains were heavy, and much of the low land was flooded. On horseback the party headed south through the San Joaquin Valley.

Almost immediately Hopper was taken seriously ill with what was judged to be typhoid fever. He held the party up, and time was valuable. Some were for going on and leaving him, but his friends would not agree. At last, they rigged a litter between two mules, one ahead and one behind. Thus they were able to make slow progress, with Hopper half dead. The mules became frightened once, and ran away, with almost fatal results. In terror that it might happen again, Hopper pulled himself together well enough to cling to his saddle and make short journeys. Gradually he recovered.

They did not find Walker's pass, if that was what they were hunting. Instead, they crossed by Tejon Pass, thus coming within some seventy miles of Los Angeles.

They swung east across desert country, without a trail. When they were in a bad way for water, Hopper had a dream that was more like a vision, and to his dying day he believed it was sent from Heaven. He saw which way to go for water, and all the landmarks. In the morning he led in that direction, saw the landmarks, and came to the spring.

They swung north, along the east side of the Sierra Nevada.

They reached Mary's River, went up along it, kept ahead, and arrived at Fort Hall. Already they had traveled fifteen hundred miles. Four men dropped out of the party there.

The nine others went on, picked up their old trail at the Soda Fountain, and followed it eastward clear to Green River. There, doubtless from some trappers, they had bad news. The Sioux war-bands were out. Rather than run ahead into disaster, they changed their plans, deciding to go by way of Santa Fe. (No one but this reckless crew of '41, you would think, would have had such a crazy idea.) Hopper undertook to guide them.

There is no information as to their route from Green River almost to Santa Fe, but the mountain-men had regular routes, and Hopper had doubtless learned something about where to go. At some point they struck the old Spanish trail which extended between southern California and New Mexico. They were on this trail at Abiquiu, where Chiles got into a tight fix with some Apaches, and was only saved by quick thinking and decisive action on Hopper's part.

At this point they were about fifty miles from Santa Fe, and from Santa Fe the trail was well established. They got to Missouri on September 9.

In about seven months they had zigzagged their way across most of the West, passing through areas which were later to be included in California, Nevada, Utah, Idaho, Wyoming, Colorado, New Mexico, Kansas, Missouri, and possibly Oklahoma. The distance ridden can scarcely have been under four thousand miles. They had suffered no deaths, and had not, apparently, endured any excessive hardship. On the basis of a trip no more extensive, Frémont could have submitted a five-hundred-page report and would have been hailed as the Pathfinder. After a much shorter trip, Parkman wrote *The California and Oregon Trail*. So little, however, of the record of this journey of '42 has been preserved that historians have even assumed Chiles and his companions to have followed the Spanish trail all the way from California to New Mexico. But history—though we seldom so think of it—is not really the story of what happened; it is necessarily the story of what is preserved in the record.

CHAPTER THREE

Chiles, having returned to Missouri vastly more experienced than when he had gone west only sixteen months earlier, was now convinced that California could be reached by wagon, and he began to prepare an expedition for '43.

A rather curious question may be raised about his motivation. If he merely wanted to live in California, why did he not simply stay there? Surely by this time he must have taken the edge off his love of adventure. Since Chiles himself left almost no record, we are reduced to surmise. Perhaps he had to return to make more permanent arrangements for his children. Quite possibly fame was the spur, and he wished to make himself known as the opener of the trail. Certainly, having become acquainted with conditions in California, he had learned that manufactured goods commanded exorbitant prices there, so that there was a chance of huge profits for the importer. Since we know that in '43 he loaded his wagons partly with goods to be sold in California, there can be no question but that he was at least partially motivated by the desire to make some quick profits. From this time on, indeed, the attempt to speculate in the California trade was a common one, and many of the more prosperous emigrants included a store of trade goods in their wagons. But, because of the great distance and because of the competition of traders shipping goods by sailing ship around Cape Horn, nothing that resembled the Santa Fe trade ever developed.

Whatever his motives may have been, Chiles at once set about organizing to go west again. His motherless children, all under ten years of age, he decided, should remain in Missouri. He turned now to William Baldridge, his close friend.

Baldridge dealt in the machinery, such as iron wheels and gears, for flour- and lumber-mills. In '30 he had spent a night in a hotel in Lexington, Missouri, and there had talked with a man named Mills, who was buying mules for a western trip. Mills was a trapper, who had been in California. He told wonderful stories about it, and Baldridge had been seized with a desire to go there.

He had planned to set out in '41, but had been involved in a deal to set up some mills. As this fact would indicate, he was a man of some substance. He was unmarried and therefore free to move easily.

Baldridge readily agreed to join his friend. Moreover, Chiles had decided that there was a great opportunity in California for setting up mills. So they would take along some sawmill irons, including three saws.

Chiles also made good on his promise to Yount, and arranged for both the daughters to come. Along with one of them, Mrs. Vines, came her husband and two small children.

Another important recruit was Julius Martin, about thirty years old, with a wife and three little girls. Moving was Martin's established habit. Born in North Carolina, he had lived in Alabama, Mississippi, and Missouri. To go west again must have seemed natural. Martin furnishes some refutation to the legend that the early emigrants were ignorant louts. He had been educated at the University of North Carolina and could quote Latin and Greek poetry.

Around this nucleus a dozen single men collected. But, as in '41, those who made the final attempt for California were not to be determined until after the first part of the journey had been completed.

Decisions as to equipment must have been made by Chiles. Basic possibilities for means of travel were three—pack trains, carts, wagons.

Chiles had gained plenty of experience with pack trains—in '41, after abandoning the wagons, and all the way east in '42. Pack trains, usually of mules, had many advantages. Yet Chiles decided against a pack train.

His reasons were probably two. First, he had women and children with him. Few women were accustomed to stand the strain of continuous riding, and the difficulties of taking young children in a pack train, though not insurmountable, were serious. Second, Chiles could remember the problems raised by Hopper's fever. In case of serious illness or accident, the pack train offered no practical solution.

What about carts? In Mexico, carts had served excellently for the magnificent sweep of the frontier northward. Chiles must have seen *carretas* in California and New Mexico. Moreover, far to the north, on the Canadian prairies, the so-called Red River

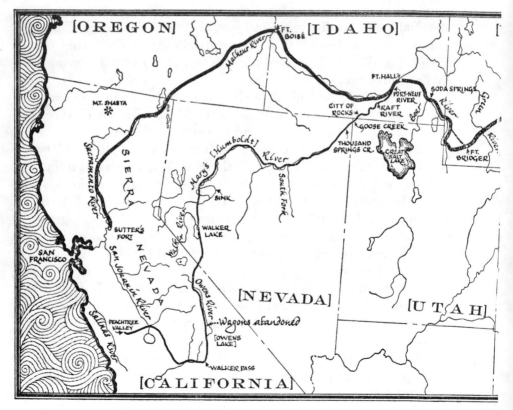

carts had become the standard means of transportation. These carts, hauled by two or three mules in tandem, were strong and highly maneuverable. They could make better time than wagons. In '41 the missionaries had had such carts, and Chiles had seen the emigrants wear down their wagon teams in trying to keep up.

But Chiles did not choose carts. The decision may have been partly based on mere traditionalism. Though carts were used on many American farms, wagons were commoner, and were probably yielded more status. Moreover, wagons were a good deal better than carts for transporting people, especially women and children. Carts could be covered and made weatherproof, but they were too small for family living.

So it would be wagons. But what kind? Chiles had seen the great lumbering freight wagons which went over the Santa Fe Trail, but such heavy vehicles would not be practical to haul over

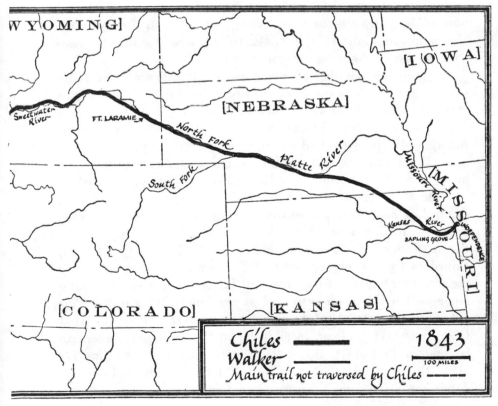

the steep and twisty mountain trails and across the sandy deserts. The wagons, then, would be ordinary farm wagons, as they had been in '41. They would be covered with canvas, as protection against the weather.

There were also three choices as to how the wagons could be pulled—horses, mules, or oxen. In '41 Chiles himself had used oxen, but he had seen horses and mules also. The prevailing opinion among early emigrants was that horses could not stand the long pull without grain to eat, and probably Chiles shared this opinion. Oxen and mules were judged to be about equally satisfactory. An often effective argument against mules was their expense, since they cost about three times as much as oxen.

Chiles's choice of mules thus shows, at least, that he was not too much pressed for funds, and like Baldridge was a man of some substance.

In making these decisions Chiles was not working entirely on his own. There had been a migration to Oregon in '42, and now in '43 many wagons were setting out. In fact, the comparative eclipse of California from '42 to '45 accounts for the more common use of the name Oregon Trail.

Again the jumping-off place was a few miles west of Independence, which was the chief supply point for the region. The start was nearly three weeks later than in '41, partly because the season itself was late. The trains could not venture out onto the prairie until the grass had grown sufficiently to support the animals. Finally, at the end of May, as one of the emigrants wrote later, "they left the frontiers with high spirits but much anxiety."

On the evening of May 31 Frémont, again starting west, camped at Elm Grove, and made note of "several emigrant wagons, constituting a party which was proceeding to Upper California, under the direction of Mr. J. B. Childs [sic]." He continued with his observations, "The wagons were variously freighted with goods, furniture, and farming utensils, containing among other things an entire set of machinery for a mill." This note as to the contents of the wagons seems to show definitely that Chiles was taking along, in addition to the machinery, goods to be sold in California. Since there were only eight wagons for about thirty people, such weight could have been carried only by dangerously reducing the amount of food.

The emigrants and the explorers traveled close together for several days' journey, and Chiles and another man acted as hunters for both companies, bagging many wild turkeys and two deer. When Frémont appropriated the hindquarters of the deer, and left the emigrants only the forequarters, Chiles became disgusted at such arrogance, and quit the arrangement.*

At the crossing of the Kansas River the party overtook the last of the more than a hundred wagons composing the so-called Great Emigration to Oregon, and in the following weeks they followed at the rear of the Oregonians. They traveled more slowly than the Bartleson Party had done in '41, because rainy weather made a muddy trail and necessitated halts at swollen streams. Chiles took thirty-four days to get to the crossing of the South Fork of the Platte, though in '41 twenty-eight days had sufficed. There the river was in flood, and the party lost several days more by having to wait for it to become safe for fording.

Once across the South Fork, Chiles stepped up the pace, and passed some of the Oregon wagons. Eighteen of these, in one of the frequent splits so common on the trail, thereupon joined Chiles. Possibly one of the inducements was the presence of some "very handsome young ladies," whom one of the Oregon emigrants noted to be with the California company. On July 17 the party came into Fort Laramie, along with many of the Oregon wagons. The emigrants, Californians and Oregonians alike, then relaxed and held dances on two successive evenings, at which "some of the party got gay." In fact, it seems to have been a very social year on the trail.

Just what Chiles was planning at this time, by what route he expected to reach California, is unknown. Everything that he had in mind may well have been changed, a little west of Fort Laramie, by his lucky chance of encountering Joe Walker, a meeting that brought together two men who had much experience and whose fields of knowledge were somewhat complementary.

* My authority for this detail is Chiles's son William, about seventy years old when I talked with him, late in 1919, on a rainy morning before breakfast in his cabin at the old toll gate on the Mt. St. Helena road. I got hungry and went to breakfast before I had got all that I might have out of him, not then knowing that I would be writing this book. But I wrote some of it down for a class exercise and Professor Herbert E. Bolton asked me to give it to the Bancroft Library. So, the other day, in 1961, I was able to read it again.

Walker, in this year, was forty-five years old. Along with Fitzpatrick, Bridger, Clyman, and a few others, we may say that he was at the head of his profession as mountain-man. His fund of experience was vast. He had led an expedition to California in '33. On his return in '34 he had discovered Walker Pass, at what was called "the point of the mountain," that is, the southern end of the Sierra Nevada. No one living was better qualified to act as a guide on the trail to California. Besides knowing something about the route, he would be useful as a hunter and for his knowledge of Indians. But Walker had traveled as a mountain-man, on horseback. He knew little of the problems of handling a wagon train.

Here Chiles was well experienced. In addition, Chiles had traveled to and from California, and his experience was more recent than Walker's.

The two, therefore, could have talked somewhat as equals, and their talk should have been interesting. Most likely, for instance, they discussed Jedediah Smith and his journey back from California in '27, when he had crossed the Sierra Nevada. But Indians had killed Smith in '31, and not very much was remembered apparently about his route. (Even Frémont, in '44, when he should have picked up all the gossip of the West, had apparently never heard of Smith's crossing.) That journey, therefore, remains essentially an isolated and romantic exploit. Knowledge of it may have influenced Walker, and memory of Smith's difficulties in crossing the Sierra Nevada may have tended to keep people away from the southern part of that range. One cannot, however, pinpoint any specific and direct influence of Smith's journey upon the later development of the trail.

Chiles certainly discussed routes with Walker. At this time, Chiles may have been intending to follow the trail of '41, though he might also have seen the possibilities of following the trail through Fort Hall, which he had traveled eastward in '42.

He and Walker may not have worked out a precise plan immediately. They would know that in the uncertainties of the mountains and deserts any plan might have to be altered to suit new circumstances. But Walker agreed, for a fee of $300, to act as guide.

The party then proceeded westward, making for the newly established Fort Bridger.

Like the meeting of the trappers and emigrants at Green River in '41, this establishment of Fort Bridger in '43 may be considered symbolic of new conditions. Jim Bridger was one of the most famous of the mountain-men. He realized, however, that the old days were over, that trapping no longer paid much, and that the emigrant trains offered a new source of income. So, with Louis Vásquez as a partner, he built himself a little stockaded post in a pleasant meadow where Black's Fork split into several small channels. This was in the country of the Snakes, who were friendly. There was good hunting roundabout. Horses and cattle could pasture on the meadowland.

Fort Bridger was about halfway between Fort Laramie and Fort Hall. By maintaining it as a supply point for emigrant trains, the partners could expect to make money. For instance, they could get worn-out oxen cheaply from the emigrants, and then could let the same oxen recuperate on the rich grass. Next year, or even later in the same season, another emigrant would come along with exhausted teams, ready to pay well for some reconditioned oxen.

It looked like a sure thing—but things were never sure in the mountain country. That very summer the Sioux and Cheyennes came raiding. They frightened off both the local Indians and the local buffalo.

The California emigrants arrived on August 13, "expecting to stay 10 or 15 days and make meat." This is the first sinister note. Chiles had not profited from the experience of '41, and had again started without sufficient supplies, once more expecting to live on the buffalo. And again he had passed through the best buffalo country before halting. Perhaps Chiles was not good at logistics, but we should remember that no one, in these early years, had learned much. To load your wagons too heavily with food at the beginning might also have seemed dangerous. But, at least, it would have been better to carry food than to carry the ironwork of a mill!

Chiles soon discovered that there was no good chance, this summer, of killing buffalo around Fort Bridger. So he moved on two days' journey farther west, breaking trail, and thus getting away from the route that the Oregon wagons were following and into country where he could expect to find the game undisturbed. Camping on Bear River, he and the others went out to hunt. But there were no buffalo. All they could get were some deer and antelope, along with an occasional bear and elk.

On August 28, still with the supply problem unsolved, the emigrants broke camp, and moved north along the valley of Bear River. After a few days they came back into the established trail. At Soda Springs they did not turn south as in '41, but kept on north, and arrived at Fort Hall on September 12.

By this time plans had crystallized somewhat, and John Boardman, who was keeping a diary, could write: "Walker is to pilot Chiles to the Point of the Mountains, in California." But the situation was not good. If the emigrants of '41 had hurried too much, those of '43 had perhaps loitered unduly. On this same day of the month two years before, the Bartlesons had been well to the west of Great Salt Lake.

Moreover, the shortage of provisions was critical, and very little could be bought at Fort Hall. A few cattle were feeding in the meadows, but Captain Richard Grant, the Hudson's Bay factor commanding the post, refused to sell at any price. We may sympathize with the captain. He doubtless needed beef to get his own people through the winter. On the other side, the emigrants were close to desperation, and Grant's being an Englishman gave the matter a sinister look. The situation was close to violence, since a man like Julius Martin was not willingly going to let his three little girls go hungry.

During a day or two the situation hung in balance. Walker properly refused to commit the company for California without a supply of food. Finally Chiles managed to purchase four head of cattle, and Walker agreed to start. But the plans had suffered a change.

Under the stress of necessity, in fact, Chiles had apparently come up with an idea that can only be called brilliant. . . . There was not enough food. Well then, he would split the company. Most of the food he would leave with the wagons, and with the wagons would go the women and children. Walker would have charge of

44

them. Chiles himself would lead a group of men on horseback, travel fast, and live off the country.

But the real brilliancy lay in the geographical scope that the plan revealed. Chiles must by now have realized that the chief barrier to wagons was not the desert but the Sierra Nevada. This lofty range, however, could be flanked at either end, and might also, though no one had yet found a pass for wagons, be crossed in the middle. Walker doubtless supplied much information and may have given advice, but the final decision must have rested with Chiles more than with any other man.

The two companies, as they may now be called, left Fort Hall on September 16. Later in the day, however, having got the women and children safely away, Martin and one of the Oregon emigrants rode back to the fort, "unable to resist the clamors of their children for food ... with the resolution of compelling Grant to sell them provisions." A small party of Americans, a section of Frémont's explorers, were camped at the fort, and these men promised support, if it came to shooting. Thereupon the fathers "boldly bearded the lion in his den and succeeded in frightening him into terms."

Though anyone is likely to sympathize with the distressed fathers, the action was little short of robbery, and another American wrote that the food was obtained "by very unpleasant means." The affair was another consequence of setting out without supplies sufficient for the whole journey.

Returning triumphantly with this additional food, Martin rejoined the wagons. That night the two parties camped together at Port Neuf River, a few miles west of the fort. . . .

In the morning the horseback party rode ahead. Under the leadership of Chiles, it consisted of thirteen young men, most of whom had originally set out for Oregon. Among them were several who were to be of some note. Pierson B. Reading, whose brief diary of the journey has survived, became a prominent citizen of California and left his name, in phonetic spelling, on the city of Redding. Samuel J. Hensley, John Gantt (a former army officer), and perhaps some of the others, had already spent time in the West. Hensley, John J. Myers, and Milton McGee were to figure in the later history of the trail. In fact, this little horseback party might be said to have served as a school for guides and explorers.

To the horsemen had been assigned two duties—first, the outflanking of the Sierra to the north; second, a reverse crossing, west to east, over the center of the range, to bring aid to the wagons in the vicinity of Humboldt Sink, and at the same time, if possible, to open a direct route between the sink and Sutter's.

Following the trail to Oregon, the horsemen reached the Hudson's Bay post of Fort Boisé on October 1. There they explained their intentions and needs to the commander. He could not supply them with much food, but he drew them a map, covering about half the distance to the Sacramento Valley. On October 3, they left the fort.

Using the map, they reached the Malheur River, and followed along its course, southwestward. On its headwaters they passed beyond the limits of their map and into an unknown region. The country was desert, and they had difficulty in finding water. Game, too, was scarce, so that they were close to starvation. On October 20 they crossed into what would later be the state of California, close to its northeastern corner. Two days later, they sighted a high snow-covered cone, far to the west, which was Mount Shasta. Buffeted by early snowstorms they struggled on, still southwestward, through rough mountain country, suffering hardships. On November 1 they entered the northern end of the Sacramento Valley. Finally, on November 10, horses and men alike exhausted, they arrived at Sutter's Fort.

In many respects the journey had been highly successful. The riders had outflanked the Sierra Nevada, as they had hoped to do. They had explored a new region, and had passed into California by a new route, some of which would later be used as an emigrant trail. In spite of all their difficulties they had averaged about twenty miles a day—as much as could possibly be expected of horsemen on so long and arduous a journey.

But they arrived at Sutter's much too late, after snow had fallen on the mountains. The trouble was that they had simply been sent on too roundabout a route, further evidence that even such mountain-men as Walker were by no means sure of their western geography. The distance by way of Fort Boisé was at least a thousand miles.

To Hensley, an experienced frontiersman, had been assigned the duty of crossing the Sierra eastward, and thus taking provisions to the wagon train. Because of the snow, he did not even make the attempt. This breakdown of the plans left the wagon train, with its women and children, on its own. . . .

The wagon train, too, had left the Port Neuf on September 17. With it were sixteen men. There were also Mrs. Martin and Mrs. Vines, two unmarried girls, and five children.

Walker was both guide and captain. Baldridge and Martin were courageous and energetic. Not much is known of the others. "Old Wheat" Atkinson was a colorful frontiersman from Texas. Charles McIntosh was a half-breed Cherokee. Major (a name, not a title) Walton had been one of the '41 party, and had ridden east with Chiles in '42. Though not outstanding and though having to care for women and children, the party could be expected to do well enough—especially since Walker was a host in himself.

There were three mule-drawn wagons, according to one account; six, according to another. The discrepancy probably indicates that some wagons were dropped off along the way.

Walker thought that he would be able to get through to California in sixty days. He must have based such an estimate on the assumption of a direct journey to Sutter's Fort, either by taking the wagons over some pass to be discovered by the horsemen or by making the last part of the journey by pack-train.

After following the Oregon Trail westward for about three days, Walker turned the wagons off to the south, at what is today known as Calder Creek. Frémont, passing that point a week later, saw the tracks and followed them for some distance, mistaking them for a detour of the main trail, until he recollected the California-bound emigrants with whom he had camped at Elm Grove. Frémont's mistake indicates how few wagons had as yet gone to Oregon—if the trail left by these few wagons suggested a main road to be traveled.

No diary has survived, and the itinerary can only be estimated by "dead reckoning." We can, however, be certain of much of the route, for at this time Walker established more than five hundred miles of the California Trail, as it is known from later years.

The question may be asked how he knew where to go. Presumably he was following a trappers' trail, that one which he himself had followed or established in '34, and that one also which Chiles followed in '42. The difficulty of the first part of the route, in fact, suggests that it had originally been developed for horsemen. In its first hundred miles the trail went up and down over three divides. Walker could have avoided all of these troublesome climbs and dangerous descents by taking the wagons two days' journey farther along the established Oregon Trail and then south up the course of Goose Creek. But, by following a known route instead of something new, he was playing safe.

Walker soon crossed from Calder Creek to the valley of Raft River. (The later emigrants eliminated this first divide by following the Oregon Trail to Raft River, so that its crossing became the separating point for Oregon and California wagons.)

Thus following what was presumably a trail already, Walker eventually reached the headwaters of Mary's River, the present Humboldt. If we assume an average rate of thirteen miles a day, good enough for wagons having to break trail, the date would have been just about the end of September. Following down along the river, he then brought the wagons to the sink about October 22.

Since almost no record is preserved of the five weeks' progress, we may make the ordinary deduction, "No news is good news," and can assume that the journey was steady, successful, and dull.

The emigrants had hoped to see Hensley already at the sink with his pack train of provisions and probably with information as to how to reach Sutter's Fort by a direct central crossing. (As yet, however, Hensley and the other horsemen were still involved with the northern mountains, and would not even reach Sutter's until another three weeks had passed.)

Walker and the others settled down to wait, undoubtedly casting many a glance westward for a cloud of dust that would indicate approaching horsemen. In any case, a rest would do much good, both to man and to beast. The meadows offered a pleasant camping-place at that time of year, and the animals could build up their strength on the good grass.

After a few days of waiting, everyone undoubtedly got nervous. Chiles's grand strategy had the weakness that always accompanies any far-flung division of forces without the possibility of communication: that is, if either party met disaster or got off schedule, there was no way to let the other know. Yet, as good generals should, Chiles and Walker had presumably arranged alternate plans, to be used if the original plan broke down, by which either party could act independently.

After eight days, about October 30, with the animals rested and somewhat fattened, the little train of mule-drawn wagons again set out. Hensley's failure to reach them was later blamed on the snow; actually, he would have had to follow the wagons to the south, if he had managed to cross the mountains after his arrival at Sutter's.

By the time of leaving the sink the party had expended about forty-five of the sixty days that Walker had estimated as necessary. Food was getting low, and there was almost no game in the desert country through which they would have to pass. Since he could not expect to reach the California settlements in fifteen days, Walker probably put the people on short rations.

He now followed in reverse his trail of '34—doubtless much the same trail that Walton had followed with Chiles in '42, the preceding year. Indeed, Walton rather than Walker may have been the better guide in many places. The route took them far to the south, so that they would really go around the Sierra Nevada, crossing by Walker's easy pass, which would probably not be blocked by snow, even in the winter.

But this route was very long. At the sink, though no one would have known exactly, they were only about 250 miles from Sutter's. By this southern route the distance was about three times as far. Moreover, though the pass itself was easy, they would have to cross, before they reached it, many desert stretches and much rough country, where wagons had never gone before. In addition, they were very short of food. Still, they cannot have been greatly worried as yet, for they did not lighten the wagons by dumping the heavy ironwork of the mill.

First they crossed the long desert stretch south of the sink— weary miles of heavy pulling. Fortunately, because of Walker and Walton, they must have known what they were up against. Also, the teams were well rested.

Probably they halted a day at the river flowing eastward, which Frémont was later to name after Kit Carson. Continuing forty miles to the south, they came to a river which was later to bear Walker's own name. They followed this river down a few miles until it flowed into a lake, which was to be Walker Lake. The slope on the east side was such that they could take the wagons along without too great difficulty. Beyond the lake there was no obvious route. They kept on south across difficult terrain. As one of them wrote later, "The country in parts seemed to be only recently erupted by the volcanoes and earthquakes. Hot springs occurred every few miles, and the route . . . crossed the most awful piles and hills of black hard, basaltic rocks." The days were hot; the nights, very cold. There were long stretches without water, and with little or no grass. Under such conditions the animals suffered. The people themselves were on reduced rations.

One incident is recorded. A young man named Milton Little, on guard one night, was bushwhacked by a skulking Indian, and got an arrow in the chest muscles. They managed to pull the shaft out, but the arrowhead remained in the wound, causing him great pain.

About November 20 they came into a southward-trending valley with high mountains to the east and an even higher range to the west. This latter, wholly blocking the direct road to California, was the dreaded Sierra Nevada itself, with snow-covered peaks towering to more than fourteen thousand feet. Its existence, however, was no surprise to Walker, and he continued to lead the wagons southward toward his pass, following a pleasant stream.

But a time of crisis was approaching. The sixty days that Walker had judged sufficient for the journey were now exceeded, and the people were facing starvation. The teams were failing. And finally the little river came to an end in a large brackish lake.

Here, at last, the exhaustion of the mules necessitated the decision to leave the wagons. In any case there was little food left to be carried. Baldridge cached the valuable machinery for the mill by burying it. Doubtless the men made pack-saddles from part of the wood of the wagons. They burned the rest of the wagons—now, certainly, appreciating a good campfire. The place of abandonment was close to Owens Lake; the time, near the end of November.

Even at this extremity these people were by no means so

desperately situated as the Bartleson Party had been in '41. They were very short of food, and had the responsibility of caring for a number of women and children. But they were only a few days' journey from a practicable pass across the mountains, and they had a reliable guide.

The four women could ride. The five small children were probably sometimes carried, sometimes stowed in saddle-bags or panniers.

A few days' travel brought the pack train to the pass, and the time of its crossing is given with remarkable exactitude as eleven o'clock on the morning of December 3. Though there was snow to the depth of six inches, the passage of the mountains was accomplished without great hardship, one mule being slaughtered for food.

Coming down into the San Joaquin Valley, Walker swung to the north for several days' journey. He then decided to cross the valley, and reach what he knew to be a pleasant camping-ground in the coast-range hills. It was a dubious decision. The region was uninhabited, and this was a drought year. During three days and nights, the party endured desert conditions, without food. (About this same time, Chiles himself, with three men, went as far as Walker Pass, seeking to relieve the party, but failing to find their trail.)

Having reached the Coast Range, the people passed from famine to feast. Camped in Peachtree Valley, they passed a jolly Christmas season, feasting on "finest haunches of venison." They also came to be very fond of the meat of the fat and young wild horses which were numerous in the area, where the name Mustang Ridge still survives. Having thus recruited themselves, the emigrants continued their journey, and reached the California settlements on the Salinas River shortly after New Year's. . . .

For good or for bad, '43 must be counted as Chiles's year. Even Walker acted as his employee. Chiles showed himself outstanding in courage, enterprise, energy, and breadth of vision. He suffered, however, from over-optimism. Though he should have known better from '41 and from the cumulative experience of the Oregon emigrants, he wrecked a good possibility of success by loading his wagons with ironwork and other goods and expecting to get through by killing buffalo.

The miscalculation as to the time the horsemen would take to reach Sutter's was also unfortunate, though here Walker, along with Chiles, must bear the responsibility. Two factors were involved. First, the distance that the horsemen would have to travel must have been much underestimated. Second, the rate at which the horsemen could move was overestimated. Throughout the earlier years of the trail, indeed, most people worked on the assumption that pack-trains could move much faster than wagons. This was true for short distances. Packers might make a hundred miles in three days, and a wagon train take a week. But, as experience was eventually to demonstrate, most of this differential vanished in the long pull.

Like the expedition of '41, that of '43 must be called a failure. Again, no lives were lost, but a very circuitous route was followed, and the wagons were abandoned. The California Trail had not been opened.

Still, it was a good try! Much more was accomplished than in '41. On the direct route to California the trail had been advanced five hundred miles, all the way to the sink. Only a gap of 250 miles still remained to be closed, though within this short distance lay a formidable desert, and the even more formidable Sierra Nevada.

CHAPTER FOUR

THUS, WHILE THE BLEAKNESS of that winter lay upon the borderlands, the score for the attempt to take wagons to California stood: successes, 0; failures, 2.

But the men waiting for spring in Missouri and Iowa could not have known one way or the other. Walker and Chiles had got to California late in the year, and no one could have ridden eastward with the news, across the snow-covered mountains. Even a ship had to sail by Cape Horn, a voyage that took months. So those who planned, that winter, were perhaps just as well off, being ignorant.

Indeed, one of the remarkable features of the remarkable expedition of '44 is its isolation from everything that had happened before. It seems to spring from some fresh impulse. Not one of its members had set out in '41.

Many of them, indeed, lived near St. Joseph, Missouri, a newly founded border town, where the gossip of the frontier circulated. They must have heard of the Bartleson Party, though what they heard would not have been encouraging. They would also have known of the departure in '43, and in recruiting that expedition Chiles would have talked as if success were certain. Since no word of failure had as yet returned, these arrantly optimistic people could have assumed that Chiles had known what he was talking about.

Moreover, anyone starting for California in '44 did so with a kind of built-in insurance, knowing that he could at least get through to Oregon, if he thought it better to change his mind at Fort Hall.

The start, this year, was from Council Bluffs at the western border of Iowa Territory. The party waited there a few days, about the middle of May, "to make repairs and perfect their organization."

About forty wagons were assembled—most of them for Oregon. The company organized under one captain to travel as far as Fort Hall.

The emigrants bound for California numbered twenty-three men, eight women, and about fifteen children. The party was thus

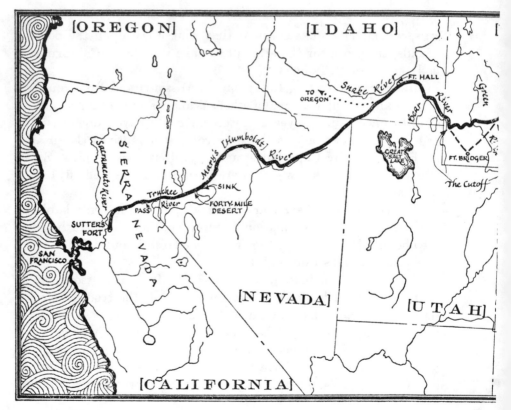

composed primarily of families, not of adventurers. In addition, two of the wives were pregnant, though one of them so newly that she might not even have known it yet. (But pregnancy was not considered a bar to starting on such a journey.)

One family with its ramifications, centering about Martin Murphy, constituted half the California company. Murphy was fifty-eight years old. Born in Ireland, he had migrated to Canada in 1820. In 1840 he moved to a farm in western Missouri, thus arriving at his third home just when the interest in migration to the Pacific Coast was beginning.

A memoir of Murphy states that he came to the United States "beneath the folds of whose starry flag perfect religious and political liberty was maintained." But he had hardly settled beneath that propitious flag before he prepared to leave—since California was then Mexican. Some of his motivation was religious.

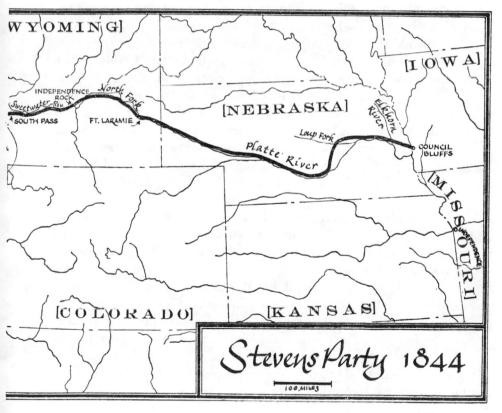

Stevens Party 1844

100 MILES

In those years the missionary priest Christian Hoecken labored along the Missouri frontier. He was an enthusiast for California—for one reason, because Catholicism was there the established religion. But Missouri too had a strong Catholic tradition, and the Murphys, in any case, do not seem to have been fanatical religionists. Though Hoecken helped persuade Murphy to emigrate, and though the idea of living in a Catholic country might be attractive to an Irishman, the influence need not be heavily stressed.

More likely, bad luck in Missouri was most cogent. An unusually virulent outbreak of malaria afflicted the whole family, and carried off Murphy's wife and three of his grandchildren.

So here he was at Council Bluffs, with three married and four unmarried children, a son-in-law, two daughters-in-law, and eight grandchildren. In addition, the wife of one son was the daughter of Patrick Martin, who was a member of the party, along with his two grown sons. The whole connection thus totaled twenty-two, with perhaps a few hired men besides.

In addition, at least five others were Irish and three were French, either Canadians or Mississippi Valley Creoles. The Catholics, therefore, numbered no fewer than fifteen of the twenty-three men and owned at least six of the eleven wagons. This strong Catholic bloc, further connected by ties of kinship and nationality, might well have elected one of themselves to the captaincy, especially since the Murphys were an energetic and able family. If Grandfather Murphy had seemed too old for the post, his son Martin—aged about thirty-seven—might well have served.

Possibly, however, too much domination by one group would have alienated the others and caused them to split off. Besides, among the other members of the party were some natural candidates for the captaincy.

Among these was Dr. John Townsend, whose title and profession gave him status. He was, indeed, no notable physician, having practiced on the frontier while also farming, as was commonly done. Still, he considered himself an important person, and thought in large and sometimes fantastic terms. He was therefore a half-and-half figure. You could not pay him too much attention, and yet you could not ignore him.

With Townsend were his wife and her brother, Moses Schallenberger, a gawky youngster, not yet in his full strength, but to be counted very nearly a man.

Also possible candidates for the captaincy were two men who had much experience as trappers beyond the frontier. One of these was sixty-four-year-old Isaac Hitchcock. Little is known of him, but one reference would indicate that he had been to California—though with what party (if, indeed, at all) must remain doubtful.

The other who had been a trapper in the West was a hawk-nosed fellow of forty years, who must have been marked by the heavy arms and strong hands of the blacksmith. Elisha Stevens (or Stephens) owned one of the wagons, but we do not know who accompanied him. He had neither chick nor child, and he was not a talkative or sociable man. In fact, he was almost a recluse. Within him, however, there must have burned some subtle fire. Years later, an interviewer wrote of him, "he was born to command." Apparently in '44 at Council Bluffs the men of the party also recognized that strange power, never quite to be explained, which some men possess and inevitably exercise.

Dr. Townsend would have expected to be chosen. So might either Martin Murphy. There was also a vast amount of experience in the head of "Old Man" Hitchcock. The Oregon emigrants, too, would have had candidates. But the vote went to Stevens.

We can hardly imagine him—tongue-tied as he was—making a speech or soliciting votes. He appears to have had little charm of manner. But this is one of the times when we can be proud of the democracy of the frontiersmen. They passed over the talkers and the men with blocs of votes, and with some sure instinct acknowledged that inner fire of Elisha Stevens—"he was born to command."

Also with the party—though not, strictly speaking, of it— were the old mountain-man Caleb Greenwood and two of his sons by his Crow squaw, John and Britain. The boys were about twenty and eighteen; the father, according to his own statement, was eighty-one. Old men sometimes exaggerate their ages, and Greenwood may have done so. He had, however, accumulated more than thirty years of experience in the West. He had even been briefly enlisted with the Astoria expedition in '10, though that would make us think him younger than eighty-one in '44, since men approaching fifty would rarely have been enrolled among the Astorians. But, at least, he was commonly known as "Old Greenwood." He was now the hired guide of the party, undertaking to conduct them as far as the Rocky Mountains— that is, perhaps, to Fort Hall.

Besides being a guide, Greenwood could be useful in many other ways, as Fitzpatrick and Walker had already been in '41 and '43, though he was scarcely of their caliber. He had, in fact, almost entirely "gone Indian," as the result of long residence with the Crows. His sons, too, were half Indian by blood and wholly so by upbringing. Probably the three kept to themselves. An emigrant girl of a later year who traveled in a party guided by the old man and John wrote of them: "They were mountain men, and dressed the same as Indians. I was more afraid of these two men than of the wild Indians."

The emigrants' camp at Council Bluffs was to the east of the Missouri River, and their first problem was to get across. One primitive flat-bottomed boat was available, and in it the wagons were safely ferried over. The emigrants decided to swim the cattle. But the swirling river was frightening, and the animals refused to take to the water. Forced in from behind, they then began to swim in a circle, each one trying to climb upon the back of the one in front. They were allowed to return to the eastern bank, where many of them stuck in deep mud, from which some could not be extricated. As a final expedient two men started across in a canoe, leading behind them one of the most tractable of the oxen by a rope tied around the horns. Once the ox was swimming, his course was easily controlled. The others, being crowded in, followed the lead of the first one, and swam safely over. Thus at the very beginning the company faced a serious problem and gained confidence by overcoming it.

The Stevens Party left the west bank of the Missouri probably on May 18. The second test came about two days' journey farther on, at Elkhorn River. It too was high. To cross, the men sewed rawhides over one of the wagon-boxes. Then they unloaded all the wagons, took the wagons themselves apart, ferried everything across, and then reassembled and reloaded. The animals, once more, had to swim. Again, with prodigious labor, an obstacle had been passed.

A boat, thus improvised, came to be a regular device among the emigrants. A waterproofed wagon-box—say, nine feet by four, with two-foot sides—could ferry a ton safely. Since a wagon rarely was freighted with more than a ton, the number of trips to ferry a small party across would not be excessive. But the total amount of work was appalling.

From the Elkhorn onward, across the plains, the journey was prosperous. The emigrants kept good discipline, setting a regular guard over the cattle at night. They had no trouble with the Indians.

The route kept to the north of the Platte River, on what would later be called the Mormon Trail. A few wagons had already gone that way, as early as '35, so that the Stevens Party cannot here be called the pioneers. Greenwood presumably knew the route.

According to one statement, they took things "very easy," during the early part of the journey, but they made excellent time to Fort Laramie. They rested there for several days. An estimated four thousand Sioux were encamped near-by, and the emigrants did some trafficking for ponies and moccasins—at the same time feeling a little apprehensive for their own scalps after they should leave the fort.

With increased precautions they traveled on, but no Sioux molested them. They halted near Independence Rock for a week to hunt buffalo and "make meat." Here they celebrated July Fourth, and also the arrival of a new member—the birth of another grandchild to the patriarch Martin Murphy. The James Millers, proud parents, named the girl in commemoration of the time and place, Ellen Independence.

The emigrants crossed South Pass, where "they saw that the water ran towards California, and their hearts were rejoiced as though already in sight of the promised land." Some of the more ignorant, considering how far they had come already, were of the opinion that the journey must now be nearly at its end!

Moving ahead to Big Sandy Creek, they camped for a day, resting for a special effort.

At this point, for the first time in the history of the trail, a party was faced with a decision of a kind that would be recurrent in future years. Should they play safe by keeping to the established route, or should they try a "cutoff," reported to be shorter?

The informant in this case was the rather mysterious "Old Man" Hitchcock. From here, he maintained, they did not need to go so far southwest and then back northwest, but could head out directly west along only one side of the triangle. One should note that the informant was Hitchcock, and not Greenwood, who was supposed to be the guide. Captain Bonneville in '32 had taken wagons over this proposed route, and Hitchcock's knowledge suggests that he had been on that expedition. On the other hand, the scantiness of his information may indicate that he had merely picked up gossip.

Doubtless there was much argument, and in the end the decision was reached, as commonly happened, by vote of the men assembled in council. In such a situation the vote nearly always went the same way. After all, if you believed in playing it safe, you never even started on this journey, but were a man who gambled on long chances. So you would vote to take the cutoff.

Hitchcock told them it would be twenty-five miles across to the Green. Thinking this to be only a long day's march, the emigrants made no special preparations to carry extra water and to cut grass for the oxen. They set out at daylight, and traveled all day "across a rough, broken country" without water. After dark, exhausted and thirsty, they made a dry camp in a desolate spot. Hitchcock must have had to do a lot of talking.

During the night forty head of young cattle went off looking for water. At daybreak, without trying to retrieve these cattle, the party pushed on, and finally came to the river at eleven o'clock. Since the distance between the two streams at this point is at least thirty-five miles by air line, the distance traveled by the wagons in getting through the broken country was probably close to the forty-three miles that a careful emigrant of a later year calculated for the same stretch.

A few men, young Mose Schallenberger among them, were sent back from the river to look for the strayed cattle. Some of them sighted a Sioux war party, from which they managed to hide. Having backtracked clear to Big Sandy, they found all the cattle there, and then set out to return to Green River, but were forced to camp for the night. The next morning a band of mounted Indians charged down upon the party, scaring them half to death, though they put up a firm front. But these Indians proved to be friendly Snakes, who were themselves on the trail of the Sioux.

From Green River, Hitchcock led on across some rough mountainous country, and eventually made good on his word by bringing the wagons to Bear River and a junction with the old trail. In spite of these difficulties the party, by taking the cutoff, shortened the route by about eighty-five miles, five or six days' journey. (This more direct route was commonly used by later emigrants, being called Greenwood's—or, later, Sublette's—Cut-off.)

After some ten days more of uneventful travel the emigrants arrived at Fort Hall, about August 10. They halted for several days. There was much to be done.

An obvious need was food. Some of the party had started with an eight months' supply, and were still well furnished. But others had already exhausted their flour and bacon and were depending upon those who were better provisioned. The emigrants bought some flour at the fort, where they had to pay a dollar a pound. They still had some dried buffalo meat. In the end they decided that the problem of food was not critical. They were driving along some extra cattle, and these could be slaughtered as need arose. Thus, narrowly, the Stevens Party escaped the difficulty that had forced Chiles to improvise new plans the year before.

Equally as important as food was the need for more information about the route, but there is no record of what they were told. The leaders would have learned about Walker's departure the preceding summer. They would also have been told of the two possibilities—the long swing to the south, and the questionable direct push to the west from the sink. Did they learn of Walker's failure? In those years there was no regular travel from California to Fort Hall. No one crossed those eight hundred miles of Indian-haunted deserts unless he had good reason. On the whole, the evidence suggests that no one at Fort Hall knew what had happened to Walker. But we cannot be sure. If the men of the Stevens Party learned about Walker, they would then have known not only that they could take wagons to the sink and even beyond it, but also that they would have to do better than Walker had done. If they learned nothing about the outcome, they would at least have started out with the pleasant illusion that they could follow his tracks clear to California. Either way, they would not have started except under the spell of that rash optimism which marked all these early expeditions.

So they left Fort Hall, and a few days later, on or about August 17, swung off to the south from the Oregon Trail, following the track of Walker's wagons.

Since this is a critical moment in an epic story, let us catalog the wagons, taking refuge in alphabetical order, since no other order is available. The eleven wagons were those of:

1. Isaac Hitchcock, called "Old Man" Hitchcock, his daughter Isabella Patterson, and her children, variously listed as from four to six in number, the older ones approaching adulthood.

2. Patrick Martin and his grown sons, Dennis and Patrick.

3. James Miller, his wife, his young son William, and three young daughters, including ten-week-old Ellen Independence. (Mrs. Miller was the daughter of Martin Murphy.)

4. Allen Montgomery, a young man, gunsmith by trade, and his wife.

5. James Murphy, his wife, and young daughter Mary. (James was the son of Martin Murphy; his wife, the daughter of Patrick Martin.)

6. Martin Murphy, the elder, and his younger children, Daniel, Bernard, Ellen, and John.

7. Martin Murphy, the younger, his wife, and four boys, James, Martin, Patrick, and Bernard.

8. Elisha Stevens (with him a man or two to help with the oxen, but their identity uncertain).

9. John Sullivan, a young Irishman, his sister Mary, and younger brothers, Michael and Robert.

10. Dr. John Townsend, his wife, his brother-in-law Moses Schallenberger, and a French hired man named Deland.

11. Owner unknown—perhaps Joseph Foster, or perhaps a second wagon owned by one of those already listed. (Certainly

the numerous Hitchcock clan should have had more than one wagon.)

In addition, there were five single men—Edmund Bray, Vincent Calvin, John Flomboy, Matthew Harbin, and Ollivier Magnent. They were working their way as ox-drivers or cattle-herders, and one of them must have been with Stevens. Bray was an Irish laborer. Flomboy was a half-breed, and Magnent was French.

Greenwood with his sons still accompanied the party, though he no longer acted as guide, not knowing the country.

In its personnel the party was excellent, and might well hope to succeed where others had failed. It included at least three men who had had extensive western experience—Stevens, Hitchcock, and Greenwood.

By this time, indeed, the whole company had a right to consider itself somewhat expert, after three months of travel. Good leadership had welded the men into a well-functioning unit. As one of them wrote later, "we had great confidence in our leader."

The company as a whole seems to have been distinguished by general good sense. The grandfathers Murphy and Martin, along with Hitchcock and Caleb Greenwood, were on the oldish side, but all of them were strong and active. Schallenberger, John Murphy, and "Brit" Greenwood were on the line between being boys and men, but generally did man's work. The other twenty were at the height of their physical power. The women ranged in age from twenty to thirty-six.

Stevens was a blacksmith; Montgomery, a gunsmith; Townsend, a physician. These were useful specialists to have along.

Food, including beef on the hoof, appeared to be sufficient. The yoke-oxen were in good condition.

Of the equipment little is known. Some goods were being carried to be sold in California. The cargo specifically mentioned is that of Dr. Townsend, who had some silks and satins—much better than Baldridge's mill gears, being valuable but not heavy enough to wear the oxen down. The doctor also had a small library, including Lord Chesterfield's letters and Byron's poems.

All things considered, the men of the Stevens Party must have swung south with some confidence, the more so because they enjoyed almost complete ignorance of what they were up against.

"Happy are the people whose annals are brief!" The same might be written of emigrants on the California Trail. And the annals of the Stevens Party during their march from Fort Hall to the sink are so short as to approach nothing at all. The longest account states only: "The journey down the Humboldt was very monotonous. Each day's events were substantially a repetition of those of the day before."

From the records of other journeys we can reconstruct the day's routine in a well-conducted train, such as this one. . . . The camp began to stir at daybreak. The cattle-guards rode in, to report a quiet night. Already the women were building the fires up. The dead sagebrush, gathered by the children the preceding evening, blazed hotly and briefly. There was coffee, bacon, and flapjacks or bread—if the supplies still held out; otherwise, jerked buffalo meat, or beef from a newly butchered steer.

Soon came the cry, "Catch up! Catch up!" The well-trained oxen docilely held still for yoking. One, or two, or three men cantered off ahead to act as scouts and lookouts. The women and smaller children clambered into the wagons. The driver of the lead wagon took his stand next to the wheel team. Suddenly his long bull whip curled menacingly in the air; its lash leaped out, and the crack was like a pistol shot. The whip did not touch the backs of the oxen, but they knew the signal, and the weight of their shoulders fell against the yokes. The wagon creaked, and lurched forward.

The other wagons took their places in the line, the one which had held the lead on the day before now bringing up the rear. Behind the last wagon two or three men or boys herded up the loose cattle.

From wagon wheels and the feet of horses and oxen the fine white dust of the desert arose. The lead wagon had the hardest time, since it was always, to some extent, breaking trail. Each driver plodded beside his oxen, cracking his whip, calling, "Gee!" or "Haw!" From the flaps in front or from the puckering-strings behind, the faces of women and children peered out. The captain and a few other men rode beside the wagons or spread out as flankers.

Nearly all the twenty-six men thus had assigned posts. One or two were probably sent off hunting. There was always a chance for antelopes, though they were hard to stalk and usually had to be knocked over by a long-range shot.

Now and then the slow progress was halted, where a rainstorm had left a gully across the way or some other obstruction blocked the passage. The men worked with shovels or axes, and then the lead team plugged on once more.

Well before the sun was overhead, the captain called a halt for nooning. People and animals rested, and all fed on anything available to eat. In fact, the place had been selected by the scouts with regard to the water and grass which it offered.

After a halt of two hours—even more, if the day was very hot—they went on. The afternoons were more tiresome, and tempers wore thin. Oxen felt the lash, and children were spanked. The blazing desert sun moved slowly to the west, shining now in the eyes. And gradually, very gradually, the afternoon wore to a close.

Well before sunset they drew near to a spot that the scouts had picked for a camp. Almost automatically, now by long custom, the teams moved into position and halted. The oxen were unyoked, and the wagons were left standing in a rough circle.

Children went off to gather brush for fires; women began to get supper ready; a teamster looked to an ox that seemed to be going lame; the captain and the scouts argued about whether to log fourteen or sixteen miles for the day; another teamster unhooked the tar-bucket from beneath the rear axle and greased a wheel spindle that had been whining; a hunter rode in with the carcass of an antelope tied behind him.

They ate supper, which was necessarily about the same as breakfast—unless they decided to eat the antelope that evening. The sun was silhouetting the jagged and treeless mountain range to the west. An evening breeze sprang up. Everyone was feeling better, and perhaps they even sang a few songs, now that the younger children had been put to bed in the wagons. The men smoked their pipes, or chewed tobacco, spitting into the fire. The older women, too, puffed at their corncobs.

Soon they all made ready for sleep, except the unlucky ones who had the first hours of guard duty.

The people made up their beds just outside the circle of wagons, no longer bothering to set up tents. Men laid their firearms handy—not expecting trouble, but just as routine. The fires of quickly burning sagebrush had died out. All was still except for a restive horse. Silence, and the darkness deepening!

We need not wonder that the chronicler remembered monotony. He did indeed recall something about the desert Indians, the "Diggers," whom he characterized as "indolent and degraded." They came into camp often, in "hundreds," as he remembered, though this figure is undoubtedly an exaggeration built up over many years of telling the story. They were friendly.

But the chronicler left no record of what it was like to follow Walker's trail. Again, this would indicate that it was no great problem. Certainly that trail had been plain to Frémont, and the passage of a year in an almost rainless country would have made little difference. Here and there flooding water or blown sand might have wiped out the trace, but it could always be picked up again by a little scouting. In fact, it could probably be made out where it went over the next rise, for such a trail often shows up best at a distance. Three wagons and all of Walker's horses, mules, and people, passing across such country, would have left a clear mark—broken sagebrush, wheel ruts in sand and dried mud, droppings of animals, stones rolled aside or banks dug down, bare spots where campfires had burned. ("Where the red dog has lain, no grass grows" is not a proverb of Americans, but they at least knew the fact.)

When the Stevens Party finally came to the wide-spreading meadows of the sink, people and animals both were in surprisingly good condition—another tribute to careful management. One pony had disappeared and was presumed to have been stolen by the Indians. Even the team oxen were in "tolerably good condition," their feet sound and hard—"except that they needed a little rest, they were really better prepared for work than when they left Missouri."

The time of the arrival at the sink was about October 1, but the chronology of this journey is vague and uncertain. Several reminiscences give the date for this arrival, but each gives it differently, from October 1 to November 10! This, however, is only what is to be expected of reminiscences, which are excellent for personal adventures, but are hopeless for dates, unless the day can be associated with an anniversary, like the Fourth of July.

Thus the same reminiscence that gives the impossible November 10 also supplies what seems a trustworthy picture of life during the week's encampment at the sink:

The cattle were let out to grass, the horses unharnessed [unsaddled], while the men and women, too, busied themselves with repairing outfits, mending damaged vehicles, washing soiled clothing, and the younger members busied themselves in shooting game, which, in the shape of wild ducks, geese, sage hens, as well as antelopes and deer, were very abundant.

Time was also needed to gather information upon which to base an all-important decision. From the sink Walker's wagons had gone south. But toward the west, also, a broad passageway between mountains lay open.

Again we can work only by inference because we are ignorant of how much the emigrants knew about Walker. Also, how much, if anything, did they know, or suspect, of a central pass across the Sierra Nevada? In later years two different trappers told—or boasted—that they had discovered and used such a pass. Trappers were often notorious liars, and there is much reason to think that these two were lying. In later years you might win some acclaim and free drinks by telling how you had discovered the pass now used by the railroad.

As far as the evidence goes, it indicates that the men of the Stevens Party, no matter how much they might have been told in a vague way at Fort Hall, knew nothing at all for certain about what lay west of the sink. Greenwood did not even pretend to any knowledge. According to one account, Hitchcock advised the company to go west instead of south—but, if he did so, we do not know the basis of his information. The best reminiscence gives a synopsis without reference to Hitchcock:

Many anxious consultations were held, some contending that they should follow a southerly course, and others held that they should go due west. Finally, an old Indian was found, called Truckee, with whom old man Greenwood talked by means of signs and diagrams drawn on the ground. From him it was learned that fifty or sixty miles to the west there was a river that flowed easterly from the mountains, and that along this stream there were large trees and good grass.

Three men—Stevens himself, Dr. Townsend, and Foster— then rode out to investigate, taking Truckee along as guide and hostage. After three days they returned, to report that everything was as had been told.

Though there was still doubt as to where or whether they could get over the mountains, they decided to move west. Merely to linger at the sink would be to let time run out.

Besides, they should be moving because of the Indians. These were present in large numbers, and very friendly—as Truckee had demonstrated. But Indians and emigrants seldom mixed well. The chief trouble at the sink was with John Greenwood, who, "being a half-breed, had a mortal hatred for the Indians." Just as well, we could say that being half Crow he could not consider himself a warrior until he had performed some exploit, and at the same time he considered the Diggers, who were related to the Snakes, as his hereditary enemies. He more than once accused them of having stolen cattle, which had merely strayed. Only by peremptory authority did the older men prevent him from shooting his Indian.

At the moment of departure the situation became suddenly tense. Mose Schallenberger missed a halter. Looking about, he saw an end of it hanging below a short feather blanket worn by an Indian. With youthful impetuosity, Mose demanded the halter, and then seized it. The Indian stepped back and drew his bow. Grabbing his rifle, Mose leveled it. Martin Murphy, in horror, rushed in and struck the rifle up. In an instant the whole camp was in confusion, with a general battle threatened. The Indians, however, were appeased by liberal bestowal of presents.

The emigrants departed immediately, carrying along in the wagons—with their usual good sense and foresight—two days' cooked rations and all the water vessels filled. A forced march till midnight brought them to some boiling springs, and there they halted to let the oxen rest.

At two in the morning the party moved on. Day broke, and the march continued, across a long stretch of deep alkali dust, wholly without vegetation. Now they no longer had Walker's wagon tracks to guide them, but only the trail that their own scouts had left. About noon, they sighted the dark green line of the cottonwoods along the river, still far ahead. After a while the cattle, most of them without food or drink for nearly two days, scented the water ahead, and became restive. The emigrants—again with good foresight—unhitched the teams and let them hurry ahead to the river. Otherwise the animals might have become uncontrollable and rushed into the stream with the wagons, wrecking them.

Because of the fine grass and water at the river the party rested for two days. In gratitude they named the stream the Truckee after their friendly chief, and it has retained that name, though Frémont had already called it Salmon Trout River.

The long desert stretch which the party had just crossed was later to be known as the Forty Mile Desert, one of the most dreaded of *jornadas;* in some years it would be dotted with dead cattle and abandoned wagons.

To this point the party had progressed at fair-enough speed and with amazing success, as the result of their own good sense, cooperation, and skill—and also because of some luck. Now, however, it was close to the middle of October, and snow could soon be expected on the higher mountains. Time was running out, and the emigrants had very little idea of where they were or of where they should go.

Their immediate move, however, was clear. The river flowed from a generally western direction; obviously they should ascend along its course.

Their luck still held—"there was plenty of wood, water, grass, and game, and the weather was pleasant." But the canyon through which the river flowed was difficult, and the men had to take the wagons across the stream about once a mile. After some days of this hard going they came out into the fine open country, later known as Truckee Meadows, where Reno now stands.

West of the meadows "the hills began to grow nearer together," and the wagons had to enter the upper Truckee canyon. Here the stream swung back and forth between precipitous walls. On one day they had to cross the river ten times to progress a mile. In places there was nothing for it but to travel in the stream bed, where the passage across rocks threatened to break or overturn the wagons. The men labored hip-deep in the cold water, and the excessive strain wore them down. Things were even worse for the oxen, whose hoofs grew soft from constant immersion and worn down by the rocks until the pain was such that the teams would not pull forward unless the drivers walked beside them in the water, urging them on. A few light snows fell on the mountain-tops roundabout, giving ominous suggestion of what might be happening on the higher mountains ahead, and preventing any halt for rest.

The party, in fact, was very close to being stalled altogether. Then, to make things even worse, snow fell a foot deep, burying the grass beyond reach. In the night the oxen bawled so miserably with hunger that the people almost forgot their own weariness and apprehension. They even gathered pine needles and offered them for fodder. Then just in time to escape disaster, the party came to where some rushes grew tall enough to stand up above the snow. The cattle ate these greedily—so much so, indeed, that two of them died of surfeit. But this food saved the teams, and thereafter the camps were always made at some point where the rushes could be found.

Thus involved with icy water, slippery rocks, rough terrain, and snowy weather, the party struggled on, each mile marking an achievement. Faces grew longer as the days grew shorter. Winter was at hand.

On the evening of November 14 they camped at a forking of the stream. As at the sink, they had reached a point of decision.

The main canyon, which they had been following upstream for so long, now turned definitely to the south. The broader valley of the tributary, they could see, led directly west, toward snowy and craggy mountains which they could suppose to be the main Sierra Nevada.

The old question—south or west? In '41 and '43 the emigrants generally chose to go toward the south, perhaps because the easier road lay in that direction, as it did here. But the emigrants of '44, if they knew what their predecessors had done, realized that nothing was to be gained by going southward. Moreover, we may say that this Stevens Party was dominated by some aggressive determination to strike straight ahead by the shortest road. Once before, at the sink, they had gone west, directly toward California. Here again, at the forking of the stream, they made the same decision. (The spot was at the mouth of Donner Creek, about a mile west of the present town of Truckee.)

But they did not, recklessly, stake everything on one chance. As one of them wrote, they took their decision "after considering the matter fully," by which he probably meant both that the leaders discussed the problem and that a general council of the men (or, at least, of the wagon-owners) voted upon it. The decision was that the main body would press ahead westward, up along the smaller stream, right at the high mountains. A party of six was selected to try the main canyon southward. Here were assigned two of the women, Mrs. Townsend and Ellen Murphy, two of the older Murphy boys, and two of the single men. They were given horses, with two extra ones for pack animals. Some of the party's now scanty provisions went with these pack horses. The women, it is recorded, "had each a change of clothing and some blankets." Each man had a rifle and ammunition. (According to another account, the separation of this party was accidental, but this seems unlikely for many reasons.)

These six were all active and young, and included two women. The emigrants of '44 were perhaps already beginning to notice what later companies learned more fully, that women could endure more than men could. Though the reason for sending this party is nowhere given, it was obviously designed to travel fast and light, unencumbered by wagons, in order to get through to Sutter's Fort as soon as possible. Captain Sutter would thus be alerted, and might send help to the rest of the company, if it should be needed.

The main body with the wagons went two miles west, and then came to the beautiful body of water since known as Donner Lake. Beyond it, they could see the mountain wall, blocking the whole end of the valley, towering up, snow-covered except where the granite rose sheer. They camped and spent several days exploring ahead in an effort to find a practicable pass. Finally they made another decision, though it must have been almost one of desperation. The result was another division. Still, there seems to have been no panic.

Six owners of wagons decided to abandon them here, and to go ahead with the other five wagons and all the oxen. The six to be left were of value in themselves, and contained some valuable cargo. Three young men volunteered to remain with these wagons through the winter to guard them against the Indians, supporting themselves by hunting. But, for the moment, these three went ahead to help.

The party then set out with the five wagons, and managed without much difficulty to work along the north shore of the lake. About half a mile beyond the lake, one can still see a little meadow, which may well be the site where they then encamped. From this base they began the laborious and almost impossible operation of getting the wagons up the steep granite slope rising more than a thousand feet above them. There was already snow on the mountains, two feet deep. Fully to appreciate the courage of this attempt, we must also remember that these people were from the flat lands of the Middle West, and had no experience with alpine conditions.

First they unloaded the wagons and carried the contents to the top of the pass. Considered among the contents were, of course, the smaller children. Then with double teams—made possible because of the abandonment of half the wagons—they started up with the wagons themselves.

Just where they went is something that no one has been able yet to determine. The present writer, for one, has spent hours clambering over the granite, and has never discovered what seemed to be a possible route. One must remember that the building of the railroad and of modern highways has destroyed much of the original appearance of the pass.

The critical point was halfway up, at a vertical ledge about ten feet high. The people were here at the point of abandoning the wagons. Finally, however, they found a rift in the ledge, just wide enough to allow one ox to pass. Unyoking the oxen, they took them up through this passageway, one at a time. They then reyoked them on the somewhat more level ground at the top of the ledge, and let chains down to a wagon below. The oxen then pulled from above and the men heaved up on the wheels from below, and the wagons were taken up, one by one.

Like the ancient Israelites, whose Scriptures many of them read so earnestly, some emigrants were quick to see divine intervention. Stevens himself, as an old man, told how at this time he prayed earnestly and was granted a vision showing him how the pass could be surmounted.

The day of the crossing was probably November 25, 1844. It may be considered the date of the opening of the California

Trail. If wagons could be taken over the pass, there was every reason to believe that they could be taken down the western slope, in spite of the canyons.

From the top the three young men turned back to establish their camp with the six wagons.

The main body moved ahead, about three days' march, downhill, over very rough country.. They must have pushed hard to reach lower altitudes, for obviously a crisis, perhaps two crises, were upon them. Winter was at hand, and one of the wives, it may be, was approaching her time.

But the west slope falls away gradually, and at the end of the third day they were still in high rugged country. That night, with a storm about to break, they camped near the present Big Bend. Perhaps at about the same time Mrs. Martin Murphy was taken in labor.

Like Ellen Independence Miller, the child then born was named commemoratively Elizabeth Yuba Murphy, the middle name taken from that of the mountain stream by which she was born. (The name may have been given later, since the parents can scarcely have known the name "Yuba" at the time of the birth.)

In a wagon train a woman expected to be allowed a few hours for her labor, and then to go on. But now, perhaps, the combination of difficulties was too much— three or four feet of new-fallen snow, a trackless and unknown country ahead, rough mountains, and a newborn baby.

Another decision was reached. At this mountain camp would be left the five wagons, with the women and children, under the charge of two men. Most of the cattle were butchered, to be left as a food supply at the camp. The weather would be cold enough, it was hoped, to keep the meat from spoiling. The men built a log cabin.

After a week in this camp, seventeen men proceeded on, floundering through the snow, driving the few remaining cattle ahead of them.

They left about December 6, and after a day or two of descent must have got out of the snow. They went ahead, apparently with no especial difficulty, and arrived at Sutter's Fort in about a week.

They found the six members of the horseback party already

73

there, having arrived a few days earlier. Their story could have been briefly told. Ascending the canyon toward the south, they had come out, after a day or two of travel, on the shore of a large and beautiful mountain lake. (They thus became the first white people to arrive at the shore of Lake Tahoe, though Frémont had sighted its waters from the mountains to the south, nine months earlier.) They went along the west shore of the lake "for some distance," and then turned westward, across an easy pass, probably at the head of McKinney Creek. They then descended along a stream, which proved to be one of the tributaries of the American River. When the big snowstorm struck, they were already low enough to escape being badly caught. With some adventures and much tightening of belts, they managed to get through without ever being reduced to an extremity.

Two sections of the badly scattered party had thus arrived. The next move should have been for the men to organize their relief expedition and go back after the women and children. But California was in the throes of a revolution, and Captain Sutter was up to his ears in it. Twenty-one American riflemen, suddenly descending from the mountains, must have seemed a heaven-sent reinforcement. To get them to join his ranks, he could entice, cajole, or even threaten. At the same time he could argue convincingly that the deep snow made an expedition into the mountains impossible, and that the women and children, with the aid of two men, could live through until spring on the food available. In any case, the twenty-one rode off to the south— Dr. Townsend as surgeon, the rest in the ranks. They left Sutter's Fort on New Year's Day.

As to what happened in the camp at Big Bend, no daily record exists. The location is a snowy one, and the cabin would soon have been almost buried. About the middle of December, the people there had a surprise. Foster and Montgomery, the older two of the three young men who had been left to guard the wagons at the lake, came stumbling in on improvised snowshoes. Young Mose Schallenberger was not with them.

These two had a grim story.... Going back to the lower end of the lake, they had all been in good spirits, expecting to pass a pleasant winter. The only animals remaining with them were two skinny cows. The three men at once set about building

74

a log cabin, making good use of the cows by having them drag logs. In two days a snug-enough little cabin was ready, twelve by fourteen feet, roofed with hides and pine boughs. At one end was a large log chimney, faced on the inside with stones. There was no window, and only an opening for a door. They did not fear the cold, since they had plenty of bedding from the six wagons that they were guarding.

Their first night in the cabin must have been that one on which the main party arrived at Big Bend. Doubtless the three young men looked forward to going hunting the next day. Like the Middle Westerners they were, they supposed that the winter would be more or less open, with the snow melting between storms and game always available. They naturally did not know that the region of the pass is one of the snowiest in the entire world.

That night the storm broke, and snow fell to the depth of three feet! The young men were surprised, but not especially worried. The weather was not very cold, and they decided that the snow would soon melt. Instead, it continued to fall. They then slaughtered the two cows, to keep them from starving to death, and hung the carcasses up to freeze. The snow was now so deep and so fluffy that they could flounder through it only with the greatest difficulty, and were barely able to get firewood. Fortunately, Foster and Montgomery knew something about snowshoes. They took some of the wagon bows, which were of flexible hickory, and bent them into shape. These they filled in with networks of rawhide thongs. The crude makeshifts were heavy and clumsy and very exhausting to use. Nevertheless, thus equipped, the three went out hunting, but saw nothing except now and then the track of a coyote or fox, when there had happened to be a little crust on the snow.

After a week of this they realized that there would be no game in such deep snow. The deer had gone to lower levels; the bears were hibernating. They also realized that the meat of their two half-starved cows would not suffice to keep them through the winter. At last, facing starvation, they decided to attempt the crossing on their snowshoes. They dried some of their beef, and each of them took about ten pounds of it, along with a pair of blankets, a rifle, and ammunition.

Progress through the snow was both slow and exhausting.

The men themselves had little skill at snowshoeing, and progressed by sheer hard work. Foster and Montgomery were in their full strength, but Mose was only an overgrown boy, having just passed his eighteenth birthday. He failed rapidly. The awkward and unaccustomed motions gave him cramps in the leg muscles, so that several times he fell down in the snow, and his companions had to wait for him until the paroxysm passed. Toward evening, he could move no more than fifty yards without stopping to rest.

At nightfall they reached the summit of the pass, cut down a tree, and managed to build a fire. At an altitude of seven thousand feet the cold was bitter, and they fed the blaze all night to keep from freezing. From cold and worry they could not sleep. They did not know the tricks of camping in deep snow, and the fire gradually melted its way down. In the morning it was sunk into a circle fifteen feet across and equally deep, to the bare ground.

They ate some dried beef, and gloomily considered what to do. Mose was so stiff that he could hardly move. If he should fail on the way, his comrades could not carry him, and he would have to be left to die. He realized the situation, and courageously said that he would return to the cabin and live as long as possible on the small amount of beef still remaining there. When it failed, he would try the mountain again. The others reluctantly assented to this plan. If they got through, they said, they would organize a relief party to come back for him.

No one said the obvious thing, that Mose would not be able, in his condition, even to get back to the cabin, and would die in the snow. Even if he should get back, what chance would he have? They prepared to leave. The English language and the American temperament supplied little equipment for such a situation. They shook hands and said, "Good-by." Foster and Montgomery went to the west, and left young Mose there, a lonely figure.

After their halt at the women's camp the two went on to the west, and with the advantage of the downgrade got through to Sutter's without too great difficulty.

The long weeks of winter passed, with the snow piling deeper and deeper upon the mountains. Sutter's "army" had joined Governor Micheltorena and gone slowly southward. Some of the Americans got tired of the whole business and "left"—"deserted" being hardly a term to use in connection with such informal

warfare. Some of them returned to Sutter's Fort, having decided that it was now time to see what could be done for the women and children. Among these men was Dennis Martin, whose old father had been one of the two men left with the women. Martin, having lived in Canada, was familiar with snowshoes and their use, and he was strong and active. Before he left the fort, Mrs. Townsend approached him, and pleaded that he should make an attempt to see what had happened to Mose, her younger brother, whom she had reared as a son. Martin gave his word.

About February 20 he left the fort on his bold solitary expedition into the snow. Going into the mountains, he first met James Miller and his young son, who had left the women's camp and were making their way out on their own. A day or so later Martin reached the women's camp. Conditions were bad. Mrs. Patterson and her children, for two weeks, had been living on hides. Such extremity implies that the basic individualism of the frontier had reasserted itself, each family using its own food without regard to the general need. At least there had been no deaths.

February had apparently been a month with few storms, so that the snow had settled and somewhat consolidated, and traveling was easier. Plans were now made to get the women and children down to the valley, and probably some of the other men followed in along Martin's track to help.

Martin himself, though there was small chance that Mose was still alive, remembered his promise to Mrs. Townsend. He gambled on fair weather, since a storm would have trapped him.

In late afternoon he crossed the summit, and a little before sunset came in sight of the camp. He then saw—a short distance from the cabin, standing in the snow—the unkempt and emaciated figure of Moses Schallenberger.

The story of that solitary wintry ordeal can be told as Schallenberger himself dictated it to his daughter forty years later.*

The feeling of loneliness that came over me as the two men turned away I cannot express, though it will never be forgotten, while the, 'Good-by, Mose,' so sadly and reluctantly spoken, rings in my ears to-day. I desire to say here that both Foster and Mont-

* For the full text of Schallenberger's narrative, see *The Opening of the California Trail,* University of California Press, Berkeley and Los Angeles, 1953.

gomery were brave, warm-hearted men, and it was by no fault of theirs that I was thus left alone. It would only have made matters worse for either of them to remain with me, for the quarter of beef at the cabin would last me longer alone, and thus increase my chances of escape. While our decision was a sad one, it was the only one that could be made.

My companions had not been long out of sight before my spirits began to revive, and I began to think, like Micawber, that something might 'turn up.' So I strapped on my blankets and dried beef, shouldered my gun, and began to retrace my steps to the cabin. It had frozen during the night and this enabled me to walk on our trail without the snow-shoes. This was a great relief, but the exertion and sickness of the day before had so weakened me that I think I was never so tired in my life as when, just a little before dark, I came in sight of the cabin. The door-sill was only nine inches high, but I could not step over it without taking my hands to raise my leg. [A short omission in the original text.] As soon as I was able to crawl around the next morning I put on my snowshoes, and, taking my rifle, scoured the country thoroughly for foxes. The result was as I had expected—just as it had always been—plenty of tracks, but no fox.

Discouraged and sick at heart, I came in from my fruitless search and prepared to pass another night of agony. As I put my gun in the corner, my eyes fell upon some steel traps that Captain Stevens had brought with him and left behind in his wagon. In an instant the thought flashed across my mind, 'If I can't shoot a coyote or fox, why not trap one?' There was inspiration in the thought, and my spirits began to rise immediately. The heads of the two cows I cut to pieces for bait, and, having raked the snow from some fallen trees, and found other sheltered places, I set my traps. That night I went to bed with a lighter heart, and was able to get some sleep.

As soon as daylight came I was out to inspect the traps. I was anxious to see them and still I dreaded to look. After some hesitation I commenced the examination, and to my great delight I found in one of them a starved coyote. I soon had his hide off and his flesh roasted in a Dutch oven. I ate this meat, but it was horrible. I next tried boiling him, but it did not improve the flavor. I cooked him in every possible manner my imagination, spurred by hunger, could suggest, but could not get him into a condition where he could be eaten without revolting my stomach. But for three days this was all I had to eat. On the third night I caught two foxes. I roasted one of them, and the meat, though entirely devoid of fat, was

delicious. I was so hungry that I could easily have eaten a fox at two meals, but I made one last me two days.

I often took my gun and tried to find something to shoot, but in vain. Once I shot a crow that seemed to have got out of his latitude and stopped on a tree near the cabin. I stewed the crow, but it was difficult for me to decide which I liked best, crow or coyote. I now gave my whole attention to trapping, having found how useless it was to hunt for game. I caught, on an average, a fox in two days, and every now and then a coyote. These last-named animals I carefully hung up under the brush shed on the north side of the cabin, but I never got hungry enough to eat one of them again. There were eleven hanging there when I came away. I never really suffered for something to eat, but was in almost continual anxiety for fear the supply would give out. For instance, as soon as one meal was finished I began to be distressed for fear I could not get another one. My only hope was that the supply of foxes would not become exhausted.

One morning two of my traps contained foxes. Having killed one, I started for the other, but, before I could reach it, the fox had left his foot in the trap and started to run. I went as fast as I could to the cabin for my gun, and then followed him. He made for a creek about a hundred yards from the house, into which he plunged and swam across. He was scrambling up the opposite bank when I reached the creek. In my anxiety at the prospect of losing my breakfast, I had forgotten to remove a greasy wad that I usually kept in the muzzle of my gun to prevent it from rusting, and when I fired, the ball struck the snow about a foot above reynard's back. I reloaded as rapidly as possible, and as the gun was one of the old-fashioned flint-locks that primed itself, it did not require much time. But, short as the time was, the fox had gone about forty yards when I shot him. Now the problem was to get him to camp. The water in the stream was about two and a half feet deep and icy cold. But I plunged in, and, on reaching the other side, waded for forty yards through the snow, into which I sank to my arms, secured my game, and returned the way I came. I relate this incident to illustrate how much affection I had for the fox. It is strange that I never craved anything to eat but good fat meat. For bread or vegetables I had no desire. Salt I had in plenty, but never used. I had just coffee enough for one cup, and that I saved for Christmas.

My life was more miserable than I can describe. The daily struggle for life and the uncertainty under which I labored were very wearing. I was always worried and anxious, not about myself alone, but in regard to the fate of those who had gone forward. I would lie awake nights and think of these things, and revolve in my mind what I would do when the supply of foxes became exhausted. The quarter of beef I had not touched, and I resolved to dry it, and, when the foxes were all gone, to take my gun, blankets, and dried beef and follow in the footsteps of my former companions.

Fortunately, I had a plenty of books, Dr. Townsend having brought out quite a library. I used often to read aloud, for I longed for some sound to break the oppressive stillness. For the same reason, I would talk aloud to myself. At night I built large fires and read by the light of the pine knots as late as possible, in order that I might sleep late the next morning, and thus cause the days to seem shorter. What I wanted most was enough to eat, and the next thing I tried hardest to do was to kill time. I thought the snow would never leave the ground, and the few months I had been living here seemed years.

One evening, a little before sunset, about the last of February, as I was standing a short distance from my cabin, I thought I could distinguish the form of a man moving towards me. I first thought it was an Indian, but very soon I recognized the familiar face of Dennis Martin.

Under the ever-present threat of a storm, which might well bring death, no time was to be lost. That very evening Martin made better snowshoes for Mose, and instructed him in their use. Next morning, they set out on the trail, and managed to get through.

At the same time, the women and children were being moved down below the snow line. Finally, on March 1, this rear guard safely entered the Sacramento Valley, a year to the day from the time when some of them had left their homes in Missouri. . . .

In the history of the California Trail the year '44 was critical, and the achievement of the Stevens Party was decisive. After these wagons followed the migration which poured yearly into central California.

This success was achieved at a minimum of cost. No lives were lost, and the party, in fact, arrived two stronger than when it had set out. Though the oxen were gradually sacrificed for food, many of the horses were taken through, and no wagons were lost. After the snow melted in July of '45, some of the men returned, driving oxen ahead of them, and with no great difficulty retrieved the wagons, even those which had been left at the lake. The goods in these latter, however, had been removed, except for the firearms, of which the Indians were afraid.

Since the Stevens Party enjoyed no special advantage of equipment, we must credit its success to the courage, energy, and good judgment of the men who composed it. Even individuals about whom we otherwise know little stand out brilliantly in some particular test—Hitchcock in taking the wagons across the cutoff, Schallenberger in his struggle for survival, and Martin in his heroic solitary journey across the snow. So also the six isolated members of the horseback party handled themselves well.

The successful outcome of the enterprise depended particularly upon two decisions: the one made at the sink; the other, at the mouth of Donner Creek. In making the first, the emigrants were guided by the information supplied by Truckee. In making the second, they seem to have been guided chiefly by a simple and primitive instinct to plunge ahead directly toward their goal.

We may also credit the success to good leadership, but as to just who were the leaders, there may be some question. Some have picked out Greenwood, and have attributed everything to him. But Schallenberger's narrative states that Greenwood knew nothing about the country west of the Rocky Mountains, and that account seldom mentions him. Greenwood was useful to have along, but there is no evidence that he exerted any leadership during the latter part of the journey. We must conclude the same about that other old-time Westerner, Hitchcock.

The Martin Murphys, father and son, were undoubtedly key figures in the party. As the heads of a large and well-knit family group, they could certainly have wielded a veto power. But they lacked Western experience, and therefore could scarcely initiate plans. Since the family was so numerous in the party and since it was later well known in California, some historians have used the term Murphy Party. Others have referred to the Townsend Party, since the doctor was a prominent member and was impressive to some people.

The official elected captain, however, was Elisha Stevens, and the party should, by established custom, bear his name. As the story of the Bartleson Party makes clear, the titular captain was not necessarily the leader. Stevens, however, seems to have been a real leader, as far as the scanty records allow us to make judgment. The few reminiscences attribute high qualities to him. But historians have not dealt generously with Stevens. Other men have been eulogized, and the party has been called by their names.

It was, of course, his own fault. The qualities which enabled a man to face and overcome the desert and the mountains, and to lead a wagon train to California were not those which necessarily enabled a man to succeed in the cutthroat competitive civilization which was soon to arise in California.

Stevens—solitary, taciturn, eccentric—could only remain on the outskirts of such a society. He worked for a while as a blacksmith. He returned to trapping for some years, living in the mountains of Santa Clara County, where a creek preserves his name. Finally, for twenty-three years he passed a hermit-like existence on a piece of land at the present site of Bakersfield, raising poultry and tending bees. His neighbors knew him as a kindly old fellow, who indulged in such harmless eccentricities as wearing his hat indoors.

In later life he may have become a little bitter. The chief gateway to California, through which he had brought wagons and which he may be said to have discovered, was called Donner Pass. The transcontinental railroad used that same pass, and in '69 was opened with a great celebration. But no one then honored the old man. He lingered on until '84, and his eightieth year.

When he died and for many years afterward, his only memorial was little Stevens Creek, which flows undistinguished into the southern end of San Francisco Bay. Yet time has its revenges. The recent increase of population in California since World War II has caused a great urban development to arise along Stevens Creek Road.*

* There was in March, 1962, a strong movement to place Stevens's name upon the summit where the new freeway (Interstate 80) crosses the Sierra, about two miles north of Donner Pass, the place of the '44 crossing.

CHAPTER FIVE

AFTER THE SUCCESS of '44 the number of emigrants traveling the California Trail increased so greatly that the story itself must reflect that change. No longer can individual wagons or even individual parties be catalogued.

In a more subtle way, also, the story is altered. It had involved, in the earliest years, almost wholly the struggle of man against the forces of nature. From '45 onward, it became more and more the competitive struggle of man against man. For, it would seem, once men have overcome nature, they inevitably begin to fight one against another.

In '45 the story started at the western end. . . . When the snow had melted sufficiently from the mountains, old Caleb Greenwood and his two sons set out on horseback. He was going partly on his own, and partly on the behalf of the great Sutter.

From his fort in the Sacramento Valley, Captain Johann Augustus Sutter held a vast land grant, almost to be compared in size with his own ancestral Switzerland. But he was land poor. He needed people to build up a prosperous colony, and he was willing to do much to get them. Greenwood, the rough old squaw man, was a curious forerunner of the suave public-relations emissaries who have since promoted California, but that was just about what he was. In addition to doing Sutter's job, he also planned to hire himself out again as a guide and thus to collect $2.50 for each wagon.

As he went eastward, he also worked out a better route. Most notably, he turned sharply to the north a mile east of Donner Lake, and swinging around through Dog Valley, rejoined the old route ten miles above the meadows. (So well did he do his work, that the main road followed through Dog Valley for eighty years, until 1925.)

As the Greenwoods came on, the emigrants were already organizing. In fact, some of them had been getting ready all winter.

There was William B. Ide, for instance, a prosperous Illinois farmer with some young children. He was almost fifty— old enough, you would say, to know better. Still, a look at his record shows that moving was the most natural thing in the world for him. Born in Massachusetts, he had lived in Vermont, Kentucky, Ohio, and Illinois, and at more than one place in some of those states. He planned to set out with three wagons.

During the winter he had personally selected the wood for two of these wagons, and had had the running gear made to order. Such procedure was common. Here and there a factory was manufacturing wagons, but most of them were still being made in local shops, where a careful man could be sure of what went into them and of how they were put together. Flawless and well-seasoned wood was essential. One of the worst things that could happen was to break a tongue or axle when you were a thousand miles out, or to have wheels go wobbly because of shrinkage.

So, we can be sure, Ide looked well to the wood, and selected the right kind for the right part—elm or Osage orange for hubs, oak or hickory for spokes, ash or beech for felloes, ash for framework, hickory for tongues and hounds. (The deacon who planned the one-horse shay was not the only man who knew his woods.) The well-built wagon of those days, though simple when compared with an automobile or airplane, was built with more sophistication than most people now realize.

Ide undoubtedly specified wrought-iron reinforcement around the tongue and hounds, and the wheel tires were of iron.

As for the wagon-beds, they did not require such specialized

84

carpentry, and Ide made them himself, as many farmers did. There was plenty of time available during the winter. He would have used maple or poplar for the wagon-beds. He also made the bows, those long strips of flexible hickory by which the wagon-covers were supported. Mrs. Ide and young Sarah sewed up the canvas covers.

Finally the wagons, including the covers, were neatly painted a light gray—an unusual touch of distinction. In bold black letters on the back of what was to be the hindmost wagon was painted OREGON, since that was the intended destination.

The Ides then set out with thirteen people, including five young men to drive teams and herd cattle "for their board and passage." There were four children, if we may include seventeen-year-old Sarah as one of them. To pull the wagons they had four-teen yoke of working oxen. They also had 165 loose cattle, and the usual riding horses. Sarah had a pony. The wagons were laden with six months' provisions. The Ides should be able to get through if anyone did, and in some comfort.

Other emigrants were the Bonney brothers, Jarvis and Truman, with their families. Truman, like Townsend of '44, was a backwoods doctor. Jarvis was a millwright, carpenter, and cab-inetmaker. They lived in a part of Illinois where malaria was bad, but Jarvis had a special reason for heading west. He loved to fish, and he had heard great tales of trout and salmon in Oregon. Considering what a fisherman will do, we may accept this as as good a reason as any for setting out on a two-thousand-mile journey by wagon.

This year, as in '44, the migration was definitely a family affair. The muster role of one party showed: men, 31; women, 32; children, 61. This party had twenty-four wagons, so that there would have been an average of three adults and three children to a wagon—definitely high. The party had 212 cattle, of which about half would have been in the loose herd.

In '45 many emigrants were taking off from St. Joseph, Missouri. There was much to be said for doing so. "St. Jo" was fifty miles farther on the way than Independence was. By ferry-ing the Missouri River there, at an established town, you elim-inated the necessity of depending upon the not-always-reliable ferry kept by the Indians over the Kansas River.

From both points of take-off the trains started shortly after the first of May. On the plains they formed a straggling caravan of several hundred wagons.

Almost everyone was bound for Oregon—naturally enough, because no one as yet was sure that a wagon could be taken to California. Still, some of them had read a little book published early that year. It was by Lansford W. Hastings, and was called *The Emigrants' Guide to Oregon and California.* It offered descriptions of both places, more glowing for California than for Oregon. It also briefly described the routes, and offered such a trap for the unwary as the statement: "Wagons can be as readily taken from Fort Hall to the bay of San Francisco, as they can, from the States to Fort Hall." Only a careful reader would notice that there is no statement that wagons "have been taken" over that route. Actually, Hastings had left California in '44, before the Stevens Party had arrived. His statements about the route to be traveled were vague and overoptimistic to the point of irresponsibility. One emigrant of '45 mentioned having read the book, and that it influenced his decision to start for California. But any careful man would have asked for more precise information, and only about fifteen wagons were, in some vague way, California-bound. On the other hand, many of the people headed for Oregon must have had California in the back of their minds. . . .

This year we have much testimony from an objective commentator, one who was physically present, but mentally removed from the emigrants by several degrees of social status. This was Captain Philip St. George Cooke, of an old Virginia family, West Point, '27. Just why he was on the plains that summer is a matter of significance in the history of the trail.

To date the government had shown little interest in the migration; even Frémont had been instructed to make general explorations, and he had not paid much attention to the road. But the newly established Polk administration was expansion-minded. So, this summer, Colonel Stephen Watts Kearny had been ordered to march a detachment through South Pass along the emigrant trail. He was to look for a site where a post could be established to protect the trail from the Indians. In addition, his march would in itself be a military demonstration. He had with him five companies of his First Dragoons, a dozen supply wagons, and a few little howitzers.

Cooke was in command of one of the companies. He was of a literary family—a brother being John Esten Cooke the novelist. We need not be surprised, then, that the captain later published a book. He was, unfortunately, overwhelmed with the desire to be literary, so that the logophily of his generalizations and philosophical reflections often becomes stomach-turning. But, in between, he produced some clear-cut vignettes of emigrant life.

On first approach he wrote, "we soon espied on a distant ridge, the wagon-tops of the emigrants—dim, white spots, like sails at sea." Coming nearer, he observed more closely:

Here was a great thoroughfare—broad and well-worn—the longest and best natural road perhaps in the world. Endless seemed the procession of wagons; mostly very light, and laden only with children and provisions, and the most necessary articles for families; and drawn generally by two yokes of oxen; some three hundred wagons or families, they said, were in advance.

Inevitably followed a comparison with the patriarchs of Israel, traveling with their flocks and herds.

The women, particularly, interested him.

Poor women, indeed! Three weeks ago they parted from every comfort—severed ties of kindred, even of country.... What privations are here; what exposure to bad weather, cooking unsheltered.

He expressed his wonder: "Is it possible that many of them *willingly* follow thus their life's partners for *all* the 'worse'?" But their cheerfulness puzzled him:

Who knows! We passed an old lady of sixty whom I have often seen dispensing a comfortable hospitality, and I *cannot* believe that she is content to give up the repose which her years, her virtues, and her sex entitle her to; but strange! She wore a cheerful smile, and said her health improved.

Again, he saw a woman driving her own oxen, and learned that her husband had died. But before being moved too much to pity, he also learned, to his amusement, that she was reputed ready to accept any reasonable offer from some other man who wished to assume the double responsibility of husband and ox-driver.

A wedding (there was the usual preacher along) piqued his curiosity. Was it, he speculated, a true pastoral romance? Or was it a *mariage de convenance*, resulting from the remarkable coldness of the prairie nights, and the well-known fact that two can sleep warmer than one? The groom, he noted, as "a driver of oxen—a homespun matter-of-fact lad . . . clad in dirty woolens." The two made up their marriage bed, not under the stars or in some sylvan grot, but in a wagon. Thereupon—when the bride could scarcely have been bedded—some friends of the groom, as a substitute for a shivaree, ran the wagon down into the hollow and left it all topsy-turvy.

But tragedy dogged the heels of comedy. "We passed this morning an emigrant camp; they were lying by,—had lost oxen, frightened off by buffalo,—several persons were sick—a poor woman at the point of death."

On another occasion two men told him of "the great discouragement of the women, who even wish to return." They said that some of the men, too, were so disposed, especially those who had lost many cattle. The men, themselves, were ignorant of what lay ahead, and scarcely knew where they were going. Then followed the inescapable comparison, to the compulsive migration of small animals like the lemmings. At the same time, the captain admired their pluck, and found them "pure democrats all, and independent as woodsawyers." Whether they went to Oregon or California, he thought made little difference—"movers they will be to the end of the chapter."

He considered also their motivation. Should we admire them as "first laborers in a great work," carrying civilization to the ends of the earth? Or should we consider them mere reckless vagrants? He confessed an inclination to the less complimentary opinion.

So the captain rode on—a year later to command the Mormon battalion on its march to California, and in due course, though a Virginian, to be a general of cavalry in the Army of the Potomac.

And tough old Colonel Kearny marched his men up to

South Pass and then, like the King of France, marched them down again. He later recommended against the establishment of a post. Preferable, to keep the Sioux in order, he thought, would be an occasional demonstration such as his own.

Yes, five companies of dragoons, each company on horses of matched color, with guidons flying, and bugles blowing! And an occasional sounding off by the loud-mouthed howitzers!

Doubtless the Sioux were impressed, but one wonders how deeply. They may have had their own thoughts.

Those big clumsy American horses could never match the Sioux ponies in rough country. Bow and lance against pistol and long-knife? It might be interesting to try, sometime!

Just now the Sioux were happy enough. To have sport and win honor they could always go and fight the Crows or the Snakes or the Blackfeet.

Their warriors were seldom sex-starved, and probably did not lust after paleface maidens, though many an emigrant girl thought that they did.

Besides, those old friends of the Sioux, the mountain-men —"Broken Hand" and the others—told them to be good to the strange people who went through, always toward the sunset, with the wagons pulled by spotted buffalo.

One imagines also that life in the tepee at times was boring, and that the Sioux had a good deal of fun watching the wagon trains and indulging in an occasional prank that scared some white people half to death.

The emigrants passed through quickly. The buffalo that they killed were not worth counting. Besides, you could do a little trading with them—ponies and moccasins for various amusing little objects, and sometimes even for that strange burning drink which gave a man such a godlike sense of being above and beyond the world. And, if you went into their camp, well armed and putting on a show of being dangerous, the white people quickly would give you something to eat.

So, whether because of Colonel Kearny and his men on the big horses, or for other reasons, the Sioux were friendly—or, if not exactly friendly, they bided their time.

Into the mountains, over South Pass, and beyond, there is little record, good evidence that the journey was a prosperous one. It was a drought year, and the parties sometimes split into sections so that the stock would have a better chance to find grazing. In compensation, the streams were low, and even the North Fork of the Platte was fordable.

On the Sweetwater some of the emigrants met and talked with Joe Walker. He may already have seen Greenwood, and learned of the success of '44. He told the emigrants that it was very difficult but they could get through to California if they lightened wagons and had good luck and were careful. Some young men traveling without families thought it sounded good enough, and decided to try for California.

At Green River a large party of Snakes barred the way. They were the most friendly of all the Indians, but they had decided that they might as well profit by charging something for safe passage through their country. The emigrants corralled the wagons, and put up a firm front, refusing to pay anything. After a day and a night the Snakes decided not to push the matter. They came in, made friends, and commenced trading horses.

Some of the parties went by Fort Bridger, and others by-passed that post by taking the cutoff where Hitchcock had guided the Stevens Party. On the cutoff, near Green River, upon a cliff of soft rock now called Names Hill, even then bearing the names of many of the mountain-men, one of the emigrants entered his name on July 25, and you can still read T. BONNEY and the date.

Possibly, old Caleb rode as far east as where the cutoff split off, and guided some of the wagons across it. At least he became associated with it in some way, so that in the next few years it was usually called Greenwood's Cutoff.

The organization of the various companies held together pretty well until they were within a few days' journey of Fort Hall. Then everyone stampeded to get there as soon as possible. At the end of the first week of August the wagons began pulling in.

At the fort some of the emigrants met Greenwood. We had better put it "the Greenwoods," for with the old man were not only John and Britain, but also Sam, aged sixteen, who had been picked up somewhere.

Among Caleb's many endowments were an effective command of language and a tongue seldom weary. He circulated among the emigrants, talking. His theme was always one, "Come to California!" And far be it from any present-day Californian to suggest that he did not have a good argument!

Among the early arrivals at the fort were the Bonneys. (Jarvis Bonney was the one who was going to Oregon because of the good fishing.) One of the Bonney boys was named Benjamin Franklin, and he was about seven. Whether he remembered what happened, or described it from family tradition makes little difference. He certainly thought that he remembered, and we can let him take the description over.

Greenwood was a very picturesque old man. He was dressed in buckskins and had a long heavy beard and used very picturesque language. He called the Oregon emigrants together the first evening we were in Fort Hall and made a talk. He said the road to Oregon was dangerous on account of the Indians ... to California there was an easy grade and crossing the mountains would not be difficult[!]. He said that Captain Sutter would have ten Californians meet the emigrants who would go and that Sutter would supply them with plenty of potatoes, coffee and dried beef. He also said he would help the emigrants over the mountains with their wagons and that to every head of a family who would settle near Sutter's Fort, Captain Sutter would give six sections [!] of land of his Spanish grant land.

Some of this was true, and some was not—or was highly exaggerated. (But if boosters had always stuck to the bare truth, the frontier settlement in the United States might still be at the Appalachians.) Greenwood's kernel of truth, however, was of the utmost importance, that is, that the road had actually been opened to California. That was correct, and no one seems to have doubted it—and it made all the difference in the world.

After Greenwood had finished, there was a free-for-all argument among the emigrants, and it almost developed into a free-for-all fight. Some said that land titles were uncertain in California, and that it was a foreign country. Others said that it would soon be a part of the United States. Then the first ones said that that would mean war, and they did not want to get their families involved in a war. Finally the captain of the train,

91

who was a strong champion for Oregon, made a flag-waving speech in which he appealed to them all to go and make Oregon for sure a part of the United States and not to go to California and aid Sutter's ambitions.

The meeting broke up in a good deal of excitement and hard feeling, and the men went back to their wagons, to talk the matter over with the womenfolks.

The next morning it was sheer melodrama. One thinks of those great scenes when some commander draws a line on the ground with the point of his sword, and asks his followers to step to one side or the other, and are they mice or men. We must grant that the words are those of Ben Bonney as he thought he remembered them years later.

Next morning old Caleb Greenwood with his boys stepped out to one side and said: "All you who want to go to California drive out from the main train and follow me. You will find there are no Indians to kill you, the roads are better, and you will be allowed to take up more land in California than in Oregon, the climate is better. [Note that!] There is plenty of hunting and fishing [here, perhaps, he turned to Jarvis Bonney], and the rivers are full of salmon."

That last touch may have done it. Jarvis Bonney, the fisherman, was the first to pull over, and behind him, his brother Truman. Then went Sam Kinney, a gigantic Texan; then a man named Dodson and a widow named Teters. When someone counted, eight wagons were lined up for California.

This was no sentimental parting. From the Oregon wagons they were yelling over, to quote the rather improbable words that Ben Bonney put into their mouths, "Good-bye, we will never see you again. Your bones will whiten in the desert or be gnawed by the wild animals in the mountains."

The wagons with the four Greenwoods moved ahead. The old man guided them for three days, far enough to get them turned off on the trail toward California and to a point from which they could not well return. Then he left them with the three boys as guides, and hurried back to pick up some more emigrants.

He did even better with the main body than he had done

with the advance guard. As one of the Oregon emigrants wrote complainingly, Greenwood told "the most extravagant tales . . . respecting the dangers that awaited a trip to Oregon." He stressed the perils of the two crossings of the Snake River and the hostility of the Indians.

The Ides now decided to go to California. The OREGON on the back of their wagon must have been fading out by this time anyway. Also for California was Solomon Sublette, leading a well-equipped and fast-moving party. He was the youngest of the five brothers who had made the family name famous among mountain-men and fur-traders. Still another to shift away from Oregon was Jacob R. Snyder, who kept a diary all the way— a conscientious but dull chronicler.

Altogether Greenwood got at least fifty wagons. That meant $125 in his pocket, not a bad sum for an old mountain-man in these bad times when you could not make much by trapping. Since he already must have totaled an enormous debit of lies in the Great Account Book, the comparatively few more that he had told on this occasion probably did not burden him.

Things for California were looking up! Fifty wagons would mean about 250 people, including children—five times as many as in '44.

South from Goose Creek and along the Humboldt the wagons straggled out over a long distance. Sometimes, even, a single wagon was by itself, as when the Ides with their family wagon camped one night all alone, with nothing but a watchdog on guard.

And Indians? Nobody paid much attention to Indians, at least for a while. These were only Diggers, anyway. Old Greenwood must have told them what miserable creatures the Diggers were. And the three Greenwood boys, proud of being half Crow, would hold them in contempt. They were not really warriors at all; they fought in self-defense, and had no interest in counting coup or taking scalps. They had neither guns nor horses.

Among the Diggers the attitude of the emigrants changed. In the country of such powerful tribes as the Sioux and the Snakes no one in his right mind did anything to provoke trouble. But who was afraid of a Digger? The emigrants, however, did not realize, and perhaps even Greenwood did not know, that the Paiutes, at least, would fight back courageously and toughly if pushed to it.

As you might expect, the Diggers seemed very curious about the wagon trains. Sometimes, by day, you could see their heads poking up from the bushes to watch. Sometimes, at night, you would hear a howling as of coyotes. Then, if you fired a gun, the howling ceased. The emigrants thought that this howling was from Indians, but since real coyotes might have behaved in much the same way, it would be hard telling. Sometimes, also, the Indians came right into camp, wanting to be fed. The emigrants usually gave them something, since it was better to be on the safe side even with Diggers.

Then—it must have been soon after the first wagons entered the Digger country—the big Texan, Sam Kinney, had an idea. Like most of the emigrants, he was moderately well-to-do. He had a big wagon, pulled by four yoke of oxen, and also a comfortable light carriage with springs, called a hack, pulled by a team of mules. Kinney's wife drove the mules, and he had a hired man for the oxen. He himself rode a mule. Kinney was formidable-looking. He was tall and weighed over two hundred pounds. He wore his black hair long, and he had long black mustaches and heavy black eyebrows. This description makes him a good deal like the villain in the melodrama, and that may be exactly what Ben Bonney remembered him as being. For he also had a violent temper, and he boasted of having killed two or three men, besides an unspecified number of "niggers." We must again remember that Ben Bonney, who wrote this description, was only seven at the time, and he must have remembered Kinney as a kind of nightmare figure. Still, another authority describes the man as what in the language of that time was a "hard case."

Kinney developed a portentous scheme. Anyone could have pointed out that Indians were not Negroes, and that slavery was not legal in Mexican territory, where they now were. But the big Texan had his own ideas.

One day his wagon was in the lead, and he saw an Indian in the sagebrush, probably just looking at the train. Kinney ordered his driver to halt, and the others had to halt behind the lead wagon. Kinney got a pair of handcuffs out of the wagon, and someone asked him what he was going to do. He said, "Where I come from we have slaves. I am going to capture that Indian, and take him with me as a slave."

Jarvis Bonney protested, for practical reasons. "The first thing you know, that Indian will escape, and tell the other Indians, and they will kill all of us."

Kinney brushed him aside. "I generally have my way. Any man that crosses me regrets it. I have had to kill two or three men already because they interfered with me. If you want any trouble, you know how to get it."

The Indian continued to watch. Kinney rode through the sagebrush, jumped off the mule, and struck the Indian on the head. He tried to run, but Kinney knocked him down, and with his tremendous size and strength soon snapped the handcuffs. He dragged the Indian back to the hack, fastened a rope around his neck, and the other end of the rope to the rear of the hack.

The other people looked on, horrified, but not daring to interfere. Kinney took a black-snake whip from the hack, and called to his wife to drive on. He lashed the Indian across the bare shoulders as a hint to follow. The Indian threw himself on the ground and was pulled along by the neck. Kinney slashed at him with the whip until he finally got up and walked along behind.

Over a period of several days, this continued. Kinney kept the Indian handcuffed and tied up at night, calling him his man Friday. In the daytime, he tied Friday behind the hack, and slashed him with the whip, as he said, to break his spirit.

At length, judging that this operation was completed, Kinney untied Friday in the daytime, and turned him over to the hired man to break in at driving oxen.

After another week or so, Kinney judged it safe to untie Friday at night, since by this time the train must have moved on into other Indians' territory; besides, Kinney had a hound dog who was wonderfully smart, and who could be counted upon to trail any slave that escaped. If Friday tried to get away, Kinney said, he would follow him with the dog and kill him, as he had killed many Negroes, to show the superiority of the white man. (In fact, one begins to think that Kinney was more interested in beating and eventually killing the Indian than he was in the doubtful project of enslaving him.)

Then, one morning, after a dark and windy night, Friday was gone. Moreover, when Kinney looked around, he discovered that a blanket was missing, a powder horn, some lead, three hams, and his own favorite Kentucky rifle, worth a hundred dollars.

He fell into a terrible fit of rage. Everyone else in the train was glad, but out of sheer terror they sympathized. Kinney called the dog, took another rifle, mounted his mule, and set out.

A fool's errand! In later years, many a white man was to marvel at the way a Digger quickly and completely disappeared into the desert. After all, it was his native habitat. Friday had chosen his time shrewdly, for during the night the wind had blown the sand about, wiping out both tracks and scent. After a futile half day, riding this way and that, Kinney returned, and the train started on.

The incident not only illustrates the problem between emigrants and Indians, but also shows the difficulty that arose from lawlessness in an isolated wagon train. This group apparently consisted of nothing more than the eight wagons which had split off at Fort Hall. They may not even have had an officially elected captain. Aside from Kinney, they seem to have been peaceful and decent people, chiefly from the free states. But they had no mechanism of law by which to restrain Kinney, and merely to have shot him down would have been to commit murder.

This particular group of wagons was destined for even more trouble. . . . With them was John Greenwood, and he, as the story of '44 indicates, had a consuming desire to kill an Indian.

A few of the young men generally rode ahead or on the flanks, as scouts and guards. On September 6, as several of them were thus riding along, an Indian suddenly stood up from the sagebrush, frightening John Greenwood's horse, which reared and almost threw him. The others laughed. John was furious at being humiliated, and cried out he would kill the Indian. There was a moment's confusion. John seized his rifle; the others protested; the Indian raised his hand in sign of friendship; someone called to him in alarm; sensing trouble, he turned to scuttle off. But the rifle spoke, and the Indian fell, face forward.

John immediately spurred his horse, and galloped ahead. The others waited for the wagons to come up. Truman Bonney, the doctor, examining the Indian, found him shot through the lung, dying.

One of the women took a quilt from the wagon, and they laid him on it. They offered him water, but he refused. Not knowing what else to do, and being fearful of reprisal, they drove on a mile, and camped.

At dusk, old Caleb and another son, who had been escorting some other wagons, came riding in. They had found the wounded Indian, and Caleb, in the simple way of the older West, had shot him through the head to put him out of his pain, and had buried the body. When Caleb rode into camp, he naturally thought that Kinney was responsible. Before he could be told anything, he said, "The man who killed that Indian must die."

Jarvis Bonney said, "Your son John shot him."

In a situation that might have served for a Greek tragedy, the old man met the test with austerity. He inquired first, and found that there had been no question of self-defense. He then assumed responsibility, as the guide and leader who had persuaded the emigrants to take this trail—these people who were now threatened with Indian reprisals because of the act of his son. He said, "I will act as judge of this trial. I order that the murderer of the Indian be killed."

He then told the men that whoever saw John must shoot him down like a wild animal. But no one was put to the test. John was not seen again.

Up to this year there had been little difficulty with the desert tribes. Now, immediately, trouble seems to have begun. Indians crept up at night and shot arrows into oxen as they grazed or lay chewing the cud. The animals were seldom killed, but in the morning the only thing to do was to slaughter the wounded ox, cut out a steak or two for breakfast, and go on. Afterward the dark and nearly naked desert people came in and ate what remained.

One morning one of the companies found a young steer thus badly wounded. In this company there was a man named Carter, a doctor of sorts, although his ethics would seem to leave a little to be desired. He took something from his medicine chest, and "poisoned" the ox, so that any Indian that ate its flesh would die. At least that was what "Doctor" Carter said, though he may have been merely trying to impress the yokels. Snyder, who recorded the incident in his diary, seems to have accepted the idea, and he indicates no disapproval of such an indiscriminate method of killing Indians.

A growing hostility during the few weeks while the wagons were passing may account for the anomaly that some of the reminiscences note there was no difficulty with the Indians, although other reminiscences, and Snyder's diary, mention hostile acts. The first parties, it may be, got through ahead of the trouble, and the later parties began to feel the results of the hatred stirred up by the reckless actions of a few whites.

There was little difficulty in the Shoshone country. Trouble began about halfway down the Humboldt, when the emigrants entered the country of the Paiutes, who were inclined to be both enterprising and truculent.

The worst trouble fell upon a small party which seems to have consisted merely of a man and his wife, together with her mother and two grown brothers. Such a group would have had only one or two wagons. According to the story, they were passing through a canyon on the Humboldt, and were there "attacked" by Indians, who killed all the stock except for one yoke of oxen. (More likely, we may think, it was not an open attack, but a stealthy driving-off of the animals at night.) Thus reduced, the three men adopted an expedient which was often to be used later. They cut a wagon down to a two-wheeled cart—not difficult since the running-gear of a wagon was essentially nothing but one cart coupled to another. They then loaded their supplies into the cart, and the people, including the women, were forced to walk.

Anyone knowing that after '45 the nagging depredations of the Indians beset the emigrants along the Humboldt is likely to blame the trouble on Kinney and John Greenwood. Certainly their actions allow of no defense. But as for their causing the Indian troubles, we must remember the cynical folk adage, "If I hadn't done it Monday, someone else would have done it Tuesday!" There is not, in fact, any certainty that the whites were the first aggressors. In '41, Bidwell recorded a horse stolen. In '43 Milton Little was wounded. An Indian took Schallenberger's halter in '44. The desert Shoshones and Paiutes were poverty-stricken and often hungry. They had little sense of private property, and lifted what they could, on the ancient principle of belly-need. On the other side, the emigrants had behind them the tradition of cruel and bitter Indian warfare from the times of Opechancanough and King Philip. Many of them regarded the killing of an Indian as being, on the whole, an act of virtue. Unless we adopt the extreme view that the whites should never have entered America at all, we can scarcely blame them more than the Indians for the bullets that flew by day and the arrows that flew by night.

Toward the end of September the head of the migration left the sink, and thrust out across the Forty-mile Desert. As the Stevens Party had demonstrated, a well-equipped and well-managed wagon train could perform this *jornada* with difficulty but without loss. But in '45 many cattle died of thirst and exhaustion in the desert. One man remembered that when he finally reached the Truckee River, he thought its water the finest he ever drank.

Going up along the Truckee, some emigrants found the Indians already hostile, probably alerted by their kinfolk farther east. A man named Pierce was killed—the first such fatality in the history of the California migration.

At some point a curious incident occurred; like Greenwood's speech-making at Fort Hall and like the troubles with the Indians it indicates the way in which the journey was already ceasing to be man-against-nature and was becoming man-against-man. . . . There was a young unmarried emigrant named Thomas Knight. He had been a storekeeper in Arkansas, but had closed out his business in '44. He built a large wagon himself, and loaded into it some goods he had left over, including a barrel of gunpowder. He also had some money, gold and silver. He put this into two little bags, and concealed it somewhere in the wagon. Such procedure was common. People would take a cleat off, and hollow out a place for coins, and then replace the cleat. Or they would make some other hiding place, which looked very well concealed to them.

When the wagons were approaching the mountains, Knight decided to join some other young fellows who were planning to ride ahead, hire pack animals from Sutter, and then ride back to get their goods, if the wagons could not be taken across. Knight

99

hired two men to take charge of his wagon while he was gone. The young men rode across the mountains, and got to Sutter's, but they thought his charge for pack animals was too much, and so started back just as they had come.

Meanwhile, the two men left with Knight's wagon drove it along until—one day—there was great excitement. The wagon had caught fire, as occasionally happened when men were careless about campfires. No one wanted to fight a fire burning close to a barrel of powder. The powder blew up, scattering the wagon and its contents all over the place.

Shortly afterward Knight returned. He went to the spot and searched everywhere for the coins, but recovered only $18.50. He himself was convinced that his hired men had discovered the money, taken it, and covered themselves by a rather ingenious and plausible trick. . . .

At last the trail, having returned to the river for a mile or two, finally left it and came to the lake. Again the wagons were hauled precariously along the north shore. Sarah Ide remembered "some of the time the water coming almost up to our feet—keeping the women in constant dread of being drowned."

When the emigrants passed beyond the head of the lake and came into the little meadow, they were appalled at the great dead-end wall of the pass that they saw ahead. The solid granite seemed to block all progress, even though they knew it had been surmounted the year before. Some of them, going ahead to scout, found no sign of a trail—naturally, since the wagons of the Stevens Party, both in the fall and in the spring, had been taken across while the mountains were largely under snow. Climbing up the pass, these scouts pronounced it impassable for wagons. But, on going back, they found that some of their own wagons were already being taken through places which they themselves had thought to be impassable!

The emigrants now had the great advantage of being accompanied by Greenwood, who had been there in '44 and could show the route then used. But Greenwood himself, who knew little about handling wagons, was for taking them to pieces and carrying them over. William Ide, who apparently prided himself on being an ingenious Yankee, proposed that they build some kind of bridge or something like an inclined railroad. The others would not listen to him, and went ahead to attack the problem by the same direct methods that had been used in '44.

Ide himself reported some comparatively level spots with steep pitches or cliffs between them. The men, by rolling stones and piling dirt in, built up narrow and steep "roadways" from one of the leveler spots up to the next. Then, with difficulty, they took the oxen up the precipitous places, one at a time, the men pulling them with ropes to help them up. At the higher level, having assembled ten or a dozen oxen, the men yoked them, and by means of a long chain attached them to an empty wagon at the lower level. But a team of six yoke was sixty feet long, and filled up most of the space. All the men could do, then, was to drive the oxen ahead a short distance—as far as they could, perhaps not more than half the length of the team. By doing so they laboriously "hitched" the wagon part-way up the steep pitch. They then held the wagon by blocking its wheels, brought the oxen back, shortened the chain, and repeated the process.

Another emigrant was David Hudson, who wrote vividly:

So we hitched up our teams and made a start, and when we came to benches or rocks six and eight feet straight up and down we would unyoke our oxen, drive them round to some low place, get them above the bench, yoke up the oxen. In the mean time some of us would cut some long poles strong enough to bear up the wagons and lay them up on the rocks. Then take enough chains to reach back to the wagons, hitch to the end of the tongue, and pull the wagon up.

Sarah Ide, who was only an onlooker, gives the feminine touch, remembering:

a long time to go about two miles over our rough, new-made road . . . over the rough rocks, in some places, and so smooth in others, that the oxen would slip and fall on their knees; the blood from their feet and knees staining the rocks they passed over. Mother and I walked, (we were so sorry for the poor, faithful oxen) all those two miles—all our clothing being packed on the horses' backs. It was a trying time—the men swearing at their teams, and beating them most cruelly, all along that rugged way.

Her father remembered two exhausting days spent in getting the wagons and goods to the top—the hardest labor of the whole journey.

Yet the men might well be willing to expend themselves and their animals at this point. The Rockies, split by the broad avenue of South Pass, had been as nothing. But there was no break at all in the Sierra Nevada. The so-called pass itself was high and steep and rough as a mountain, only a little notch between towering crags in a saw-toothed ridge hundreds of miles long. . . .

The difficult journey down the canyon-seamed western slopes was largely a go-as-you-please affair, each group of wagons on its own. Sarah described these days:

Up-hill and down; fording streams in the small valleys, with muddy bottoms, and small rivers, with large boulder rocks at the bottom; so large as almost upset the wagon; driving over rocky roads.

As David Hudson remembered:

In coming down the mountain we had frequently to tie trees behind the wagons. Sometimes we let them down with ropes with a turn around the tree. On side hills we tied ropes to the tops of wagons, and some men would walk up above them and hold onto the ropes to keep them from turning over.

To add variety, there were several rough river crossings, some steep uphill pitches out of ravines, a few long pulls to the tops of ridges, and some canyons to be crossed. Sarah Ide particularly remembered the canyon which was to be called Steep Hollow the next year. This was one of the places where trees had to be dragged behind the wagons. There also, as she remembered even more clearly, she was riding her pony down the steep slope, and the girth slipped, sliding the saddle forward. Fortunately the pony was gentle, and stood still while the girl disentangled herself.

But Sarah remembered Steep Hollow tearfully for another reason:

Our best milch-cow died the next morning. We did all we could to doctor her. We supposed she was poisoned by eating laurel leaves —grass being so scarce.

Provisions were getting low by this time, but any real trouble was averted by the arrival of a relief party with food, sent out by Sutter, according to his promise as reported by Greenwood at

Fort Hall. Once at Steep Hollow the emigrants were well below the level where they could be caught by a snowstorm. Between the middle and the end of October the wagons, a few at a time, came straggling into Sutter's Fort.

From our modern point of view it seems a hard and even dangerous experience. But one of the '45 emigrants merely remembered "a comparatively pleasant journey of five months." Many people, at least in retrospect, considered the crossing their equivalent of a Grand Tour, and looked back upon it as pleasurable and exciting. This was particularly true of boys and girls, who felt little sense of responsibility and remained a part of a strongly knit family group. Sarah Ide wrote: "I was with my dear parents then." She recognized their problems: "They had care and toil all the way. My father was broken of his rest and sleep a great deal—taking charge of the cattle late and early." But she also declared: "To me the journey was a 'pleasure-trip'— so many beautiful wild flowers, such wild scenery, mountains, rocks, and streams—something new at every turn." Thus a young girl remembered. . . .

The shift from '44 to '45 is thus tremendous. In the former year one small party, having to break trail over the last hard 250 miles, had barely managed to survive and had not got their wagons through until the succeeding spring. But in '45 a number of parties with about fifty wagons, using the trail thus established for them, made the whole distance from Missouri to California in less than six months, without severe hardships. Overland migration by covered wagon might now be called practical.

The year '45 was also notable for two horseback parties. . . . One of these was led by Frémont, whom the historians rightfully record as a great explorer of the West. He had been traveling widely in the region traversed by the covered wagons in every year since '42.

None the less, the curious fact is that the history of the trail can be told without more than passing references to Frémont. Either he traveled, as he often did, on roads which the wagons had already established, or else he traveled through out-of-the-way places where no one wished to go. In '43, for instance, he had ridden along nearly the entire length of the emigrant road to Oregon. He had then, from the lower Columbia River, headed south and southeast. At some point he must have crossed the fresh trail of Chiles's horseback party. It may, however, have been obscured by snow; in any case, he did not mention it. Continuing on into what is now western Nevada, he discovered and named Pyramid Lake, went still farther south, wandered about considerably, and finally struggled across the Sierra Nevada in midwinter. At this time Frémont was close to what was later known as Carson Pass. The whole country, however, was under deep snow, and he apparently did not grasp the possible significance of his discovery for the emigrants.

A year and eight months later, about the middle of October in '45, Frémont was exploring in a region close to the southern shore of Great Salt Lake. He headed toward the west, where much of the country was unknown. Without serious difficulty he crossed the Salt Lake Desert, directing his course toward a lofty mountain, to which he gave the name Pilot Peak. At its foot, he came to the springs where the Bartleson Party had passed with eight wagons only four years earlier. He continued to the west, gave the Humboldt River its final name, and then crossed into California, in very tame fashion, over the now-established emigrant road.

Perhaps we should consider Frémont as an early advocate of "pure research," not wishing to be concerned with anything so practical as the working out of the route for wagons. The establishment of the trail we owe to Walker, Chiles, Stevens, and other little-known men who followed them.

Frémont, however, gained the title of the Pathfinder. We might say cynically that he was exactly that. He found not roads, but paths—generally rocky, tortuous, and unimportant paths. Only in two sections, each for a distance of about a hundred miles, did the emigrants ever follow his trail. Neither of these became an important route, and they would better have been left untraveled altogether. One of the two was the stretch across the desert to Pilot Peak. . . .

The last party of '45 left Independence on August 17. It consisted of ten young men on horseback, with a few pack mules.

The leader was Lansford W. Hastings, the author of *The Emigrants' Guide*. He was already well-traveled in the West. A young Ohio lawyer, inordinately restless and ambitious, he had gone to Oregon overland in '42. Dissatisfied there, he had gone to California. Apparently he saw opportunities; under weak Mexican rule the rich country was politically unstable. As in Texas, a local revolution, spearheaded by American settlers, might detach California and set it up as an independent republic. There would have to be leaders. A young man, inordinately restless and ambitious, would sense the possibility.

Hastings went east in '44 by sea and across Mexico. Early in '45 he published his book. Then he was off again for California; there he would have to do his work.

It was much too late to be setting out, but Hastings had always been lucky. The ten riders got to Fort Laramie in good time; there, however, they were delayed because of Indian trouble. At last, chancing it, they detoured first to the north, and then swung far to the south, to Fort Bridger. Beyond that point they ran short of food, and got into Fort Hall half-starved. By now it was so late that any prudent man would have wintered there. But Hastings was never prudent, and apparently his companions were like him.

They reprovisioned, and went on along the emigrant road to California. The chances were all for snow on the pass. Perhaps Hastings believed that without wagons he could get across even through the snow, as Frémont had done the year before. Perhaps he figured on going all the way south on Walker's old route.

His luck held. The storms kept off, and a few days before Christmas the horsemen were approaching the pass. The snow was not deep enough to be of much hindrance.

Here they passed a small log cabin, which would certainly have aroused their interest, since it was the first habitation of white men that they had seen since leaving Fort Hall. Quite possibly, somewhere along the trail, they had heard the story of Mose Schallenberger. If so, Hastings would have known that the snow sometimes came early and lay deep, and he would have realized that emigrants thus trapped would face disaster.

He went on, and crossed the pass without difficulty. On Christmas Day—there would ordinarily have been heavy storms on the mountains six weeks earlier—he got to Sutter's Fort.

Hastings's luck had held, though a gambler might have said that he was expending it recklessly. Thus he came to California again. If he had not made it, the most famous episode in the history of the California Trail would presumably never have occurred.

INTERCHAPTER ONE

HOW THEY TRAVELED

Dᴜʀɪɴɢ ᴛʜɪs ᴡɪɴᴛᴇʀ when '45 shifted to '46 we sense a pause, as if between an end and a beginning. Behind lay five years of adventure and uncertainty, of accumulating skill and knowledge, culminating in success. Ahead lay—or seemed to lie—years of normal development, since no one at the time imagined the cataclysms that would soon affect the trail. Since this is, then, a point of rest, we may let the story also pause and consider the materials and techniques of the covered-wagon migration, that amazing phenomenon. . . .

By this time the methods of travel had been well established. For instance, the idea that you could expect to live off buffalo had been well disproved. Buffalo hunting took too much time and energy, and was too uncertain. You could hope to kill buffalo or other game for a welcome bit of fresh meat, but you should have enough food in your wagon to support the family all the way through.

In such matters, the experience of the Oregon and of the California emigrants was confirmatory. The emigration to Oregon, up to '45, had been much larger than that to California, and its problems of travel were almost identical. In fact, the two trails were the same for more than half the distance, and many people set out for one objective and then shifted to the other. When, at a campfire, two men shared their experiences and both gained knowledge, neither was much concerned that the one might be heading toward the Columbia and the other toward the Sacramento.

Experience gained on the Santa Fe Trail was comparatively unimportant, and might be misleading. Conditions there were very different. The distance was only half as far, and the country was nearly all open and level. Even more important, as the expression "Santa Fe trade" indicates, that trail was used by traders and not by emigrants. When the Oregon and California emigrants imitated the Santa Fe traders, they nearly always came to grief—as in using big wagons, forming large companies, and organizing in military fashion.

On the other hand, the emigrants made use of a general backlog of experience with teams and wagons. Every farmer knew a good deal about that sort of thing, and he had probably made journeys of several hundred miles. What had to be faced, to get to California, were the new conditions—the tenfold-long pull, the untamed Indians, the lack of supply points, the difficult country of deserts and mountains. But in the handling of the wagon itself most of the men were already proficient, and this proficiency was essential to success of the covered-wagon migration. . . .

Lest those words "covered-wagon migration" seem to beg the question, we may reiterate that by this time the wagons had gained the decision. A few people chose to travel by pack train, making use of mules—occasionally, of horses. The advantages of the pack train were obvious. The greater speed of movement meant that the time, with good luck, could be cut by a month or more, and that the dangerous desert stretches could be passed more safely. Pack trains forded streams and crossed mountains and rough country much more easily than did wagons.*

But the disadvantages of the pack train, though less obvious, were extreme. It was not to be chosen by a man who had small children or a pregnant wife. And there were other handicaps. As an ox-driver noted:

The pack-mule companies are a pitiful set of slaves. They have to sit on their mules roasting in the sun all day. If they get down to

* On the use of carts, see pp. 38–39.

walk or rest themselves, they must be bothered leading the animals. When they stop at night, they must unpack everything. In the mornings they have to repack everything.

Finally, as the case of Hopper had shown in '42, the packers faced disaster if one of them fell ill or suffered an accident. A man with a broken leg or a case of dysentery could be trundled along, although uncomfortably, in a wagon. But in a pack train, there was no humane solution. Such companies, therefore, nearly always consisted of young men, willing to risk their chances of getting through quickly against their chances of not getting through at all.

As for the wagon, its disadvantages were obvious—slow, heavy, cumbersome, subject to breakage, hard to take across rivers and ravines and mountains and through rocky or sandy country. But it served as a home on wheels, required little daily trouble of packing and repacking, permitted more pounds to be transported per animal, could be used as an ambulance, and offered a fortress against attack when properly set into formation. The covered wagon thus became the standard means of migration, and developed eventually into the symbol.

Since it has become the manifestation of a heroic tale, there has been an inevitable tendency to build it up to epic proportions. Its image has been exaggerated into a massive wain, on the model of the Conestoga—the great six-horse freight wagon developed in southeastern Pennsylvania about the middle of the eighteenth century. The Conestoga had a huge boat-like body, and a sway-backed cover that overhung front and rear. It was adapted for use on the Santa Fe Trail, where the problem was merely one of attaching a large number of animals to the wagon and plugging ahead.

But the California emigrant could not use large numbers of animals to a single vehicle, because on twisty and hilly roads such teams could not pull effectively. If he had a large family, or wished to transport a considerable weight of goods, he could do better by using two or three small wagons.

The vehicle was known simply as a "wagon" or a "farm wagon," and was designated as "one-horse" or "two-horse," though such description was retrospective, and in the actual journey the wagons were not pulled by horses and always by more

5 FT.

LIGHT WAGON COMMONLY USED BY EMIGRANTS

MEDIUM-SIZED WAGON WITH SLOPING SIDES AND ENDS.

CONESTOGA WAGON (RARELY USED IN THE MIGRATION)

Types of Wagons

than one or two animals. In addition, the term "light" was gener‐ally applied to both sizes of wagons. Such vehicles could carry a ton or more, but three-fourths of a ton was considered enough of a load to start with. Even the romantic name "prairie schooner" —almost never used by the emigrants themselves—makes the analogy not with a big three-master, but with a small, maneuver‐able, and almost homelike vessel.

Granted that there were some individual variations, the ver‐bal descriptions of the wagons and some contemporary drawings show a strong generic similarity. The wagon must be considered as having three parts—bed, top, and running-gear.

The bed was a wooden box—often, indeed, called a box— nine or ten feet long, about four feet wide, with ends and sides about two feet high. On ordinary wagons the sides and ends of the bed went up perpendicularly, but on some of the larger wagons they flared outward, as if imitating the Conestoga in miniature.

The bed could be caulked, or covered with hides or canvas, and then used as a boat. Many people built a false floor, a foot or so from the bottom of the box. The lower space was divided into compartments and used for storing supplies. The boxes served their purpose, were subjected to no particular strain, and gave no trouble. They are seldom mentioned in the diaries.

The top or cover was the most conspicuous part, and has supplied the distinguishing adjective in the phrase, "covered wagon." This top was of canvas, or of some cloth which had been waterproofed with paint or linseed oil. The five or six bows sup‐porting the top were of bent hickory. They merely followed the line of the beds, and on the usual straight-sided bed the bows therefore went straight up before curving over. There was thus no overhang at front or rear, and no "sway-back." Flaps at the front and a "puckering-string" at the back allowed opening and closing. Inside, the wagon was a tiny room, with sides partly of wood and partly of canvas rising almost straight to a height of four or five feet and then arching over to make an inverted U in cross section. A man could stand upright along the center line. On wagons with flaring beds the bows, again following the lines of the sides, produced a more cylindrical effect with a front and rear overhang and perhaps a slight sway-back.

The top served its purpose well, protecting goods and people

110

from the weather. In an upset the canvas might be torn, and some of the bows broken. In forested country the overhanging branches might catch the top and rip the cloth, but there was not much country of that kind. When going head on into the strong westerly winds of the plains, an occasional company put the tops down to reduce pressure. But the tops produced few incidents.

Not so, the running-gear! In the surviving instructions to emigrants there is the admonition that the wagons (that is, the running-gear) should be light and strong. Obviously the two qualities were somewhat incompatible, and even the best material and workmanship did not always produce a vehicle that went through without breaking.

Strength was attained by careful selection of wood of the proper kind for the particular part. A reliable wagonwright would have his shop stocked with well-seasoned maple, poplar, hickory, ash, Osage orange, beech, elm, and oak.*

The tires were of iron, and iron was used for reinforcement at critical points. But very liberal use of iron was not advisable, since lightness too was essential. There was no point in having a wagon that was unbreakable, but so heavy that it wore the teams down by its dead weight. The result, inevitably, was a compromise. In the end, breakages were frequent, so that many a crisis and many a tragedy thus began, though probably fewer than would have occurred with heavier, team-killing vehicles.

Tongues snapped on sharp turns; front axles gave way on sudden down-drops. These were the commonest accidents and were taken almost as routine. "Occasionally we break a tongue or an axle-tree," wrote one emigrant, taking it all in the day's work. Some people carried extra axles, but this built up the total weight, and so it was doubtful practice. More often the nearest suitable tree supplied timber, though "nearest" was sometimes a day's journey distant.

Not many were as unlucky as one man who snapped both axles at the same stream crossing. Fortunately he was with a large, well-equipped company, and so the accident meant only a day's delay.

Wheels were extremely tough, and seldom collapsed altogether. Many a one began to give way because of shrinkage in the

* See also pp. 84 85.

111

dry air of the desert, but usually wedges could be driven under the tire to tighten it. Eventually the tire might have to be taken off, heated red hot in an improvised fire-pit, and reset on the wheel.

Front wheels were smaller than rear wheels, but generally not by much. These large front wheels cut down the maneuverability of the wagons, and such wagons could not turn at an angle of more than about 30 degrees. Wagons with small front wheels, though more maneuverable, were harder to pull. Only an occasional wagon had wheels so low that they could swing under the bed, and thus permit right-angled turns.

The ordinary wagons had neither brakes nor springs. The harder-riding quality resulting from the lack of springs was not serious. Since the rate of movement was only about two miles an hour, the jouncing would not be severe, and on very rocky stretches the people would walk. Many of the breakages, however, must have resulted from the absence of springs to ease the shock.

Lack of brakes never seems to have caused concern. At the top of slopes the wagon was halted, and a wheel, or more than one, was locked. On steeper slopes wheels were "rough locked," by means of a length of chain on which the tire rested, thus producing a rough surface on which the wagon could cut into the dirt. In forested country a tree might be dragged behind the wagon to supply breakage, or else the wagon was lowered bodily by a rope snubbed around a trunk.

Essential equipment was the "tar bucket," hanging from the rear axle. The term "tar" was highly indefinite. Often the bucket contained tar or resin, mixed half-and-half with tallow. Since the contents were expended steadily to grease the wheels and kingbolt, the supply ran short, and before the end of the journey a man might be using anything that came handy, such as the grease fried out of a fat wolf. Some emigrants found an oil seep, and filled their buckets at it—thus being among the first Americans to make use of a petroleum lubricant.

In those days a man had an appreciation for a good wagon. On the street in Cincinnati, a wagon caught the eye of a young emigrant starting west. He sized it up as he might a horse or a woman—"light, strong, short-coupled." Then and there, though the wagon was in use, he made an offer for it. He had it shipped to the frontier, and later was able to write proudly, "I made no mistake," after he had finally taken it clear to California. . . .

Granted, then, that the wagon was to be the vehicle, how was it to be hauled—horses, mules, or oxen? The question was one of some complication.*

The horse, indeed, was scarcely in the competition. Though that noble animal moved faster than the ox and pulled more than the mule, he was not as tough as either of these to endure the long haul, the constant work, and the insufficient food to be gained by his own foraging. Only in later years was a technique developed that permitted the common use of horses.

As between mule and ox there was endless argument around the campfires, punctuated by tobacco juice spit into the embers:

"Mules move faster."

"Yes, but oxen pull more."

"Oxen don't stampede so easy."

"But when they do, they run worse."

"Mules bog down worse in mud."

"But they can live on cottonwood bark."

"The Sioux steal mules, but don't want oxen."

"Oxen get sore feet when mules don't."

Individual emigrants, fortunate enough to have a good team, became greatly attached to their animals, of either kind. One of them wrote enthusiastically of his mules:

It was a noble sight to see those small, tough, earnest, honest Spanish mules, every nerve strained to the utmost, examples of obedience, and of duty performed under trying circumstances.

But another man wrote that he found the oxen "greatly superior." He continued with a eulogy:

The ox is a most noble animal, patient, thrifty, durable, gentle, and easily driven, and does not run off. Those who come to this country will be in love with their oxen by the time they reach here.

The long-continued case of mule vs. ox could never be really decided. With good luck and good handling, either could be highly satisfactory, and with bad luck or bad handling, either could cause trouble, or even disaster. There were always compli-

* See also p. 40.

cating factors, and there was no possibility of running a scientific control to determine which animal was the better.

The mere numerical verdict was strongly in favor of the ox. A weighty deciding factor was the expense. One contemporary price list gave the cost of a mule at $75 and of an ox at $25. In time "ox-team emigrant" became a generic term.

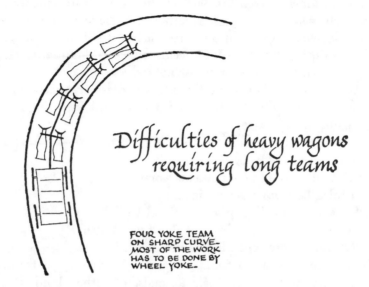

Difficulties of heavy wagons requiring long teams

FOUR YOKE TEAM
ON SHARP CURVE.
MOST OF THE WORK
HAS TO BE DONE BY
WHEEL YOKE.

Modern representations notwithstanding, oxen were not driven by means of reins held by people sitting on the wagon seat. Instead, there were no reins attached to yoked oxen, and the driver walked alongside, controlling his team by shouting (and often by cursing), by cracking his long-handled and long-lashed whip, and sometimes by applying it. Oxen recognized the commands, "Giddap!" "Gee!" "Haw!" and "Whoa!"

FIVE YOKE TEAM
AT SHARP CREST.
TWO FRONT YOKE
CANNOT PULL.

114

The number of animals to the wagon varied with the size and weight of the wagon and its load, and according to the temperament and wealth of the owner. Four oxen, that is, "two yoke" was the minimum. Three yoke was common, and was generally recommended. Thus equipped, if you were unfortunate enough to suffer the loss of two oxen, you could still move the wagon. Besides, when there were three yoke, the animals were able to walk rather than having to pull, and so did not wear themselves down rapidly. In the early years four yoke was unusual. . . .

As '44 and '45 had proved, light wagons with moderate loads and adequate teams could be taken through or across any obstacle that the West could offer. Much of the country, indeed, presented what was often called a "good natural road." Thus the wagons could roll easily across the grass-grown plains, through many broad mountain valleys, even across much of the desert.

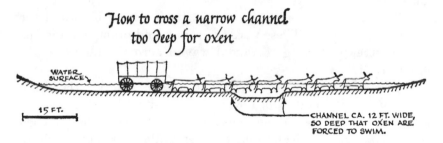

How to cross a narrow channel too deep for oxen

WATER SURFACE

15 FT.

CHANNEL CA. 12 FT. WIDE, SO DEEP THAT OXEN ARE FORCED TO SWIM.

Difficult stream crossings, often in ravines, were the commonest obstacles, encountered daily. There was the steep down-pitch on one side, and the equally steep up-pitch on the other; between them was the stream or stream bed where the bottom might be muddy and where the water might be deep enough to cause trouble. But, by locking one or more wheels, the teamster could take the wagon down the slope, and then, if necessary, he could double teams and with cracking of whip and shouting could take the wagon through the water and mud and up the slope on the other side.

Since the wagon-beds had a clearance of about two and a half feet, streams with combined water and mud no deeper than this could be crossed without special preparation. After the beds had been raised by blocks placed on the axles, streams of three and a half feet, or even a little more, could be forded. In water any deeper than this the animals themselves could scarcely keep their feet or pull. A few streams had to be crossed by ferries, by rafting, or by floating the wagon-beds and swimming the animals.

Stream crossings occasioned many a broken axle, an occasional overturned wagon, and at times a halt of a day or so until a flood subsided, but never seriously impeded the migration.

The mountains, except for the Sierra Nevada, presented surprisingly little difficulty to the passage of wagons. But, if necessary, wagons could be taken up or down very steep slopes.

The emigrants, however, found certain types of country and certain situations to be laborious or dangerous, and these they therefore avoided. So-called "badlands," where the terrain was nothing but a maze of ravines, had to be detoured. At Scott's Bluff, for instance, a stretch of such land pushed the trail away from the bank of the Platte, and sent the wagons through Robidoux Pass.

The trail kept away, if possible, from stream beds and the bottoms of canyons. These were too rough and cramped, and too boulder-strewn. Trying to take a wagon across boulders might mean disastrous breakage.

Side slopes were hazardous. The wagons had a rather high center of gravity, and tipped over all too easily. To aid in passing along such stretches of dangerous hillside, ropes could be attached to the upper side of the wagon, and men could walk along pulling on them. But this technique was not practical on very steep hillsides or for long distances.

Since both stream beds and hillsides had to be avoided, the road often followed the ridges, as it did notably in some parts of the Bear River Mountains, and on the western slope of the Sierra Nevada.

Thickets and brush-grown areas were by-passed when possible. To open a trail in such country the men had to cut out a passageway with their axes, and this meant much work. Fortunately, the arid West offered little such country, and even the forest of the Sierra Nevada was generally open, with room for the passage of wagons among its large trees.

The deserts were difficult, primarily because of the distance between spots offering water and grass, but also because of the heavy pulling sometimes necessitated by the soft surface. The wagon wheels cut in deeply, and in places the animals sank to their knees in the light dust and effluorescent soil of the ancient lake beds.

All in all, we might think that some malevolent demon had arranged the difficulties in climactic order. The first part of the journey, when teams and people were fresh, was comparatively easy. The test came at the western end, after teams and people had been worn down by long travel. Then they must face, one after the other, the Forty-mile Desert, the Truckee Canyon, the ascent of the pass, and the descent of the rough western slope of the Sierra Nevada. But after '44 everyone knew that it could be done. Even the obstacles thus arranged were not sufficient to stop the small, strongly built wagons pulled by well-toughened teams, driven ahead by skillful and stout-hearted men. . . .

In addition to wagons, teams, and necessary harness, the journey demanded much else. . . . Extra cattle were usually driven along in a "loose herd," for spares and for a supply of fresh meat. Herders then had to be assigned, one man to thirty cattle. Herding was trying and disliked work. The cattle frequently strayed and occasionally stampeded, and always they had to be guarded against the Indians. Some people judged a loose herd to be more nuisance than it was worth.

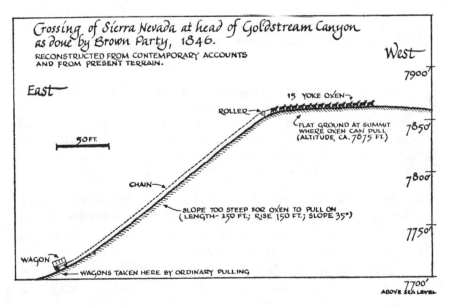

Crossing of Sierra Nevada at head of Goldstream Canyon
as done by Brown Party, 1846.
RECONSTRUCTED FROM CONTEMPORARY ACCOUNTS
AND FROM PRESENT TERRAIN.

West — 7900'

East —

15 YOKE OXEN →

ROLLER →

FLAT GROUND AT SUMMIT
WHERE OXEN CAN PULL
(ALTITUDE, CA. 7875 FT.) 7850'

50 FT.

7800'

CHAIN →

SLOPE TOO STEEP FOR OXEN TO PULL ON
(LENGTH- 250 FT.; RISE 150 FT.; SLOPE 35°)

7750'

WAGON

WAGONS TAKEN HERE BY ORDINARY PULLING

7700'
ABOVE SEA LEVEL

117

Generally some of the cattle, especially in trains that included children, were milch cows. These were usually just driven along, but in emergencies they were put under the yoke. They then did well enough as draft animals, and still continued to give milk.

The owner of a wagon regularly had at least one riding horse. A horse was useful, not only for transportation, but also for scouting and hunting, and for rounding up strayed cattle. Many well-to-do emigrants provided horses or ponies for their wives and older children. Though these animals were given special care, many of them failed on the road, particularly if they were broken down by too-enthusiastic buffalo-running. They were then sometimes killed or abandoned, and sometimes traded off with the Indians for ponies.

The ordinary party was accompanied by a number of dogs. Some of these were pets, and others were valuable for hunting and herding and keeping watch at night. But in addition to these well-trained animals there were the worthless curs, fighting, yapping, and snapping, pestering the cattle and horses by day, and keeping people awake by night with senseless barking and howling. Dogs were often a cause of quarrels among the people, and one company tried to outlaw dogs entirely, decreeing that they should be shot.

No special clothes were required; the emigrants wore just about what they would wear on their farms at home. One listing recommended:

Sack coat and pantaloons of stout sheep's grey cloth—very large and strong. Deer skin hunting shirt and pants—do. Blue twilled cotton or linsey woolsey. Duck trousers. Striped twilled cotton or hickory shirts. Red flannel shirts. Cotton socks. Stout pegged shoes or brogans—broad soles and large. Stout white felt hats—no glazing. Good palm leaf hat.

Requirements for sleeping were blankets, and usually a tent. Children, especially the smaller ones, could sleep in the wagon, but the box was not large enough to give bed-room to more than two adults. A tent could then be used for shelter and privacy.

Arms and ammunition were essential, though usually the emigrant found much less use for them than he had imagined.

118

(The tonnage of powder and lead that was transported all the way to California was considerable!) The rifle, already for nearly a century the American's trusted weapon, was standard equipment. Many of these were old weapons already well used for hunting. Others were new, specially bought for the trip, at a price of around $25. A few people preferred the old but well-proved flint-lock, but most of the rifles were of the new percussion-cap type. Most emigrants burdened themselves with a brace of pistols or, in later years, a revolver. Many people had shotguns as well.

Since the trip involved transporting a whole family, and since the only chances of resupply were a few inadequately stocked posts, such a variety of articles had to be taken along that a well-equipped covered wagon rivaled a country store. A list of recommended "useful articles" included knife, whetstone, ax, hammer, hatchet, spade, saw, gimlet, scissors, needles, palm and pricker (for sewing canvas), last, awls, nails, tacks, needles, pins, thread, wax, twine, shoe leather and pegs, staples, ropes, whip-thongs, cotton cloth, beeswax and tallow, soap, candles, opodeldoc (a linament), herbs, medicines, spyglass, lantern, patent-leather drinking cup, washbowl, and campstool.

Modern representations of the covered wagon often show a good-sized keg carried on a small platform at the side of the bed. Throughout most of the journey, such a keg would have been mere useless weight, especially if filled with water. This ox-killing monstrosity was probably unknown to the early emigrants.

The question of spare parts for the wagon was a difficult one. One emigrant recommended extra kingbolts, linchpins, and chain, but was doubtful about a spare axletree and oxbows because of the extra weight.

In most wagons the greater part of the load at starting consisted of food. T. H. Jefferson, who based his *Brief Practical Advice* on his own experiences in '46, recommended: "Take plenty of bread stuff; this is the staff of life when everything else runs short." He advised two hundred pounds per adult, most of it to be carried as flour. A careful housewife (or, may we say, wagon-wife?) took yeast along, and baked bread in a Dutch oven when she had the chance. Otherwise, hot biscuits (that American delicacy) could serve excellently.

A part of the breadstuff was regularly carried as crackers or hardtack. Corn meal also served for variety, and we may suppose that the emigrants from the Southern states may have carried more corn meal than wheat flour.

Difficulties of cookery influenced the selection of foodstuffs. Along the Platte and in the desert fuel was scarce, and in high country water boils at a low temperature. Rice, therefore, was taken only in small quantities. The same was true of beans. These foods could be cooked only when the train laid over for a day at some place where fuel was abundant.

The second staple of food was bacon, though the term was then more broadly interpreted than now, and included side-pork. The bacon gave much trouble. In the extreme heat its fat melted and oozed away, and what remained was then scarcely edible, especially since it often became rancid. Nevertheless it remained the standard meat ration, probably because the emigrants were used to eating it at home, and because it was cheap and readily obtained.

Though supplementary to breadstuff and bacon, some other articles of food were considered essential: salt, sugar, coffee, and dried fruit. In addition, each family was likely to carry along something in the way of special delicacies—tea, maple sugar, vinegar, pickles, smoked beef.

One would imagine that most wagons had a bottle of whisky stowed away somewhere, but it seems to have been considered a medicine or something reserved for snake-bite or other emergency. Except for an occasional bust at Fort Laramie, there was little drinking on the trail.

Canned goods of many kinds were available, but they were expensive, and few emigrants were accustomed to use them. Beef, sardines, fruits, and cheese were sometimes so carried.

With the staples thus assured, the emigrants supplemented their diet by what they could get from day to day. A train, in the earlier years, could expect to be in buffalo country for more than a month, and buffalo steak would often be sizzling in the pans, though sometimes at a considerable wearing down of horseflesh. Antelopes were numerous, but they were individually small, and were difficult to approach. Deer, mountain sheep, and bear were bagged occasionally. If the arrival at Humboldt Sink coincided with the southward flight of waterfowl, there was a sudden abundance. The unpalatable jack-rabbit was not altogether despised, and in sufficient emergency almost anything that walked or crawled was eaten.

There was a good deal of fishing, because each train was likely to contain a few men who enjoyed it. The prairie streams yielded sizable catfish. The mountain rivers provided trout. Most of the fish were caught by angling, but some parties used seines, or sometimes attempted to improvise them from the wagon tops.

The country also supplied berries of various kinds, wild onions and some plants which were cooked as greens, especially lamb's-tongue.

Though these backwoods people had no knowledge of scientific dietetics, they had folkways which served them well. Aside from actual near-starvation, there seems to have been no dietary trouble in these early years. There is no mention of scurvy. Toward the end of the journey, after the delicacies had been exhausted, the diet was monotonous, and perhaps for this reason, some emigrants arrived in California with a longing for pickles.

These were generally not poverty-stricken people who were content with a "hog-and-hominy" subsistence. Many of the wives prided themselves on "setting a good table." One man, invited to supper at the tent of a friend near Fort Laramie, recorded that he sat down to hot biscuits, fresh butter, honey, rich milk, cream, venison steak, and tea and coffee—and there were green peas, gathered that day from the wild vines along the trail. . . .

In addition to physical equipment the emigrants took with them their mental equipment, essentially that of American farming people and villagers.

As to their motivation in going at all, one can add little to the discussion already offered for the emigrants of '41,* except that the decision, now that the journey was known to be practical, can be considered a more reasonable one. Often mentioned are the adverse economic conditions of the Mississippi Valley, the hope of better things in California, and the poignant desire to escape from a malarial country. Not mentioned, but still, we may think, important, are the motivations of restlessness on the one hand, and of mere boredom on the other.

Most of the people were Americans—either native-born or

* See pp. 9–10.

so long resident in the country that their foreign origin was no longer important. In '44 the foreigners totaled more than half the company, but usually they amounted, it would seem, to hardly more than a tenth. They were chiefly English, Irish, and German. The French-speaking Creoles, though they had been important in the fur trade and had predominated in Frémont's expeditions, were negligible in the covered-wagon migration.

Missouri supplied a large number of the emigrants, but nearly all of those had been born farther east. Illinois was another great recruiting ground.

Except for Sam Kinney and his man Friday in '45, slavery failed to become an issue, even though the Missourians and many others were from slave states. But slavery was illegal in Mexican territory, and California was not known as a cotton-growing region. Free Negroes also fail to make much appearance. Few of them were sufficiently well-to-do to be able to set out on their own, and there was probably a prejudice against hiring them as teamsters to travel in an otherwise white company.

Life in a wagon train was much like life in a village, though in a village existing under abnormal conditions. The people, at least at the beginning, found the life highly interesting and stimulating. Most of them had lived on isolated farms or at mere crossroads settlements. Now, in a good-sized train, they came into daily contact with a hundred or more people and found themselves in an unprecedented situation. They met new men and women, talked with them, absorbed new ideas. There was a certain vacation spirit about the whole affair, though most of the people, indeed, could scarcely have known what the word "vacation" meant.

This might be considered a village, but it was a village that was not doing its regular work. There was no plowing or reaping, no buying or selling, no building or milling. There was, indeed, a good deal of work to be done daily, by both men and women. But much of it was not the ordinary kind of work; it was certainly not done under ordinary conditions, and so it had a kind of play-spirit in it. The men did whatever work was involved in moving the wagons forward a proper distance daily, and they herded the loose cattle, did odd jobs of repair, and sometimes went hunting and fishing. The women did more nearly what they did at home.

They tended the babies and looked after the older children; they prepared the meals; they washed and mended the clothes; occasionally, we may be sure, they had a wagon-cleaning. But the meals were necessarily simple, and there must have been a general relaxation of housekeeping standards, just as there is in a summer camp today.

The psychology would have been that of the traveler—and there is no more pleasant state of mind for most people. When anyone is traveling, life is reduced to a simple and solvable daily problem: to make the required distance. If the people in a wagon train totaled their fifteen miles westward, they could sleep peacefully. They did not even need to consider what they would do when they got to California, or whether they had any valid reason for going there. They had already committed themselves, and what they would do after their arrival could be comfortably left in abeyance.

So the life was that of a village, though of a village much changed in its folk habits. There was endless talk, some of it degenerating into gossip, but some of it attaining a higher plane, as when one observer recorded that three older men were discussing points of theology. The same diarist noted the resemblance to a village:

Our camp this evening presents a most cheerful appearance. The prairie, miles around us, is enlivened with groups of cattle, numbering six or seven hundred, feeding upon the fresh green grass. The numerous white tents and wagon-covers before which the camp-fires are blazing brightly, represent a rustic village; and men, women, and children are talking, playing, and singing around them with all the glee of light and careless hearts. While I am writing, a party at the lower end of the camp is engaged in singing hymns and sacred songs.

This lighthearted scene, it must be admitted, was recorded in the early part of the journey, when people were still highly stimulated and had not grown travel-weary.

Moreover, this pastoral paradise was not without some serpents. Young men and women being what they are, there certainly must have been, now and then, a bit of hanky-panky in the bushes at the bottom of the campground. Some of the numerous marriages may have been, indeed, both *post hoc* and *propter hoc*.

123

On the whole, however, the diarists tell us very little about what we might call the problem of sex. (There were indeed Lucinda and "the widow." Of them, later.)

There was sickness too. Old malaria flared up, and there were bouts with diarrhea and dysentery, though health on the whole was good in these earlier years. As for accident, a few people, especially small boys, got themselves caught beneath the wheels, though we may wonder how even a small boy could manage to be run over by a vehicle going two miles an hour.

A surprising number of people, of whom the unfortunate Shotwell of '41 may be considered the prototype, shot themselves accidentally. Though every emigrant considered it his duty to arm himself to the teeth, some of them knew little about handling firearms, and there was no general instruction in rules of safety. The result was what seems, as we read the diaries, a continual fusillade of accidentally discharged rifles and pistols. Sometimes the bullets passed into the indestructible prairie soil, but not infrequently they were intercepted by the body of an animal or person.

Drownings, also, were numerous for a country which produced few rivers large enough to make drowning possible. Quarrels generally did not get beyond mere fisticuffs, but occasionally there were knifings. Naturally, quarrels were more common toward the end of the journey, when everyone was tired and the novelty had worn off, and "cabin fever" had developed.

One wonders what the sanitary arrangements may have been. But the records are silent—whether from prudish reticence or from mere assumption that everybody would know about such matters and not care to be informed. There was certainly a problem involved in a mixed company traveling through a country which was often flat and lacking in vegetation. Did they rig up a canvas screen at the campground, or were there slop jars in the wagons? These may have been easygoing backwoods people, but the period was highly prudish. This is, however, scarcely a matter of concern for an epic tale; Homer does not tell us of the arrangements in the Greek camp along the Hellespont. . . .

The problem of government in this strangely uprooted village arose often, created many a crisis, gave rise to a great number of makeshift solutions, and was never finally solved. The men of each company regularly held a meeting for organization. They elected a captain and other officers. This meeting, or later ones, might also pass various regulations.

In practice, the captain exercised greater or less authority in accordance with his prestige and strength of personality, but never possessed much real power. He could pick the spot for encamping and assign men to the various watches. In the morning he could give the commands to "catch up," and to "roll." He could settle minor disputes, if any were brought to him. But he could be deposed by a simple majority vote, and often was.

More important decisions, such as the choice between two routes, called for a general council of the men, or of the wagon-owners. But even this decision could not be enforced.

The ultimate power of action remained with the individual —in particular, with the owner of a wagon. The company may thus be compared to an alliance or confederation of sovereign powers, not to a unified nation. Outside pressure, which usually meant fear of the Indians, made for greater cohesion. Difficulties of travel caused dissension and often dissolution, as groups of wagon-owners split off with no one to restrain them. The busy years of the trail that followed '45 were to provide many such examples.

Crime, that rebellion of the individual against the group, raised special difficulties. The emigrants of '45 had been faced with John Greenwood's killing of the Indian and the possible theft of Knight's money. As the example of "Talbot Green" had shown in '41, criminals sometimes took to the trail to escape. But the percentage of such individuals must have been negligible. There was, in fact, little crime on the trail.

Most of the emigrants, ordinary people of their time, accepted a philosophy of retributive punishment given religious sanction by the Old Testament. But a wagon train lacked the authority of law. If Preacher Williams had hesitated about his right to perform a marriage ceremony, we can understand that others might flinch from acting in a case of homicide. Each crime or alleged crime was thus likely to create a crisis and to result in an interesting story that would be noted in the journals and retold, years later, in the reminiscences. . . .

The covered-wagon migration across the plains and mountains was wholly American and is almost unique in history. The Great Trek in South Africa supplies the closest parallel. In numbers this exodus of the Boers was probably less than one tenth of its American counterpart, and the distance traveled was generally less than half.

The Great Trek began in 1836, only five years before 1841. There is no evidence that it had any influence upon the American migration. The people of the United States may, therefore, rightly regard the covered wagon as one of their most cherished symbols—and may do so proudly.

INTERCHAPTER TWO

WHERE THEY WENT

In '44 THE TRAIL was opened; in '45, it was slightly relocated and more firmly beaten down. Thus was established what we may call the "original" California Trail.

The whole distance may be broken down into eighteen sections—or "legs," as the common word was. Mileages can be given only in round numbers, since the emigrants rarely made exact measurements, and since the distance traveled might vary from season to season, even from party to party, according to whether the guide took a short cut to save distance, or lengthened the distance by going around a hill instead of climbing over it.

1. Independence to Kansas River ferry—100 miles. Although both St. Joseph and Council Bluffs were being used, you could still consider Independence the conventional point of departure. You would set out, generally, in early May. Over the first fifty miles you followed the well-worn Santa Fe Trail, and then at the forking, you kept to the right.

This leg necessitated about six days' travel, and was largely a shakedown experience. Weak pieces of equipment broke and were repaired; skittish animals settled to their work; men learned how to take a wagon across a stream bottom; women began to make themselves comfortable in camp. Since the start was made early in May, there was usually rain, and the feelings of these first few days were often as gloomy as the weather, with uncertainty and some apprehension, discomfort resulting from inexperience, and homesickness.

Ferries across the Kansas River were maintained by the Shawnees and Delawares, Eastern tribes which had been transported to the West.

2. To the Platte River—220 miles. At the ferry the trail shifted direction from west to northwest. Now everything was rolling properly, and no one as yet had had a chance to grow weary. The country was beautiful in mid-May—a rolling plain of emerald grass set with wild flowers. Stream crossings, with water still high from the spring rains, offered the chief hazard. You heard rumors of raiding Pawnees from the north, but the Pawnees never caused much trouble. (A decade earlier they had been dangerous, but the tribe had been stricken by smallpox and now offered little threat.)

This leg, about two weeks of travel, was likely to be the pleasantest of the whole journey, though there was no spectacular scenery, and the only unusual animal was an occasional antelope skimming along the horizon.

At length the wagons reached "the coast of Nebraska." Many people have taken this to be a figure of speech continuing the frequent analogy between the prairies and the sea, and such people have been likely to wax eloquent at the thought of the "prairie schooners" approaching the coast. But the phrase is a translation of the French *la côte de la Nebraska*, in which "*Nebraska*" serves as an alternate name for Platte, and "*côte*" is a term to indicate a line of bluffs along a stream.

3. To the South Fork of Platte River—135 miles. During a ten-day pull the emigrants traveled westward along the south bank, never far from the stream. They could now fairly consider that they were entering the real West. The land began to display the marks of aridity, and seemed strange to people who had lived amid the lushness of forests and cultivated fields. Here the broad grasslands stretched away, and there were no trees except along the riverbank and on islands. The hills and bluffs showed outcroppings of rock. The grass could still be called green, but hardly emerald. By now it would be June, and the grass was maturing.

So you went ahead, looking out to the right at the broad, shallow, brown river, and to the left at the low, grassy hills. Between the river and the hills an ample plain allowed the wagons to move easily westward.

Indians were rare. You were moving, so to speak, through a corridor between the Pawnees to the north and the Cheyennes to the south.

Antelopes no longer raised much comment. The first prairie-dog town was visited as a curiosity. And "Buffalo!" was on every tongue. Already people were using the dried buffalo dung—euphemistically called "chips"—for fuel.

Then, sooner or later, came the cry, "Buffalo!" In excitement women and children hurried to a place to see, and the hunters mounted in haste. This first sighting would probably be only of a few bulls. Even if the unskillful hunters managed to bag one, the meat was dry and scarcely edible.

But in a few days there would be more buffalo—and more and more. The hunters came in with steaks from fat cows, and people lived high.

The ford of the South Fork was fearsome-looking. The river was reported at different times as anywhere from six hundred yards to a mile and a half in width. To enter the water was like taking your wagon out to sea. Besides, an article of faith among the emigrants was that any wagon which became stalled in the crossing would be swallowed up by quicksand. (Just how they knew this to be true is hard to discover, since there is no record of any wagon ever having been so swallowed.)

Actually, in ordinary conditions, the river was not over two feet deep. Moreover the bottom was not very soft. So the crossing was usually accomplished without incident. If the stream was high, however, you would have to wait for it to fall.

4. *To Fort Laramie—180 miles.* Once across the South Fork, you angled over to the North Fork, and followed up along it. By mid-June the country was more brown than green, except in the moister bottomlands. But the animals ate the brown grass and

throve on it. The days were hot and the nights were remarkably cool; the more knowing people realized that this was because the trail had imperceptibly risen to higher altitudes. The sky was generally cloudless and the weather dry, but along the Platte the trains were usually struck by at least one severe hailstorm.

Here you were in the country of the Sioux; and the Sioux, those warrior horsemen, were potentially a serious threat. So the circle of wagons was made up more carefully at night, and the guards were set with stricter instructions. Yet, very likely, you still met no Indians at all.

By this time buffalo had become commonplace, and were generally reported in herds of many thousands. Another great source of interest to the emigrants, who were inveterate sight-seers, was the remarkable series of formations that began with the descriptively named Courthouse and Jail rocks. Then came the even more remarkable Chimney Rock, in sight for more than a day's journey; it was frequently compared to a funnel set upside down. The line of rock formations continued until it ended in towering Scott's Bluff.

After about twelve days on this leg the wagons pulled into Fort Laramie. At that fur-trading post a few supplies might be purchased. Considerable numbers of Sioux usually camped nearby; they might have ponies, moccasins, and skins for sale or trade. It was a place to settle back a little, take stock of things, and do some summing up. The distance traveled, thus far, was about 635 miles. You found that you had taken some forty full traveling days, and you would also have used up a few days resting here and there. You would expect to be at Fort Laramie, then, toward the end of June.

5. *To the North Fork of the Platte River—130 miles.* The road was rougher beyond Laramie, and you could no longer follow close to the river. This meant much work up and down hills and reduced the average distance between camps. You would take about ten days getting to the upper crossing.

They would be days of hard work, not very eventful or interesting, as the trail passed through what were known as the Black Hills. As the name indicates, they were not large or grand enough to be called mountains, and they were somber in color, because of pines and cedars.

This was all Sioux country, and the Indians often came into camp to trade or to ask for food. They were friendly, or seemed so. You did well to be friendly too, but to be on your guard, not to let requests for handouts turn into bullying, and to make a good show of firearms.

The upper crossing was a problem. In an ordinary year the water was too deep for fording, and the emigrants had to improvise at ferrying. The diaries often recorded the drowning of animals—sometimes, of people.

6. To Independence Rock—50 miles. Three days' travel brought you to a great gray mass of rock, like a stranded whale, rising above a broad valley. This leg, though short, was difficult and was likely to cause trouble. A bad canyon forced the trail away from the river; and so, for the first time, you faced the double problem —lack of water and bad water. Some pools were so heavily charged with alkali that cattle might die from drinking there. The name Poison Spring preserves this memory. Also, for the first time, you saw the dry beds of shining white which in the rainy season would be shallow salt lakes. These alkali flats were a fascinating curiosity, and some people scraped up a little of the white stuff and found that they could use it, like saleratus, for making biscuits.

Independence Rock itself was one of the notable landmarks. For years mountain-men had been inscribing their names there.

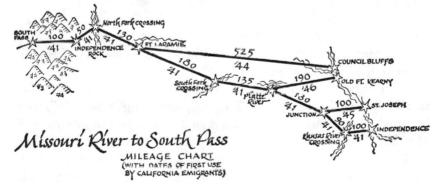

Missouri River to South Pass
MILEAGE CHART
(WITH DATES OF FIRST USE
BY CALIFORNIA EMIGRANTS)

Emigrants continued the custom, carving their names, or painting them, or crudely marking them with axle grease. He was an unenterprising fellow who did not make the easy climb to the top and take a look around. You could see an alkali flat and many strange-shaped and huge rocks, and, just at your feet, the little Sweetwater meandering through its broad plain. Off to the west were sharp and high mountains, suggestive of harder things to come. Close at the bottom of the rock would be the circle of the wagons, with the smoke rising from the fires of buffalo chips. Farther off in the valley you might see yellow spots that were antelope, and black mounds that were grazing buffalo.

7. *To South Pass—100 miles.* The valley of the Sweetwater formed a surprising topographical feature which any emigrant of religious convictions could ascribe to a Providence favoring American expansion. Here, in the middle of the Rocky Mountains, with high and rough peaks and ridges all around, the over-size valley of the small stream offered an easy passageway toward the west. It also assured water and grass, easy grades, and antelope and buffalo. It even supplied some fine sight-seeing—Devil's Gate, Split Rock, Sweetwater Rocks, and Ice Slough. This last was a boggy place where you could dig down through a foot of muck and come to layers of ice, even in summer.

The most surprising of all these was Devil's Gate, where the river had cut down perpendicular walls with high cliffs on either side. Fortunately you did not have to try to take the wagons through the gorge. There was, again as if providentially, an easy pass in the hills, just a half mile to the south.

Eight days should take you along the Sweetwater. It was Sioux country primarily, but you might hear tales of raiding Crows from the north, and even of Blackfeet, as well as of Snake war-parties from the west.

An easy day's climbing, after you left the stream, took you to the famous South Pass. This pass, also, might be attributed to Providence. Here, at the summit of the Rocky Mountains, the very backbone of the continent, the grade was easy, and the pass itself was more like a broad plain, so level that you were never sure when you crossed from the Atlantic to the Pacific watershed. A conventional spot to consider the top was a place where you went between two rounded knolls, startlingly white. (The true summit was a mile or so farther west.)

Crossing the pass, at the height of summer, you would marvel at seeing snow on the Wind River Mountains off to the north. Also, at this altitude of eight thousand feet, you might have a white frost at night and a skim of ice on the water-bucket. Once more everyone would be saying, "What a strange country!"

Another common source of astonishment was the tendency to underestimate distance. People were continually setting out to some place that they thought to be a mile or two off, and discovering that they might walk for half a day to get there. The misjudgment as to distance was usually credited to the clear air of the West, though the air was often, in fact, hazy. People who live in a wooded country without high mountains, we must remember, seldom get a chance to see for long distances. In the West, however, you often looked out across broad treeless valleys for twenty or thirty miles, and sometimes could distinguish a peak from a hundred miles off. Without experience to make them careful, people naturally underestimated.

8. *To Little Sandy Creek—20 miles.* From the pass it was only a long day's downhill journey, but it must be considered a leg in itself, because at Little Sandy came the forking of the trail. To the left, southwestward toward Fort Bridger, went the road where wagons had gone since '41; straight on to the west went the cutoff, the main route after '44. Since the country was open and easy, the trail developed branches, so that the wagons bound for Bridger's split off at various places, both east and west of Little Sandy.

9. *To Bear River, over the cutoff—110 miles.* First, you spent a day resting, either at Little Sandy or a few miles farther on, at Big Sandy. You cut some grass to take along in the wagons, and you were sure to fill all the jugs and kegs with water. After Big Sandy there was nothing, all the way to Green River. On no part of the trail was there more uncertainty about the distance and more variation in the estimates. In round numbers, forty-five miles was probably about right.

This was the hardest going yet encountered. You experienced, for the first time, a broad expanse of desert and distances from water that were frightening. Nothing like this at home! Generally this stretch took a day, a night (spent resting, though there was no water or grass for the cattle), and most of another day. You might well expect to have some of the weaker oxen give out, and then you could do nothing but abandon them to the wolves. Finally you came to the bluffs above Green River, and then made a difficult descent to the joyousness and safety of water and grass.

You crossed the river, usually by ferrying but by fording in a dry year. Then you followed the stream down for some miles, until you left it and entered the roughest mountain country yet encountered. But, after the desert between Big Sandy and the Green, these high ridges were a relief, with their pine forests and good streams and springs. This section of the cutoff ended, after about seven days' travel, when you came down to Bear River and rejoined the old trail.

At South Pass the buffalo range had ended. Now you could expect only antelope in the open country and a few deer in the wooded sections.

As for Indians, the desert was a borderland where you could meet war parties of either Sioux or Snakes. Fortunately the Indians would be more interested in fighting each other than in fighting you.

10. *To Fort Hall—125 miles.* At Bear River the trail swung sharply northward. The going was good, except in a few places where canyons forced the wagons away from the stream across hilly country. The principal scenic attractions were in the vicinity of the soda springs. One of them was named Beer Spring, but many people thought that it did not come up to its name, and in fact tasted too much of sulfur. Here also was Steamboat Spring, so called from the chugging noise that its waters made.

After this, it was a dull pull into Fort Hall. This leg altogether might take nine or ten days.

All this country was held by the friendly Snakes. They were horse Indians and lived chiefly by hunting, much as the Sioux did.

Fort Hall itself was a minor fur-trading post of the Hudson's Bay Company. Fewer supplies were generally available even than at Fort Laramie. Still, it was a place to rest a day or two, let the stock graze on the good grass, repair wagons, and bring your diary up to date.

From Fort Laramie to Fort Hall was the second major leg of the journey, to be reckoned at 535 miles. Altogether that would make it 1,170 miles from Independence—call it 1,200. You were a little more than halfway to California.

By now the date would be well into August, and you might tot up that you had been eighty-five days on the trail. If so, you would have averaged—by dint of steady plugging and some good luck, and including a few days when you had not traveled at all—about fourteen miles a day. That would be very good, and many companies would not do so well. In fact, by Fort Hall the different parties, some of which were late in starting, had strung out until there would be some weeks between leaders and tail-enders.

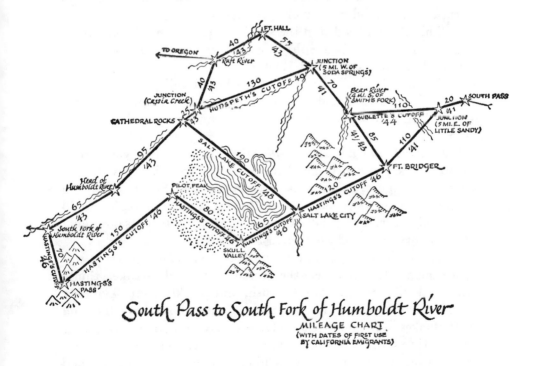

South Pass to South Fork of Humboldt River
MILEAGE CHART
(WITH DATES OF FIRST USE
BY CALIFORNIA EMIGRANTS)

11. To Raft River—40 miles. From Fort Hall the trail went westward along the south bank of the Snake River, which flowed through a canyon with perpendicular sides of dark lava and at American Falls tumbled spectacularly over a rock barrier.

The Indians here were Bannocks, closely related to the Snakes, but not so friendly. You would do well to watch out in Bannock country.

Two or three days brought you to the crossing of Raft River —a landmark, though the stream itself was so small that you could not imagine how anyone could have used a raft on it. But this was the point of the major split in the trail. Ahead, went the way to Oregon; to the left, California.

12. To Goose Creek—65 miles. The California Trail ascended along Raft River, southward, keeping close to a stream, as it always did when possible. Then it took off along the course of a tributary which is now Cassia Creek, but which in those days turned up in a wild variety of spellings.

This stream headed in the spectacular City of Rocks. At its southern edge high twin spires towered up, and these eventually gained the name Cathedral Rocks.

Beyond, the trail dropped into a broad valley, then climbed another high divide, and dropped again, very sharply, to Goose Creek. You used up five or six days of travel on this leg.

13. To the Humboldt River—95 miles. From where you struck Goose Creek you had to go about five days' easy journey, nearly southwest. Again, as with the Sweetwater and South Pass, you might call it providential, that in this rough and dry region could be found a series of small streams, offering easy passage along their valleys, with sufficient water and grass.

It was, however, uninteresting country. Although there was grass along the streams, the uplands were desertlike, thinly scattered with dry grass, sagebrush, and prickly pear. The only large animals were a few antelope. Jack-rabbits, coyotes, and rattlesnakes were more characteristic. By now, moreover, time was getting on. The vicious heat of the desert sun of late summer was taking the life out of everything. The oxen were gaunt, and

136

the people too. Everyone was tired—in mind, if not in body. In any long journey, there comes a point of weariness, beyond which new impressions make little effect. With the California emigrants this seems to have been reached at Goose Creek.

The Indians here were Shoshones, but the Americans know them merely as "Diggers," a derogatory term supposed to be derived from their digging in the ground for roots. These Shoshones were unwarlike, and were not greatly to be feared. Still, they had no scruples against stealing, and you did well to keep watch. Though an emigrant himself, at this stage, was generally far from clean, he regarded the Diggers as paragons of dirtiness and of general miserableness. They had no horses, and wandered about naked, or nearly so. The emigrant, in added disgust, noted that the Diggers seemed to eat whatever they could lay hand on, such as grasshoppers and rats. (Modern anthropologists make out a better case for these desert tribes.)

14. To Humboldt Sink—365 miles. The emigrants were just beginning to call it the Humboldt after the publication of Frémont's map. Before that, it had been Mary's River, or occasionally Ogden's. Anyone who was inclined to attribute things to Providence would have classed the Humboldt as a major miracle. Without it the covered-wagon migration to California might have been impossible. Seemingly endless, it marked off the longest leg of the whole journey. You could count upon spending three weeks along its valley.

First, you followed it toward the southwest, some seventy miles. Then a tight canyon forced the trail away from the river, and you camped for one night among the hills. You returned to the river, and followed it west and northwest. Then you followed around the big bend, and went southwest again, a hundred miles and more, to the sink. Sometimes the trail followed the right bank and sometimes the left. There were half a dozen crossings, but they were not difficult.

In fact, there was nothing really difficult anywhere along the Humboldt. There was always water and grass. It was merely a long pull— monotonous, monotonous to the point of wearing the nerves thin. The meadows along the stream might still show some green, but the hillsides were gray with sagebrush. Sometimes the mountains showed picturesque shapes, but by now you had seen plenty of strange formations.

The Indians were all called Diggers, but somewhat east of the big bend, the trail passed from Shoshone into Paiute country. The two tribes, though not closely related, lived in much the same way, because the desert permitted nothing else. The Paiutes, however, were more aggressive, and trouble was likely to start when the emigrants entered their country.

By the time the trains were approaching the sink, they were separated by long distances, depending upon luck and their policy as whether to push hard or take it easy. The head of the migration might reach the sink in the first half of September, and the tail end be a month or more later.

In either case, there was usually the halt of a day or two at the sink, where the river ended in a maze of sloughs, swamps, marshy meadows, and salt lakes. Grass and water were plentiful, and preparations had to be made for the hard pull just westward.

15. To the Truckee River—55 miles. From where you had camped near the sink there would be a dry stretch of about fifteen miles and then a place where a little brackish water might be found. Beyond that lay the Forty-mile Desert. There was no grass anywhere on this whole leg. In addition, there were some stretches of very hard hauling. All around, this desert presented by far the most difficult test which you had as yet had to meet. In addition, you came to it when the teams were already worn down by long travel, and when the Paiutes might have stolen or killed some of the cattle.

But it could be done. You halted long enough at the sink to cut a supply of grass to carry along in the wagons. You filled all the water containers, but there was never enough water, even so, to supply the oxen. Then you started early in the morning. You took the whole thing as one long pull—never camping, though making one or two halts to rest the oxen.

After sunset you kept plugging ahead into the darkness. Somewhere in the night, you came to the hot springs. If men had been sent ahead on horseback to dam the flow back, the water would have cooled enough for the oxen to drink it.

Even the most jaded sight-seer was a little stirred at coming to the springs. One of them threw up boiling water in a geyser-like way to a height of some feet. All around, other springs bubbled and gurgled and steamed, and there was a smell of sulfur in the air—as some people decided, a kind of outpost of hell.

Some miles beyond the springs came the heaviest hauling of all, through sand across a low ridge, where the animals sank knee deep. Few parties got across without losing some oxen.

Then, on the downgrade the pulling was better, and you caught sight of the cottonwoods along the river, some miles ahead, down the sagebrush slope. When you came to the trees and the water, it was as close to heaven as you had ever experienced.

16. *To the pass—70 miles.* A week or a little more took you up along the Truckee. Though you had the advantage now of water and enough grass, it was steady upgrade pulling, and hard most

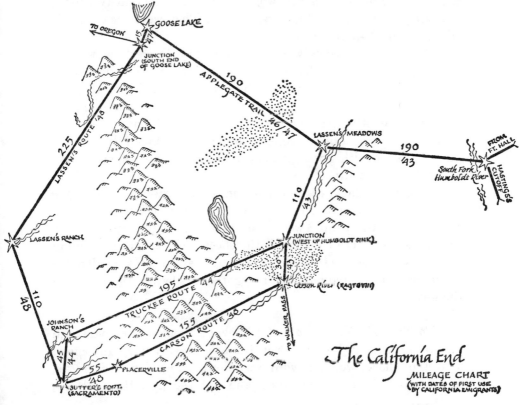

The California End

MILEAGE CHART
(WITH DATES OF FIRST USE
BY CALIFORNIA EMIGRANTS)

139

of the way. You had to cross that river many times by rough boulder-strewn fords through icy swift water. You might end by cursing the stream that you had so recently blessed.

When you turned away from the river above the meadows, by the road through Dog Valley, the pulling was hard, along mountainsides, with ups and downs. But here you had left the troublesome Paiutes behind and were in a region where you rarely encountered Indians.

The country itself was pleasant and forested, with big pines standing wide apart so that the trail wound its way among them. There were grassy glades also, with deer flitting among the trees along their edges.

Then, at last, you stood on the shore of the lake, and looked ahead at the pass!

17. To Bear Valley—across the pass—30 miles. The distance might not be more than you would expect to cover in two days, but here you would count on five, at least. They were the climactic miles, the hardest of all.

Two or three days would be necessary to get the wagons to the top of the pass, by every hook and crook that you could master. Then, on the west side, there was rough downhill going with danger of broken tongues and axles. Finally, you eased the wagons down into Bear Valley (at a place still known as Emigrant Gap) by snubbing ropes around trees. The valley was a pleasant place with good grazing, and most people spent a day or two there, resting.

A general lack of reference in the diaries to the scenic beauties of the Sierra Nevada is one of their striking features. By this time the people were simply too tired to enjoy things. As far as they were concerned, the sheer pass and the gleaming crags above it and the sapphire lake at its base—they were all nothing more than a hated barrier to be got across before snow blocked the way.

18. To Sutter's Fort—85 miles. Beyond Bear Valley you still had to work hard, but it was in the bag now! You might spend a week or more, working your way down along forested ridges, and up and down two canyons, and out through the foothills, and across the level Sacramento Valley. It would be mid-October, or later. In a year of early rains the valley would already be showing the green of sprouting grass. . . .

Then you sat in the autumn sunshine by the adobe wall of Sutter's Fort, and the train was about to break up. You talked with the others, and there was a sadness, for throughout many days and nights, you and those others had experienced greatly together, and now it was as if the veterans of a long campaign, or sailors who had voyaged far in the same ship, were parting company.

Then, figuring up, you would find that you had been on the trail for about five months. Let's see—to Fort Laramie, 635 miles; from there to Fort Hall, 535; from Fort Hall, 805; then, for the whole distance from Missouri, 1,975. Well, call it 2,000! Who could tell more closely—with all those twistings?

CHAPTER SIX

As in '45, the story began at the western end; from this time on, two-way traffic was to be the rule. Westward surged the full stream of migration in white-topped, ox-drawn wagons. Eastward trickled, on horseback and with pack animals, every year, some dozens of men, with a few women and children. These were chiefly the ones who, in the idiom of that day, "had seen the elephant," and were going home. Mingled with them were a few who intended to meet the westward-moving emigrants and offer their services as guides, and others who wished to visit "the states," pick up families or friends, and return west.

A company left from the Sacramento Valley in mid-April —nineteen men, three women, three children, with many horses and mules. Among them was Hastings, his restless spirit driving him on.

He saw two opportunities, or one opportunity that would lead to another. First he would be Moses, to guide his people through the wilderness; second, he would be Joshua, to lead them in the conquest.

He could explore a new route as he went east, and then lead the wagon trains along it. Beyond doubt, the trail should be relocated. It had never been planned for travel to California, but was a makeshift use of the Oregon Trail as far west as seemed practical. To go by Fort Hall was reasonable for people heading to Oregon, but for those California-bound this route meant an irritating detour far to the north. In '41 the Bartleson Party, trying to avoid the long way round, had headed west from Soda Springs. But they had met with no luck, and no one wished to follow their route.

Hastings had stated in his book that the California emigrants would find "the most direct route" by leaving the established trail about two hundred miles east of Fort Hall and "bearing west southwest, to the Salt Lake." But was it practicable in that direction for wagons, or was the way blocked by mountains and deserts? About such matters Hastings was totally ignorant when he wrote that vague passage. But his luck, as so often, held or appeared to hold, because his theory seemed to be confirmed by Frémont's explorations in '45.

That great Pathfinder had at least one quality in common with Hastings, that is, he was optimistic to the point of being irresponsible. He had, moreover, very little experience at travel by wagon. Nevertheless, having arrived in California at the end of '45, he confidently declared that the route which he had just explored was "decidedly better" for wagons, almost a thousand miles shorter and "less mountainous, with good pasturage and well watered." With such backing, Hastings had good reason to believe that his original idea had been remarkably right, and that the game was in his hands.

When he started eastward, his first problem, therefore, was simple, and his first opportunity was great. He would backtrack over the route publicized by Frémont, look at the country with an eye to wagon travel, and meet the emigrants. Then, if everything worked out properly, he would guide them to California. Thus, to be Moses!

But also to be Joshua! That too looked simple enough. Once he had established himself as the leader of the emigrants, he would arrive in California with a force strong enough to establish an American republic, after the model of Texas. He talked about the matter openly. One of his companions reported that Hastings was "looking for some force from the states with which it was designed to revolutionize California."

The writer of these words was James Clyman, mountain-

143

man, notable keeper of diaries, and all in all as shrewd and sensible an old-timer as you would ever meet. When the party came to the point at which the new trail branched off, Clyman was for continuing to Fort Hall, as some of the company did. In the end, however, he turned off along with Hastings. As they progressed, Clyman's skepticism grew into disbelief that anyone should attempt to take wagons across this hard desert country. Even Hastings must have begun to have qualms. But by now he was too far committed to withdraw easily. . . .

The second eastward-bound party of '46 left from southern Oregon in May—a dozen young men on horseback, prepared to move fast and to live largely off the country. Jesse Applegate, their leader, by whose name they have generally been known, later declared their object as purely altruistic, to work out a better wagon road to Oregon.

Going east and south, they somewhere crossed the trail made by Chiles's horsemen in '43. Still farther east they apparently picked up the trail where Frémont's expedition had passed in

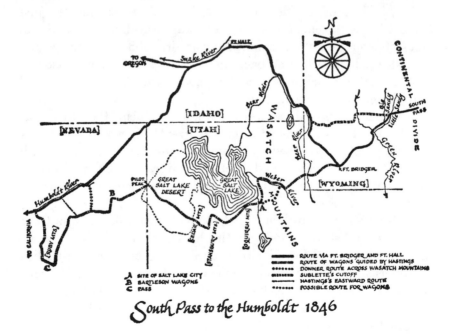

South Pass to the Humboldt 1846

the last days of December in '43. After following it for a hundred miles, the Oregonians boldly struck off on their own. Once, at a loss for water, they observed trails left by rabbits. Shrewdly thinking that these would converge toward water, they followed them, and thus discovered what is still known as Rabbithole Spring. Then pushing still farther east, they struck the California Trail, below the big bend of the Humboldt.

It was a bold and imaginative bit of exploration, skillfully executed. Moreover, these Oregonians took their work seriously. They traveled back and forth for considerable distances, working out what would be the best route. Eventually some of them rode on to Fort Hall to intercept the wagon trains. They had worked out a new way of reaching Oregon, but they had also, unwittingly, discovered the greater part of another branch of the California Trail. . . .

While the Hastings and Applegate parties were coming east, the emigrants had mustered, chiefly in the vicinity of Independence. One party, however, was preparing to cross the Missouri about forty miles south of Council Bluffs and to use what was later called the Nebraska City road. Thus, as early as '46, there were four possible places of take-off—Council Bluffs, the as yet unnamed point, St. Joseph, and Independence. There was also the military road leading westward from Fort Leavenworth, but this had little influence on the migration. All this plains country was, in fact, so level and open that a wagon could be taken across it almost anywhere. There was even some advantage in being the first. Once the passage of many wagons had broken through the sod, the road was likely to alternate between mudholes and deep dust.

The people who were preparing to set out in '46 faced a situation vastly different from that of any earlier year. Information about '44 was available, and perhaps even about the great success of '45. People now knew that there was a trail to California, plain to be seen, practicable to be followed. They also knew something about how much time would be required and about the conditions to be encountered. They could, therefore, make plans based upon experience and reason, with good expectation that these plans would be brought to realization by a prosperous journey and a timely arrival.

An interesting sign of this new confidence is a general lack of interest in hired guides. What was the use of paying out good money to someone, when the trail was already beaten down for anyone to see?

Moreover, guidebooks were available. Hastings's had been the first, although it was actually neither detailed nor reliable. Frémont's great report also was in the hands of some of the emigrants. Published in '45, it gave a description of the road to California as far as Raft River, supplied a good general map, and included also a detailed map for almost a hundred miles along Bear River. Overton Johnson and William H. Winter published their excellent *Route Across the Rocky Mountains* in '46, though perhaps too late for it to be of use to the emigrants of that year. These, however, were only the printed guides. Undoubtedly many people had letters from friends who had already gone to California, or had notes, taken down from conversation. . . .

This year a holiday spirit prevailed, as if people were setting out upon an extended picnic. Jessy Quinn Thornton, who recorded much about the California migration, though himself bound for Oregon, noted the men who "cracked their whips and cracked their jokes." As it seemed to him at one point, "All were filled with high hopes and expectations . . . all were animated in their conversation." At another time he honestly noted some that were careworn and many that seemed sad, and one wagon that went by with four or five children "crying in all possible keys." To balance these was the man "whistling as though his mouth had been made for nothing else."

Thornton's descriptions of those first days carried a suggestion of the idyllic. The people, he thought, were "plain, honest, substantial, intelligent, enterprising, and virtuous." Again, he noted:

All persons were remarkably cheerful and happy. Many were almost boisterous in their mirth. We were nearly all strangers, and there was manifestly an effort on the part of each to make the most favorable impression he could make on the others.

He reiterated: "All were obliging and kind; and there was even an extraordinary absence of selfishness." Still, since he did not publish his book until two years later, he felt constrained to add, as foreshadowing, that this was before suffering and want had "blunted the moral perceptions."

Most of the wagon-owners, this year as in earlier years, were prosperous farmers, and with them traveled their families, their hired teamsters, and an occasional hired girl to help with the cooking, washing, and child-tending.

Noteworthy among such family groups was that of George Harlan, from Michigan. He left home with eleven wagons and at least twenty-six people. The party moved in style, each wagon with its driver's name painted on it.

Samuel Young, Tennessee-born but lately of Missouri, had two wagons, twelve yoke of oxen, four cows and some heifers, a pair of mules, an extra horse, and a light carriage for his pregnant wife. (He could expect to get her to California before the baby would be born.) Also of the prosperous-farmer group were George Donner and his brother Jacob, from Illinois, each with three wagons.

But the emigrants of this year differed a little from those of earlier years, in such a way as to show that the image of California was changing. A reporter for the St. Louis *Republican* (by this year the migration had become important enough to attract newspaper coverage) noted the presence of "clergymen, lawyers, physicians, painters and mechanics of every trade." He generalized that the emigrants were "of as much intelligence and respectability certainly as ever wended their way to a new country," and he further concluded, "the integrals [elegant word!] are representatives from almost every state in the Union."

Justice, however, requires the admission that some of the "integrals" did not altogether attain respectability, and might even have to be classified as non-churchgoers. There was, for instance, Bluford K. Thompson, known as "Redheaded" or "Hellroaring" Thompson. A historian has described him as "a coarse, profane, reckless fellow, a gambler by profession, with some pretensions to gentlemanly manners when sober."

To offset such a character, one of the emigrants could even be considered a celebrity. This was Lilburn W. Boggs, known as a Western trader and a former governor of Missouri, famous for having loosed the state militia against the Mormons in the bloody little "Mormon War." He was by far the best-known person who had yet taken the trail to California.

There were others who stood out from the crowd—"Colonel" William Henry Russell, a former United States marshal; James F. Reed, a manufacturer of furniture; Edwin Bryant, late editor of the Louisville *Courier*. With them we might mention Charles Stanton, a businessman from Chicago, and Andrew Grayson of Louisiana, talented as an artist—perhaps the "painter" of the *Republican* account. Also to be noted, though little is known about him, was T. H. Jefferson, whose unusual abilities produced a detailed and accurate map of the trail.

These men, though they may be grouped together, differed widely in character. Of them all, Boggs and Bryant best showed the good sense and energy which were necessary for success on the trail. Stanton touched heroism. Reed also had a streak of the heroic, but his judgment could be erratic, and his temper was quick. Grayson was so quarrelsome that he got along with practically no one. Russell, as his nickname "Owl" might indicate, was a good deal of a natural-born fool, an amiable egotist who wanted to be beloved of all men and ended up by being scarcely beloved at all.

Two, at least, of the women deserve mention. There was Mrs. Reed, semi-invalid and plagued by migraine headaches, but in an emergency capable of passing through ordeals in which strong men quailed. There was Mrs. George Donner—that Tamsen who was to display more than a touch of the heroic. A schoolteacher before her marriage, she shows a mind at work in a few letters that are preserved. The destruction of her journal is possibly a real loss to American literature.

To be noted this year were some elderly people, one of them ninety years old and blind. Like pregnancy from the first years of the migration, old age was now considered no bar.

The foreign element, Irish and German, was more prominent than in '45. One notable German was Lewis Keseberg—tall, handsome, blond-bearded. He spoke four languages, and may well have been the best-educated person in the whole migration. He had two wagons; his wife carried a small baby, and was so far gone with another that she would obviously be brought to labor somewhere on the trail. (But deep within Keseberg lurked a demon. Of all who were making the journey he was to descend the lowest.)

Also to be mentioned are "the five German boys"—Lienhard, Thomen, Ripstein, Zins, and Diel. So poor that they could barely scrape together money for an outfit, they traveled five to one wagon. Pigheaded and quarrelsome, yet courageous and efficient, they are unforgettably pictured in Lienhard's journal.

This young Swiss was not the only scribbler. In fact, literature was in the air. Bryant was planning a book, and so was Tamsen Donner. Jefferson, also, must have been thinking of the publication of his map and commentary. As for Thornton, his work finally appeared in two volumes, so that he doubtless had it in mind from the beginning. A most literate and literary year!

Yet we have still to mention the best-known writer of all. This year the young Francis Parkman of Boston and Harvard College was on the plains. He made use of his experiences to write a book which the publishers were to sell as *The Oregon Trail* or *The California and Oregon Trail*, as the market veered. By either title the book is mislabeled, because its author was little interested in the trail and was blind to the significance of the migration. He was romantically interested in Indians, and associated with emigrants only when he could not help it. Yet, if we judge the book by its subtitle *Sketches of Prairie and Rocky Mountain Life*, we find it fresh and youthful, and can then accept as a bonus the occasional vivid pictures of the covered wagons. . . .

As the custom was, the emigrants went a little way beyond the frontier, and then assembled to effect their organization. Most of the Californians who left from Independence held their meeting on May 11, and elected as captain the amiable but ineffective "Colonel" Russell.

The next day there was an inspection by an appointed committee. The summation was:

Wagons	63	Breadstuffs (lbs.)	58,484
		Bacon (lbs.)	38,080
Men	119	Powder (lbs.)	1,065
Women	59	Lead (lbs.)	2,557
Children	110	Guns (mostly rifles)	144
Total people	288	Pistols	94

The number of animals was estimated at 700 cattle and 150 horses.

Thornton commented in summation: "The cattle were numerous, fat, and strong; the tents, new and clean; the food, of good quality and abundant in quantity and variety." The reporter for the *Republican* ventured a generalization: "The mode of travel is light wagons universally drawn by oxen and usually about three yoke to a wagon."

These emigrants were thus excellently equipped. Counting children at half-rations, we find each adult well supplied, with 250 pounds of breadstuff and 155 pounds of bacon.

If anything, these people had erred by overloading their wagons. The total poundage of breadstuff, bacon, powder, and lead was 100,000, or better than three-fourths of a ton to each wagon. In addition, the oxen must haul the women and children, other food supplies, bedding, camping materials, and whatever miscellaneous articles were being taken along for practical or sentimental reasons.

On the other hand, to compensate for this weight, the number of oxen was ample. At three yoke to a wagon, only 378 animals would be needed, and about 300, including some milch cows, would be left "loose."

The careful summation of weapons and ammunition suggests military organization, and in another tabulation we find the term "fighting men." Such a state of mind was natural to a time of war. On May 16 the company was overtaken by a horseman bearing a newspaper with an account of the opening of hostilities with Mexico along the Rio Grande. Although the emigrants were setting out for California, a part of Mexico, there was no particular alarm about the outbreak of war, and almost no hesitancy about continuing. Apparently these people knew enough about the situation to have confidence that from San Francisco Bay northward the Americans would be dominant.

Other reports also incited the emigrants to keep their powder dry. The Mormons were reported moving westward. By frontier standards of conduct you could only expect that they would be thirsting for revenge against Missourians in general, and especially against Russell's party, which harbored their archenemy, Lilburn Boggs. A report (given support by a letter from Colonel Kearny, commanding at Fort Leavenworth) was that Mormons to the number of almost two thousand were crossing the Missouri at Council Bluffs and St. Joseph, and would thus be ahead of Russell's party and in a position to intercept it. Another rumor upped the number to five thousand.

There were also the usual tales of Indian restlessness, and a special rumor to fit with this troubled time. Bryant noted the report that five Englishmen, emissaries of their government, had started along the trail to stir up the Indians to attack the trains and to "rob, murder, and annihilate." The dispute over Oregon gave credence to such a story, and also the fact that two British subjects, one of them an ex-officer of the army, were really on the trail. Far from being sinister agents, however, they were traveling for sport and adventure in company with Parkman, and they were as much afraid of Indians as anyone else was. In fact, Parkman's pen has turned them into comic-opera Englishmen, opinionated and bumbling. (Bryant's reference to them, slight as it is, has its interest as being the only passage in which any of the numerous chroniclers referred, even obliquely, to Parkman's party. If he ignored the emigrants, they equally ignored him.)

Russell's huge company, unrestrained by rumors, ferried across the Kansas River on May 18. That same day, as if to furnish symbols of prosperity, lusty twin boys were born to the wife of one of the emigrants. They were named Rupert and Russell after the attending physician and the captain, but the proud father called them his prairie wolves.

Large as it was, this company did not include all the emigrants leaving from Independence, and others were starting from other points. The California wagons of this year cannot be put as fewer than two hundred, and may well have been somewhat more numerous than that. The total of men, women, and children must therefore have been close to a thousand. (In '45, there had been only fifty wagons.) About three hundred wagons for Oregon were also on the trail.

The progress of this great migration, as far as the approaches of South Pass, was most notable perhaps for the bickerings among the emigrants themselves. The large companies with their military organization began to go to pieces in a few days, as soon as the emigrants realized that the daily journeying and camping were of much more importance than fighting theoretical hostile Indians and non-existent hostile Mormons. Russell's company, which had once been reckoned at 128 wagons, was soon down to 46. In addition, the organization of companies was frequently disrupted as captains were deposed and new ones chosen. One party, as a practical joke, elected a pompous egotist to be captain one day, and then by prearrangement voted him out the next day.

Sometimes the splits and reorganizations were accomplished peacefully and with good feeling; sometimes, with rancor. Parkman in his journal described the confusion when a disgusted captain suddenly resigned: "the hurly-burly—women crying—men disputing—some for delay—some for hurry—some afraid of the Indians."

The overtaking and passing of one party by another often led to hard feelings and sometimes to altercations. Since the trail was generally single-tracked and since one ox did not move much faster than another, such passing was attempted at noon halts, or by continuing the journey longer in the evening, or by the surprise tactics of getting up before dawn and taking to the road earlier than usual.

Parkman commented of the emigrants:

But, in fact, they have no leader—each man follows his own whim, and the result is endless quarrels and divisions, and all sorts of misfortunes in consequence.

The cream of the jest here is that Parkman had himself become infected with the spirit of schism. Adopting the early-morning technique, he deserted his English companions.

Normally some quarrelsomeness was to be expected during the later weeks of the journey, but in '46 it started almost at the beginning. Families and groups of neighbors generally continued together, but others joined, split, rejoined in other combinations, and then split into new groups, until the whole conception of a "company" came to be of little significance.

By experience, most people concluded that a group of ten or a dozen wagons was the most efficient. Such a party, totaling fifteen or twenty men, was numerous enough to be moderately safe against Indians, and to rotate guard duty at night. Larger companies were merely cumbersome, and slow-moving. Smaller companies might move more rapidly, but they either took chances or else the men burdened themselves with long hours of guard duty.

Still, many little groups went it alone this year, at least for a part of the way. "Uncle Billy" Graves, a farmer from Illinois, thus traveled for long distances with his three family wagons and only four men, counting himself. Andrew Grayson quarreled with everybody, and traveled for a while with his wife and single wagon.

These quarrels occasionally resulted in the flailing of fists, and even in the drawing of knives and the leveling of firearms. In sudden anger Zins, one of the young Germans, pushed a cocked rifle against Lienhard's chest. Lienhard knocked it away and grappled, and the two of them rolled on the ground in a wild free-for-all of hair-pulling. The height of the ridiculous was reached when two men, traveling together, quarreled violently, and yet found themselves connected more inseparably even than by marriage. One of them owned the oxen, and the other owned the wagon!

As usual, the Indians proved to be a threat and a minor nuisance, not a real hazard. The Pawnees, however, cut off and killed at least one straggler from one of the last companies. The Indians caused most trouble by crowding around and demanding to be fed. As the Mormons were later to discover on a larger scale, it was cheaper to feed them than to fight them. So the emigrants, partly in fear, cooked up messes of bacon and flour, and were happy to avoid trouble.

Stampedes of cattle, generally at night, were regularly blamed on Indians, but were probably more often attributable to nervousness caused by the smell of buffalo, or else to the plain cussedness of the bovine critter. One large company thus lost 123 oxen and had to purchase animals from other parties.

To offset such troubles some comic relief was furnished by Lucinda Jane Saunders. The Hoppe family had been unfortunate enough to bring her along as a hired girl, but she turned out to be what we may consider a low-grade moron with nymphomaniac tendencies. She was a thorn in the flesh of respectability, and most of the emigrants were highly respectable people. But even the unattached young men were afraid of Lucinda. She married one of them on one occasion, but after one night he resolutely refused to have anything more to do with her.

One incident illustrates much about both the ignorance and the toughness of some of the emigrants. On June 5 a boy of nine or ten fell from the tongue of a wagon, and the wheels passed over one of his legs, crushing it badly. His family laid him in the wagon, without even dressing the wound—doubtless considering, fatalistically, that he would either die or get well. After nine days of what must have been great pain he said that he could feel worms crawling in the leg, and his mother found the flesh swarming with maggots. Now alarmed, she tried to locate a doctor, but the best she could find was Bryant, who had once been a medical student and had gained some reputation among the emigrants for giving good advice about illness.

Protesting that he was no surgeon and that he lacked instruments, Bryant nevertheless rode some twenty miles to do what he could. He found gangrene so far advanced that there could be no hope of saving life by an operation. He so explained, but the mother, now swinging to the opposite extreme, insisted on an amputation.

Present in the company was a French-Canadian who had served as a surgeon's assistant. He assembled a butcher knife, a carpenter's handsaw, and a shoemaker's awl to take up the arteries. The boy was given laudanum, but with no apparent effect, and was tied out on an improvised operating table.

The amateur surgeon then commenced to amputate below the knee. The boy, though giving evidence of extreme pain, scarcely even groaned, and gave some words of encouragement to the one working upon him. This well-meaning fumbler had almost severed the partly putrified leg when he decided that he should amputate higher up. By this time Bryant could tell that the boy was failing. Still, the operation was continued, and the leg was severed above the knee. After an hour and three quarters, when the work was nearly finished, it was observed that the boy had mercifully died.

That same evening, within the limits of the same encampment, a marriage ceremony was performed and a baby was born —a demonstration of "Life goes on!" that did not pass without comment among the diarists.

154

The fording of the South Fork, because of high water and the large number of wagons, supplied more than the usual excitement. The men of the Young company raised the wagon-beds as high as possible, and then took the planks forming the bottoms of the beds and nailed these on top of the side boards. On this platform they lashed beds and bedding. Women and children sat precariously on top. The ox team was made ready, a man to each yoke—some with a man mounted on one of the oxen—and a man or two on horseback to ride on the upstream side with a rope tied to the upper part of the wagon to keep it from being overturned. Other horsemen rode alongside to steady the oxen, and the whole assemblage of oxen, horsemen, and wagon entered the water on a slant downstream. At this point the description breaks into a kind of Whitmanesque poetry:

If the wagons should be turned over, or the teams refuse to pull, or become uncontrollable!—The rushing of the waters against the wagons and teams, the excitement of the teamsters—to be placed at a safe and convenient distance, where you can see the wavering of the teams, to hear the loud hallooing of the teamsters, the excitement of the women and children perched on the top of everything, looking as if a breath of wind would capsize the wagons and plunge the helpless passengers in the turbid river, would make the hairs on the head stand as erect as if they were made of porcupine quills.

One of the later companies, finding the water still high and many teams ahead of them, continued on along the south bank, and located another ford about twenty miles farther up. Although this part of the route was known as the Oregon Trail, this new ford was called California Crossing—and, later, Lower California Crossing, after Upper California Crossing, twenty miles still farther west, had come into use. . . .

Throughout these weeks Hastings and his company had been riding eastward. In mid-June they crossed South Pass, and came down along the Sweetwater. Ironically, at this very time the American settlers were revolting against Mexican rule in California, and Hastings was not there! Instead, Frémont was grasping the opportunity.

Some of the party halted at Independence Rock, and among these must have been Hastings. There he would await the coming wagons—lurking, if we may use an old simile, like the spider for his prey. Shrewd old Clyman and some others rode ahead, about forty miles farther, and then, on June 23, they met the head of the migration, eleven Oregon wagons.

Riding on, that same day, Clyman came to the crossing of the North Fork of the Platte, and we can quote his own journal, spelling and all:

we had the Pleasant sight of Beholding the valy to a greate distance dotted with Peopl Horses cattle wagons and Tents, their being 30 wagons all Buisily engaged in crossing the River which was found not to be fordable and with the poor material they had to make rafts of, it took two trips to carry over one waggon with its lading.

Clyman continued eastward, meeting wagons for ten days, recording their numbers, and making additional notes. His is thus an unusual picture—the migration as seen from west to east. From his record the total spread can be calculated as nearly six hundred miles, that is, when he met the first emigrants some miles west of the crossing of the North Fork, the last emigrants still had five or six days to go before reaching the crossing of the South Fork.

On June 24, Clyman rode on eastward and met three small companies, about twenty wagons. But the next day he recorded —with obvious exaggeration, though it must so have seemed to an old mountain-man—"one continual stream," a total of 83. Then on June 26, when he was nearing Fort Laramie, his figure jumped to 117. Arriving at the fort, he found a large number of emigrants encamped, and his count hit its maximum of 128.

On the succeeding days, as he continued past Scott's Bluff and on, his figures were: 52, 15 (plus a party of packers), 22, and 6. Finally, at Ash Hollow on July 2, he met the last of them —19 wagons of Mormons.

His total count, which must be fairly accurate, was 503, with the packers to be added.

Clyman often wrote "squad of wagons," thus indicating that most of the emigrants had already split into small groups. He noted that most of the people were in good health and spirit, but their motivation puzzled him:

It is strange that so many of all kinds and classes of People should sell out comfortable homes in Missouri and Elsewhere pack up and start across such an emmence Barren waste to settle in some new place of which they have at most so uncertain information. But this is the character of my countrymen.

As Clyman rode along, company after company—especially those that were California-bound—hailed him and his companions as heaven-sent harbingers. What was California really like? What about Indians? What about the trail? Many emigrants were beginning to show some trepidation, realizing at last that the journey was more difficult than they had thought, and that not nearly as much was known about the trail as they had supposed.

Clyman, talking with them, was amazed at their ignorance and also at their foolhardiness at thus setting out with so little certain knowledge. As his conscientious keeping of journals would indicate, he was far from being the ordinary rough-and-tumble mountain-man. Not only was he intelligent, but also he had a sense of social responsibility. He did not think much of California as a place to live, and said so. (History seems to have proved him wrong, but he could only talk according to his lights.) Also he did not think much of Hastings's new route, and said so. What his companions were reporting, we do not know. Most likely some of them recommended the new route, or even praised it highly, being under Hastings's spell—possibly, in his pay.

From these conversations Clyman himself must have gone away with a certain sense of irritation and futility. Though he knew what he was talking about, people were apparently not believing him. Perhaps we may thus account for Clyman, in his turn, setting the emigrants down in his journal as an ignorant lot and thus, curiously, agreeing with Parkman, his complete opposite.

Yet, on the other hand, why *should* they believe him? He was merely a rough-looking customer whom they had happened to meet on the trail. They had never heard of him before. But Hastings—that was a great name! He had written a *book!*

So it went with Edwin Bryant, as intelligent and fair-minded a man as you would meet in many a long day's riding. At Fort Laramie he heard Clyman telling his story and wrote him off as another liar—"he had a motive for his conduct, more powerful than his regard for the truth."

That evening, however, Clyman had a better chance, for

he had met an old comrade, who might be expected to pay him more attention. This was James Reed, who was traveling with his friends, George and Jacob Donner. Their wagons were with what remained of "Owl" Russell's once great company. Boggs was the captain now, and there were forty wagons, probably still the largest party of all.

Reed and Clyman had served in the same company during the Black Hawk campaign, along with a certain tall and thin Illinoisan called "Abe." As old comrades, the two men fell on each other's necks—figuratively, that is. In reality, they probably shook hands somewhat formally, and said, "Why, you old son-of-a-bitch!" That evening they talked.

"Several of us," wrote Clyman, "continued in conversation until a late hour." Besides Clyman and Reed, there was Boggs, captain of forty wagons, feeling his responsibility. Thornton may have been another, and almost certainly the two Donner brothers. They were old men to be going to California, in their sixties—solid, well-to-do farmers of German ancestry, apparently not unintelligent, but probably not quick-witted either. Lacking experience, they probably said little. Thornton, also, who was bound for Oregon, would have been wise to keep out of the conversation. It must have been mostly three-cornered—Clyman, Boggs, and Reed.

There was liquor still to be had. Reed even had some choice brandy in one of his wagons. We may guess that they kept a bottle on the rounds.

Doubtless they talked of many things, but the serious business must have been the discussion of Hastings's route. Clyman gave his talk against it, in words that he later summarized, "Take the regular wagon track and never leave it—it is barely possible to get through if you follow it—and it may be impossible if you don't." Boggs was impressed.

Reed spoke up, as Clyman remembered, "There is a nigher route, and it is of no use to take so much of a roundabout course." Impetuous and strong-minded, Polish and Scotch-Irish mingled, it was like him to choose the "nigher" route, to plunge straight ahead toward the goal!

Clyman argued back, telling of the great desert to be crossed,

158

and suggesting, "a straight route might turn out to be impracticable."

But the final decision did not need to be made that night, and eventually they all went off to bed.

Yet, already among the emigrants of Fort Laramie there was a sense of the pressure of time. Against that, as well as against the prestige of Hastings, Clyman was arguing. As early as May 24 Bryant had been worrying:

I am beginning to feel alarmed at the tardiness of our movements, and fearful that winter will find us in the snowy mountains of California, or that we shall suffer from the exhaustion of our supply of provisions.

Now, at the end of June, to be merely at Fort Laramie was not too good. Bryant, Russell, and half a dozen others were so much concerned that they were buying mules, to travel by pack train.

The next day was June 28. And, curiously, four important chroniclers of '46 happened to be then at Fort Laramie. Thornton and Bryant were going west; Clyman was going east; Parkman had ridden in the eighteen miles from his camp.

That day Parkman saw some interesting sights. For instance, he saw the now-deposed Russell "drunk as a pigeon." The "Colonel," at the lacrymose stage, seized the fastidious Parkman by the leather fringes of his hunting shirt, for want of buttons, and poured out his soul.

His men, he said, had mutinied and deposed him; but still he exercised over them the influence of a superior mind; in all but name he was yet their chief.

In spite of Russell, the emigrants at Fort Laramie impressed Parkman a little—"more educated men than any I have seen." Perhaps he stumbled into Bryant and Thornton, though Thornton does not mention Parkman, and he was snobbish enough to be likely to mention meeting a Harvard graduate.

Parkman also wrote in a letter:

A party that passed yesterday, left at the Fort a woman, who, it seems, had become a scandal to them, and, what had probably much greater weight, caused them trouble to feed and take care of her. She is now lodged among the squaws of the traders—in a most pitiful situation; for it is quite impossible that she will be able to get to the settlements before many months at least, and, meanwhile, she is left alone among the Indian women, and the half-savage retainers of the Company.

Parkman, though we may pardon him in view of his youth, here displayed himself unfortunately. Quick to impute the worst motives to his despised emigrants, he himself did nothing to relieve the woman. His interpretation, moreover, is refuted in the account given by Lienhard, with whose party the woman had traveled. She had originally been with a man supposed to be her husband. But he had deserted her, having remarked, it was gossiped, that he wanted to have some rest during the night. Moreover, she then had two children with her. Lienhard wrote of her at Fort Laramie, "the notorious widow declared that she had decided to stay in the fort if no man would take care of her." In spite of this, at least one emigrant was much concerned. He tried to persuade the five German boys to take her in—surely an arrangement fraught with scandal. When those upright lads refused, he tried others, and finally he himself offered to take the responsibility for her. To this his wife put her foot down. The good man gazed at her in amazement for her lack of Christian charity but was unable to do anything more. One may feel some sympathy for the wife. The cramped confines of a wagon offered little chance for privacy, and to have added such a person to the ménage might well have seemed to court disaster.

The case raises interesting questions about the social organization of a wagon train. What, for instance, became of the two children? Did the emigrants, acting as a juvenile court, decide that they should be removed from the custody of an unsuitable parent?

As to the widow's ultimate fate, we may be permitted after this lapse of time some cynicism. Her career suggests mental deficiency; she had already been acting the wanton and possibly the prostitute. Such a woman was unlikely to starve in the early West, with its surplus of men. . . .

Moving on into the Black Hills, the California emigrants, many of them now feeling the pressure of time, began to face what may be called the great decision, since for some of them it would mean life or death. Should they go by Fort Hall, or take Hastings's route?

Most of them got their first word of it from Clyman and his companions. Later many of them encountered Hastings himself and his smooth tongue. After he had gone back to Fort Bridger, the emigrants met a messenger bearing an open letter. With the official and almost imperial sweep that Hastings so well adopted, this manifesto was dated at the headwaters of the Sweetwater, addressed to the California emigrants on the road. It hinted at political troubles, and everyone knew already about the war with Mexico. The suggestion, therefore, was that the emigrants should band together in large companies. And who but Hastings would be the leader of such companies? And would he not naturally conduct them by way of his newly discovered route?

It was shorter; all sources of information agreed about that. As to just how much shorter, there was tremendous variation in estimate—from 150 to 500 miles. Besides, the new route was reported to be better for wagons than that by Fort Hall. Well, yes, there was—to be sure—a desert to be crossed. Yet hope was held out that a route might be discovered to avoid this stretch. In any case, it was only forty miles! That was no longer than from Big Sandy to Green River on the cutoff.

Moreover—and this too was an aid to Hastings—the decision came, so to speak, in two installments. Your original commitment was not irreversible.

The first choice came twenty miles west of South Pass. There, if you took the cutoff, you went to Fort Hall. If you took the old trail, you went to Fort Bridger, about eight days' travel. There, by keeping to the old trail, you could still go by Fort Hall, and not lose much by rejecting the cutoff. But there, also, you made your final decision.

The plan was that Hastings would wait at Fort Bridger until the wagons had assembled. There you could rest your cattle, and let them feed fat on the rich grass of that pleasant spot. There you could repair wagons, and the women could wash the clothes. If you needed more oxen, you could buy them there.

Although the evidence is scanty, the indications are that most of the earlier California emigrants rejected Hastings's proposition. This was natural. Having got thus far early in July, they were not worrying about time and did not need to take chances. Those at the rear of the migration must have felt by that very fact that they were late. Everyone knew of the danger of being trapped by snow in the mountains, as had happened with the Stevens Party in '44. Any possibility of saving time would therefore have seemed important. In the end, some eighty wagons took Hastings's route.

Among the last to be thus diverted were about twenty wagons which had been part of Boggs's company. Their owners made this decision at Little Sandy Creek on July 19. Among them was Reed, who had not taken Clyman's advice. Accompanying Reed were his friends the Donner brothers. Each of them, and Reed too, had three wagons. The Irish-born Patrick Breen had three wagons for his large family. Keseberg, the big and handsome German, had two wagons. The others were modest one-wagon outfits, small families or single men traveling together.

They elected a captain. Reed would have been a natural choice, but he was somewhat aristocratic and arrogant and was not popular. Captain or not, he would remain for a while the most influential member. The election, however, went to the elderly George Donner, and the West thus was endowed with the name which has become one of its symbols for disaster and horror—the Donner Party. . . .

As Bryant wrote, "the great bulk" of the California migration went by Fort Hall. Some of these went by Fort Bridger, but most of them by the cutoff. Their journey, on the whole, was prosperous.

One of these companies, captained by Elam Brown, was horribly plagued by sickness, most likely typhoid fever. The epidemic struck before the company had reached South Pass, and rode with the wagons through Fort Bridger and Fort Hall, and down the Humboldt. One opinion was that the disease resulted from the large quantities of milk being drunk, and it may have actually been thus disseminated. At one time half the people were down. Two desperately ill men were left behind at Fort Bridger, each with a well man to care for him.

The company, afraid to delay because of the lateness of the season, pushed on as best it could. The men were worse stricken than the women, and at one time nine women were forced to drive teams. To relieve the emergency, drivers were hired from other trains. Among the dead were four heads of families—in one family, both father and mother. In Digger country the company followed the custom of burying the body in the trail itself, and then driving all the wagons across to hide the spot from the Indians.

As such a custom would indicate, there were troubles along the Humboldt that summer. Thornton wrote of the Diggers:

They steal the cattle, and conceal themselves behind the rocks and bushes, from which they assail the emigrant and his stock with their poisoned arrows.

As usual, the Shoshones were comparatively inoffensive, even coming into camp in friendly fashion and calling out, "Gee!" "Haw!" and "Whoa!" to show that they had encountered emigrants before. Still, they had to be watched, for they would steal anything from a shirt to a poorly guarded cow.

The Paiutes caused most of the trouble. The culminating incident occurred close to the big bend of the river, when the twenty or thirty men of a wagon train discovered what seemed to be a large band of Indians hidden in the reeds of a marshy place, as if in ambush. Though outnumbered, the emigrants had rifles and pistols, while the Indians had only their bows and arrows. The emigrants decided to attack. The Paiutes were soon routed, suffering—in the probably exaggerated opinion of the victors—a large number of casualties. Two emigrants were wounded, one of them so severely that he soon died.

This poor fellow was named Sallee. He was buried, but the Indians dug his body up. Later emigrants reburied him, but he was dug up again, so that the process had to be repeated. "Sallee's grave" became a lugubrious landmark of that year's migration.

The emigrants who had fought the battle left a note for later comers. The Indians generally did not disturb such notes, perhaps thinking them bad medicine. As a result, the companies following were warned.

But we should not consider the journey down the Humboldt in terms of guerrilla warfare. The Paiutes were nowhere numerous; they had no sense of organized hostilities; they doubtless had more interest in getting the emigrants through and out of their

163

country than in delaying their progress. As a result, Indian depredations were haphazard. There were even some friendly contacts, especially with Chief Truckee, who had aided the Stevens Party two years before. He again offered his services as a guide, and the emigrants once more admired his skill at drawing maps in the sand.

The Forty-mile Desert caused some hardship, and so also did the numerous fords of the Truckee. Still this group of companies pressed on.

In the end their numbers were augmented by the Brown Party. These typhoid-stricken unfortunates had decided to make for Oregon over the new Applegate Trail. At the proper point they turned off, abandoning the river which for so many miles had been their guarantee for water and grass. Immediately they entered a waterless country, scattered with a thin growth of sagebrush. After a hard day's journey, mostly uphill pulling, they came to the point at which they had been told they would find a spring, and discovered only a miserable trickle, not enough to water the cattle.

The explorers had conscientiously left a note here, but its information was discouraging, even appalling—that the next water was twenty-two miles farther on, and beyond that it would be twenty-eight miles to both grass and water. The note read like a death sentence.

In despondency the women got supper ready. As the people were eating, a woman suddenly said, "Let's go to California!" Once voiced, the new resolution swept through the whole company:

We knew that there was war in California, but as soon as we were done supper, we started back to the place where we had left in the morning, and reached it at one o'clock at night. We stayed there a night and day, and then started our journey to California.

Some other emigrants, including Thornton, took this route to Oregon, but met great hardships. . . .

Thornton and those others would later have much to discuss in common with the emigrants who followed Hastings and gathered, that summer, at Fort Bridger.

The fort was not proving to be as well located as its owners would have wished. The trouble was that most of the emigrants were using the cutoff. If they continued to do so, the fort would be by-passed and would have no trade. Obviously, then, Bridger and Vásquez would tend to be in alliance with Hastings, whose new route went their way. As in '45, the migration might feel the influence of the profit motive.

Bryant and his companions, arriving at the fort with their pack mules on July 16, found it a busy place—many emigrants encamped, besides five hundred Snakes and some mountain-men, including Joe Walker himself. The great Hastings, too, was there, and we can well imagine that he was living life as he thought it should be lived, knowing himself the leader and dominating spirit.

The chief topic of conversation must have been the new route. Not only Hastings and his men but also Bridger and Vásquez were talking for it, so that the general atmosphere would have been definitely favorable. But not everyone was convinced. Walker, for one, did not favor the new route, and in conversation with Bryant he "spoke discouragingly" of it.

From what he learned, Bryant adopted a compromising but reasonable position about Hastings's route. He decided to go that way himself. As he explained, "We were mounted on mules, had no families, and could afford to hazard experiments, and make explorations." But he was convinced that people with wagons should not risk it: "I wrote several letters to my friends among the emigrant parties in the rear, advising them *not* to take this route." One of these letters must have been addressed to Reed.

On July 20, Hastings started with about forty wagons and two hundred people, including the numerous Harlan clan. Doubtless he sighed in relief to have the matter assured. Once committed to the new road, the emigrants would be unlikely to turn back. Moreover, the word that many wagons had started already would be reassuring to the people coming later.

On the same day, Bryant's party of nine left the fort, and with them rode some others, who were Hastings's men and whose duty it was to explore a way for the wagons. In short, with negligence that was not short of criminal, Hastings was starting out with forty wagons, and at the same time was undecided where they should go. Moreover, he knew that there were difficulties ahead.

Right across the way rose the Wasatch Mountains—high, rugged, cut by canyons. Hastings had crossed these mountains when he came east, by a route which he must have considered questionable for wagons. He was hoping that a better way could be discovered.

Even on muleback, Bryant and his companions had a hard time getting across the Wasatch, and Hastings's scouts explored in all directions, constantly appalled by the difficulties of the canyons.

Meanwhile Hastings led his people westward to Bear River, doubtless following the route of Chiles's wagons in '43. During these same days other emigrants with about twenty wagons pushed out from the fort.

West of Bear River no wagons had previously gone, but the country was easy enough for several days' journey. Then trouble started for the head of the column. Hastings had decided not to retrace his eastward route, but to follow down the canyon of Weber River, where his scouts had done some exploring. But whether they had followed the canyon all the way through is doubtful. The river, just before it emerged into the plain near Great Salt Lake, cut through a frightful canyon, with high and in some places perpendicular walls of rock. The wonder is that the leading emigrants, seeing that canyon, did not simply turn around and go back, hanging Hastings to the nearest tree. Doubtless he talked himself out of it, at the same time persuading them to do things with wagons that wagons should really not do.

The first company spent several days at trail building, and then went over the rim of the canyon. At one point a wagon with all its oxen slipped off a seventy-five-foot precipice and ended in tangled destruction.

The next company hesitated to risk it. They halted and spent two days exploring. One scouting party rode clear back, twenty miles, and investigated part of the route by which Hastings had come east. Finally the company decided to take the wagons right down the river, as uncertain an expedient as taking them over the top. The water was swift, the river bed strewn with boulders. But this proved to be the right decision, and the wagons got through safely.

The next following company was Hoppe's, which included

166

the German boys. This company too decided to take to the water, and Lienhard left a description of what may be called the river voyage.

There were places where we unhitched all the oxen except the wheelers—then we tied both rear wheels. One man drove; the others held up the wagon. Then we glided swiftly down the foaming water. Then we again hitched up the oxen which had been freed, and now we went through the foaming river-bed filled with large boulders, the wagon threatening to tip over, first to one side, then to the other. At times we had to turn the wheels by their spokes; then we were forced to hold them back again with all our might, so that the wagon would not rush too fast upon a lower-lying rock and be dashed to pieces.

Thus, on the evening of August 6, after the taking of unreasonable chances, about sixty wagons (with the loss of one wagon) had been got through to the plain lying to the east of the lake. On this same day the Donner Party, having left Fort Bridger on July 31, came to still another point of decision.

That they were on Hastings's route at all can be attributed to double deception. First, they had been lured by his salesmanship. Second, Vásquez had failed to deliver to Reed the letter through which Bryant had attempted to give warning. In his reminiscences, Reed did not mince matters: "Vásquez, being interested in having the new route traveled, kept these letters."

On August 6, then, the party came to a place where Hastings had posted a notice. This note, apparently left before the wagons had successfully passed through Weber Canyon, advised that the emigrants could camp where they were and send a messenger forward to Hastings, who would then return and point out a better road for them.

Such news was disconcerting. But having already committed themselves, they could scarcely do otherwise than accept Hastings's advice. The company went into camp; Reed rode ahead.

He passed the difficult canyon, and finally overtook Hastings and many of the emigrants at the south end of the lake. By this time, it would seem, Hastings was losing what little judgment he had ever had, and possibly his nerve had broken. He would not make good on his word to go back and point out the new route.

Instead, he rode only to a high spot in the mountains, and vaguely showed the way by which he had ridden eastward. Apparently he did not recommend the canyon.

Reed got back to where the company was camped, having been gone five days. Except in so far as the rest may have recruited the cattle a little, these days were dead loss.

On Reed's testimony the decision was now made to leave the canyon and cross the mountains.

But this route offered difficulties which had not apparently been noticed by Hastings and Reed when they were passing through on horseback. In many places the way was thickly overgrown with bushes and small trees. Through every foot of such country the emigrants had to cut their way with axes. They numbered only about twenty men, and some of these were not skilled at such work.

On the third day of this labor, the three wagons of Franklin Ward ("Uncle Billy") Graves came up. With this accession, the Donner Party reached its maximum—eighty-seven people in twenty-three wagons.

Aided by four fresh men, the emigrants got back to their clearance. But the difficulties remained excessive—thickets, rugged terrain, high and steep slopes. Not until August 22 did they finally get free of the mountains. They were then about two weeks' travel behind the closest wagon in front of them. . . .

While the Donners had been struggling through the Wasatch, the emigrants with the sixty wagons which were more or less under Hastings's personal guidance had gone through their second ordeal. They had spent about a week in an easy journey around the southern shore of the lake. Then, turning a point of mountains, they had gone sharply southward, leaving the lake, and ending the day's march at some desert springs with good grass and water. Here they must begin the dry drive.

The word had first been that it would be forty miles, or might even be avoided altogether. But now the distance had stretched out a bit. The emigrants were apparently told to prepare for two days and two nights without water or grass. The more experienced men must have looked doubtful. Oxen were not camels. A day and a night without water was possible. A day and a night and another day—it *could* be done. But two days and two nights!

That was stretching things to the brink of disaster. The cattle might not make it.

Still, what to do? They filled all the water receptacles and cut what grass they could to carry along in the wagons. They left the springs in the morning. After a twelve-mile pull across a barren valley, the latter half of it steadily uphill, they came to another "spring," but found it a mere trickle of brackish water. Though the spot offered small comfort, they rested a while. Setting out again, they found themselves forced to climb stiffly over a waterless mountain range. The crest of the pass was a thousand feet above the level of the valley.

Through that night they pushed on, descending from the mountain, crossing ten miles of desert plain, and ascending a low ridge of sand, which made for hard pulling. Occasionally, as the slow hours passed, they rested the oxen, fed them a few bunches of grass from the wagons, and gave them a little water, if any was available.

From the top of the sand ridge—by then it might have been daylight—the emigrants looked out upon the appalling sight of a level desert of sand and salt, stretching away for more miles than anyone could estimate, finally ending in the dim distance against a high mountain.

Through the second day they pressed on northwestward. The oxen were tired and suffering from thirst. There was by now probably neither grass nor water to be given them. The desert sun beat down, and was reflected back from the sand and salt. Sometimes the pulling was very heavy because of the sand, and sometimes the wagons rolled easily across a hard and level surface of shining white salt.

As night fell for the second time, the emigrants were still in the middle of the desert, seemingly not much closer to the mountains on the other side. By this time, after thirty-six hours, the oxen were suffering badly, and progress through the night dropped to a crawl. Sensing trouble, some captains sent scouts ahead on horseback, to report back on distance and conditions. Dawn showed the mountains still far away.

This morning of the third day brought the time of crisis. The oxen, forty-eight hours without water, were beginning to lie down and with difficulty being prodded to their feet. At this point differences in weight of wagons and strength of teams became important, and all pretense of maintaining companies vanished under the pressure of necessity. Many people were close to panic, especially the mothers with children. Even groups of family wagons could no longer keep together; each individual wagon progressed as best it could.

Throughout the morning wagon after wagon came to a halt, as the oxen failed. About the same time the scouts began to ride back, telling that the distance to water was still twenty-five miles!

The only solution was to unyoke the oxen and drive them ahead, in the hope that they could reach water. The wagons were left standing in the desert, with the women and children looking out from them in terror at being thus abandoned.

The threatened disaster, however, did not quite materialize. Freed from the weight of the wagons, nearly all of the oxen managed to get to the good spring just at the base of the far-off mountain. Having been rested, watered, and fed, the animals were strong enough to be driven back to retrieve the wagons.

The crossing, which in the beginning had been about the same for everyone, came to present great diversity in the end. A few emigrants got through without having to drive the oxen ahead. Among these was Hoppe's company, which included the diarist Lienhard.

These wagons started about nine A.M. on August 17, and completed the crossing a little after four P.M. on August 19. This time of fifty-five hours may have established a record for speed. During that period the oxen had not been unyoked. They had been rested the first night, and for short intervals afterward. Each had had a water ration of about a gallon and a half. Lienhard attributed the success to the care with which the oxen had been handled, but he was also ready to admit some luck.

The diarist James Mathers was less fortunate. His party left on August 15, and at midday on August 17 they were forced to abandon many wagons. Mathers stayed with one of these. The oxen did not arrive back at the wagon until the evening of August 20, and Mathers did not reach the spring until eleven A.M. on August 21. He had thus taken five days, twice as long as Lienhard.

170

A comparison of dates shows that Hoppe's company passed Mathers's wagon while it was standing in the desert. Actually the people guided by Hastings, though under several captains, during this stage of the journey were so close together that they often mingled.

The whole distance, far from being the originally reported forty miles, was at least eighty miles, and might reasonably be set at eighty-three! An ox team moving at two miles an hour would therefore have taken forty-one and a half hours to make the crossing—without resting at all. The achievement of Hoppe's company in taking only fifty-five hours thus seems all the more remarkable. . . .

The rigor of the desert crossing was slightly eased by the continuing low comedy of Lucinda. The respectable farmer with whose family she had been traveling was finally outraged beyond measure at some vagary of her conduct. Bundling up her scant possessions, he threw them out of the wagon, just as it was leaving. "The man-crazy Lucinda," as Lienhard called her, took up her bundle and wept. Then followed great argument as to who should take her in, since everyone agreed that she could not be left there. Eventually someone was found to assume the responsibility—"reluctantly."

As often, the resiliency of the emigrants was remarkable. In spite of the "misery" which even Lienhard admits they had suffered, the young people of his company had a dance on the very afternoon of their escape from the desert. Someone played a violin, and "they danced till the dust flew."

On the next day, while wagons were still being brought in from the desert, the dance was renewed. Lucinda then joined with the young girls—"like a devil among angels." Becoming excited, she threw a chunk of wood at her former "husband," just missing his head. But in spite of snubs Lucinda remained at the dance.

Although the crossing ended in a kind of rout, no lives were lost and none of the wagons had to be abandoned. There was, however, a toll of oxen. One unfortunate man with a large family lost his seven yoke and was able to continue only by borrowing teams.

By now, even the most stupid of the emigrants must have realized that Hastings's judgment was not to be trusted. But he had a talking point left. He could still say that by taking this difficult route they were gaining much time and distance on the emigrants who had gone by Fort Hall. . . .

In due time, the Donner Party started across the desert on August 30. Perhaps their oxen were already worn down by the hard struggle in the mountains; perhaps a certain ineptness dogged the party; perhaps it was merely bad luck. They lost a large number of oxen, and had to abandon four wagons. Worst of all, they lost more time. In crossing the desert, hunting for cattle, and recuperating, they expended ten days, and thus fell still farther behind. . . .

But even the companies with Hastings were not making as rapid progress as they had hoped. When the teams had recovered after a few days' rest, Hastings had led on, still across a barren country necessitating long marches between water and grass.

At one spring the emigrants, to their great surprise, saw some fragments of wagons. As it happened, however, one man of this company had a copy of a little pamphlet written by John Bidwell about the Bartleson Party, and from this account the wagons were identified as those abandoned on September 16, 1841. The owner of this pamphlet jotted a note in the margin, "We cooked our supper and breakfast with fires made from the remains of these wagons." (By a lucky chance this particular copy of the excessively rare pamphlet is preserved in the Bancroft Library.)

A few days' journey farther on, Hastings made another major mistake. At this point a long day's march due north, across easy country, would have brought the wagons to the established trail at the head of the Humboldt River. Hastings, ignorant of the geography, kept on southwest.

Already, he must have been wondering what he was going to do, and how he would get the wagons out of the blind end into which he seemed to be leading them. Scouts, we may guess, had been sent ahead. For by now Hastings surely realized that he could not expect wagons to go where horses had gone. On his way east, he had ridden right over a high range of mountains, but this range now blocked the wagons. He had missed his chance to go north, and now he had no recourse but to turn sharply in the other direction.

172

He took the wagons three days' journey south, with a high range of mountains blocking the way to the west. Probably by this time a scout had ridden back with the word of a break in the range. On the fourth day, Hastings turned west, took the wagons through an easy pass, and then turned north. During three days the emigrants marched north, having on the east the mountains which they had just had on the west, and leaving the marks of the great detour upon Jefferson's map. Finally they swung off northwest, went down a rough little canyon where the German boys upset their wagon, and at last rejoined the main trail.

The first to reach it soon picked up a note, left by another party. They thus discovered that for all their hardships and dangers they had only lost time. Even the party captained by Governor Boggs, which had been far behind at South Pass, was now five days ahead.

As for the Donners, they were now just getting ready to leave the spring at the western end of the desert crossing, and they too would have to take the long detour south and then back north again....

At this time, in the second week of September, an over-all picture is possible.... In this year the distance had, so to speak, been shortened by the establishment of Johnson's ranch, about forty miles north of Sutter's Fort, and the emigrants began to date the end of the journey by their arrival there.

The owner of this new outpost of "civilization" was described by one emigrant as "a rough sailor, dwelling in a dirty, little hut, and surrounded by naked Indians—a fact which we understand caused some confusion among the ladies of the train." Nevertheless you could sometimes buy beef on the hoof at Johnson's, and on arriving there you considered yourself out of the woods.

Bryant and his companions on muleback, traveling fast and being able to avoid the detour to the south, had suffered no trouble or delay, and so arrived at Johnson's on August 30. There they "learned the gratifying intelligence, that the whole of Upper California was in possession of the United States." Again, the luck of the Americans had held.

Next in the line of the migration came the two wagons of John Craig and Larkin Stanley from Ray County in western Missouri. Along with the owners were half a dozen young men.

The party had started from St. Joseph on May 1 for Oregon, and had always been among the leaders.

On July 2, at Big Sandy, Hastings visited their camp, and doubtless because of his persuasion they went by way of Fort Bridger. But they resisted the temptation of Hastings's cutoff. On July 19 they were at Soda Springs, having covered 1,100 miles in eighty days, at something less than fourteen miles a day. This was good but not remarkable. At this point Craig and Stanley decided to push ahead by themselves, their goal now being California. Traveling with only two wagons and unhampered by women and children, they stepped the pace up.

On July 23 they passed through Fort Hall, not even stopping overnight. Bryant and the fast-moving packers did not overtake them until August 18, at the sink. On August 21 the two wagons came to the Truckee River, having traveled 665 miles from Soda Springs in thirty-three days, for an average of better than twenty miles a day—remarkable going!

In the difficult terrain of Truckee Canyon and the Sierra Nevada the daily average dropped to ten miles. The party lost some oxen from exhaustion and starvation, and others either strayed off or were stolen by Indians. One wagon was reduced to a single yoke. Still, the party arrived at Johnson's on September 13.

This success illustrates the adage, "He travels fastest who travels alone"—or at least—"travels in a small company." It must be attributed to good management, good teams, and good luck. All along the Humboldt they had been the leaders, and so had got through before the Paiutes were alerted and alarmed. Their time over the 1,935 miles from St. Joseph to Johnson's by way of Fort Bridger—136 days, at fourteen miles a day—was as good as anyone could expect to do in '46.

On that date the closest emigrants behind were just approaching the pass. The most advanced that can be located, though probably not the leaders, comprised the twelve wagons captained by Joseph Aram, which were then somewhere along the Truckee. Behind them, scattered at intervals of a day or two, came other parties that had used the Fort Hall road. Small companies now were the rule. The largest for which the number is reported, fourteen wagons, was that captained by Governor

Boggs. (This was the final remnant of the great company which had organized under Russell, and had once comprised 128 wagons.) At this time Boggs was near the big bend of the Humboldt.

Behind Boggs, four or five days' journey, came the first of those who had followed Hastings. After them came the others, split into several parties, and extending probably over forty or fifty miles of trail. To their chagrin, along with them came a small party which had left Fort Bridger a fortnight later but had gone by Fort Hall. . . .

Just resuming the march after the desert crossing, the Donners were separated from the preceding wagons by a gap of nearly three hundred miles. By then they had begun to realize that they were in serious trouble. Many oxen had been lost in the desert; food supplies were low; time was running out. On September 10 they encountered the sudden flurry of a little desert snowstorm—the worst of omens. . . .

Far ahead, the Aram company was close to the pass. That wall of granite at the head of the lake had always been the worst barrier on the whole trail. At this time, though we have no definite record, there may already have been companies trying to get their wagons across, so that a bottleneck had developed. In any case, the Arams halted, and spent three days exploring.

As a result, they did not take their wagons along the north side of the lake, but went up the next stream-course to the south. The pass that they had found there was about seven hundred feet higher than the one at the head of the lake, but the approach to it was easier. With no great strain on their teams, they took their loaded wagons up to a point within a hundred yards of the summit. There, moreover, they were not faced by granite ledges, though the slope ran up at an angle of 35 degrees, too steep for oxen to do much pulling. The Arams, setting out to cross this summit about September 16, used ten yoke of oxen to each wagon. Five yoke were attached directly, and the other five, having been taken to the level spot above, pulled on a long rope which had been let down to the wagon below.

This new route, by Coldstream and Emigrant canyons, displaced the older one. All of the later parties in '46, as far as the record shows, crossed by it. The devices used to surmount the steep pitch at the summit were varied. The differences resulted

175

not only from the greater or less mechanical ingenuity of particular emigrants, but also from different conditions. Some had more and stronger oxen, and lighter or heavier wagons. Others, in spite of pooling their resources, did not have enough rope or chain to serve.

One party constructed a roller to keep the chain from dragging on the ground. The men first planted two forked trunks of trees securely. In the crotches, doubtless somewhat rounded out, they placed a round tree trunk, its ends chopped down to a smaller dimension. Rubbing the crotches with axle grease, they then had a moderately efficient device.

Some emigrants, who must have been well supplied with chain, seem to have used an even more complicated mechanism. They looped the chain around the roller, thus enabling some of the oxen to pull downhill. At the same time, doubtless to take some of the strain off the roller, they kept other teams pulling from the top. A diary states: "we made a roller and fassened chains to gether and pivoted the wagons up with 12 yoke oxen on the top, and the same at the bottom."

One company, lacking enough chain, cut small trees, notched the trimmed trunks at either end, and fastened them together with short lengths of chain. Some people made props or drags, and attached them to the rear axle to hold the wagon if the chain broke, as sometimes happened. Some companies assigned a man to each wheel. At best it was a difficult and hazardous crossing.

The last of the Fort Hall parties got over the pass around September 26; the first of Hastings's parties, about five days later.

On October 16 the company including the wagons of Samuel Young (the last of all, save the Donners) arrived at the approach to the summit. Snow was falling "at a fearful rate." Not only did the storm create a special hazard, but the people were jittery besides. On the lower slope of the mountain a chain had snapped just behind the wheel team and the wagon had gone over the side, ending in total wreck. In addition, there was the problem of Mrs. Young and her new baby. Hopes of getting to California in time had faded with the disappointments of Hastings's route, and the child had been born six days before. Young himself now had a special reason to be among those who were bitterly angry at Hastings. The mother was still in a weakened condition.

The carriage which had been provided for her comfort was now worked up the slope as far as possible, and eighteen yoke of oxen were attached to it, making a team so long that the lead oxen had footing on the level ground at the top. A man stood by each yoke.

Then the still-shaky mother and her baby were placed in the carriage. Mrs. Young could not help remembering the wagon that had just gone over the mountainside.

At a signal each teamster shouted at his oxen. In their anxiety the men were too vociferous, and confused the oxen instead of encouraging them. The long team wavered back and forth in snake-like motion, the drivers shouted the more, the oxen fell into further confusion. Mrs. Young was terrified and cried to be taken out and to be allowed to walk.

When some order had been restored, her friends expostulated that for her to attempt to walk up to the summit would be certain death. She insisted.

With her husband giving what assistance he could, she struggled up the steep snow-covered slope through the snowstorm. When she became exhausted, she sat down in the snow to rest. Wearily reaching the top, she found a tent set up and a fire built for her. She drank some hot tea, and spent the night in the storm at an elevation of almost eight thousand feet. In the morning she was none the worse for the experience. . . .

Once over the pass, the emigrants felt themselves almost arrived. Actually, they had a week of their hardest and most dangerous travel ahead. A team belonging to Boggs went over the side of a canyon, and team and wagon were saved from total destruction only because the wagon caught against a fallen tree by the side of the road. The oxen were held suspended by their own chains, with the tips of their feet just touching the ground.

Two days after crossing the pass, Nicholas Carriger noted, "Distressing bad road," and on the next day, "Laid by." The reasons for the halt were made clear by the next entry. On that day, by ironic coincidence, the diarist had to mourn for the death of his father, and to rejoice for the birth of his daughter. . . .

177

And still, though there was snow on the pass, the Donners were far behind. Not until September 26 had they emerged from the cutoff and come to the Fort Hall road.

They then split into two sections. In spite of failing oxen, they toiled on as rapidly as possible, having every reason to hurry. They had already sent two horsemen ahead to get provisions from Sutter and come back for their relief.

Inevitably, as happened with most companies, nerves were wearing thin, and there were quarrels and backbitings. October 5 brought a crisis.

At a difficult sandy hill, there was an altercation as to which of two teams should go first. With the one wagon was James Reed; with the other, a young fellow named John Snyder.

Snyder struck with his whip butt; Reed, with his knife. Reed, hit on the head, went to his knees; Snyder staggered and fell.

"Uncle Patrick, I am dead," he cried out, as Breen came hurrying up.

At last it had happened! In an isolated emigrant train, far removed from all machinery of justice, not even within the United States, one man had killed another. In a way, it had happened before, and not so far from this very spot, when John Greenwood had killed the Indian. But that was somewhat different. Now it was one of their own people against another. In a well-organized train, prosperous and with high morale, the deeply ingrained American sense of government might have asserted itself. But in this little group there were only about ten wagons, and scarcely more than that number of adult men. Moreover their natural leader was the killer himself. The Donner brothers were with the other section, a day's journey ahead.

The section now faced with emergency included the Graves and Breen families, each with three wagons; there were also William Eddy, whose family now shared a wagon with the Reeds; Keseberg with one wagon; and probably some other Germans with one or two wagons. Snyder had been driving a wagon for Graves. Though not a member of the family, he had been a popular young fellow, one of the clan.

The company immediately encamped. The simplest solution would have been for Reed, like John Greenwood, to take to his horse and gallop ahead. But to have done so would have been to desert his family, and also to expose himself alone in a country of hostile Indians.

We can imagine the talk during the day, the gathering into little groups, the looking to pistols. The Graves were crying for justice—not to call it vengeance. With them joined the Breens. Keseberg, who hated Reed for his own reasons, was the most violent of all. Eddy courageously stood by Reed. With Reed also was his teamster, Milt Elliot. All three were heavily armed. Reed was naturally courageous and was now desperate; Eddy was the best shot in the company.

Keseberg, crying out for what would have been nothing less than a lynching, propped up his wagon tongue with an ox yoke for the hanging.

But as long as the three on the other side stood firm, Reed could not be seized without casualties, and the result might be the crippling of the party and the death even of the women and children.

At last, through Eddy, it was arranged that Reed was to be banished from the company. When the others promised to care for his wife and children, he acquiesced.

From this time on, the march of the Donner Party degenerated until it became like the rout of a shattered and beaten army. Over its people hung the threat of death—from starvation, from snow in the mountains, from the Indians. As was likely to happen to stragglers, the Paiutes closed in. They took a steady toll of cattle. Men venturing to go hunting had arrows shot at them from ambush.

By this time the oxen were so few and so weak that only the people who were wholly unable to walk were being carried in the wagons. A single man named Hardkoop, aged about sixty, straggled on the trail, and never rejoined. Perhaps the Indians got him. But he was known to have been in a weakened condition, and some people thought that he might have been saved if anyone had ridden back to help him. But those who wished to do so had no horses, and those who had horses refused to wear them out in what might well have been a fruitless search.

At this time the Reeds' family wagon was abandoned if, indeed, it had not been one of those left in the desert. This was the wagon which has since been called the Pioneer Palace Car, though no such thing as a palace car was known in '46. It was huge and high-built, its false floor so far above the other floor as to make the wagon seem two-storied. It had spring seats, entrances with steps at the sides, and a sheet-iron stove with a stovepipe going out through the wagon cover. In it Mrs. Reed's old mother had ridden for some weeks, until she quietly died. There the hired girl had cooked, washed, and even churned butter, as the wheels rolled on. But the wagon was so heavy that it required four yoke of oxen. The wonder is that Reed was able to bring it as far as he did. Other unusually large wagons were to appear on the trail in the next few years, but the fate of this great lumbering van must be considered prophetic of what was to happen later.

By now the men were so exhausted and demoralized that they kept only ineffectual guard over the cattle. Night after night some loss occurred. More wagons had to be abandoned until the whole company could muster only about a dozen.

A disastrous loss of twenty-one oxen at the sink left Eddy with only one ox, and a German named Wolfinger was in an equally bad state.

The weather had turned hot, and the crossing of the Forty-mile Desert was sheer horror. The wagons were hauled by mixed teams of scrawny oxen and cows. Eddy and his wife walked, carrying their two small children. Each family fended for itself.

Wolfinger had stayed behind to cache his property, now that he could no longer move his wagon. Two other Germans stayed to help him. A few days later the two rejoined without Wolfinger. They said that the Indians had killed him, but the story had an ugly look and the two were not free from suspicion.

Laboring up Truckee Canyon, the emigrants had a moment of joy when Stanton (one of those sent ahead) rejoined them with two Indian *vaqueros* and seven pack mules laden with food. Stanton brought the word that Reed had got through safely.

To recuperate the oxen, the company halted at Truckee Meadows, where the grass was rich. They waited several days, though the weather was threatening and they could see some snow on the mountains already. At this camp a man was killed by the accidental discharge of a pistol.

Though many parties crossed without fatalities, the Donner

Party at this point had lost no fewer than five men. One of these had died from disease. Death from an accidental pistol discharge might also be counted as almost "natural." But there had also been a homicide and two unexplained and mysterious disappearances. Already the survivors must have begun to feel that they were marked for disaster.

They faced it surely a few days later. . . . The Breens with a few others and four or five wagons came to the pass on October 31, attempted to cross, found themselves blocked by the snow, and had to turn back.

Thus to be stopped by an early snowfall was the decisive bad luck. In '45 Hastings had crossed the pass toward the end of December; in '44 the Stevens Party had taken wagons over in the latter part of November.

At two places, near the lake and some miles farther back on the trail, the men built log cabins or erected shelters of brush and canvas. The site near the lake was that at which Schallenberger had spent the winter, and the Breens made use of his cabin.

These emigrants, like Schallenberger and his companions, had hopes that the snow would melt, or that they could get through the winter by eating their cattle and killing game. The snow, however, piled up deeper and deeper, and in a violent storm most of the cattle wandered off and were lost. Eddy risked his life to kill a grizzly bear, but no other large game was seen. Lacking traps, the people were unable to catch coyotes and foxes as Schallenberger had done; even so, such game would not have supplied eighty people.

To record here the full story of the Donner Party would be to expand an episode out of proportion.*

Hunger and cold, deep snow! . . . firewood harder to get as the men grow weaker . . . the first death—a young man gone, not from starvation, but from malnutrition or mere despondency . . . other deaths . . . desperate attempts to escape across the pass on improvised snowshoes . . . the dogs killed and eaten . . . always the necessity of cannibalism pressing closer.

Little Stanton, exhausted by the snow trail, sitting at the campfire, smoking his pipe, saying, "Yes, I am coming soon,"

* For a full account, see my *Ordeal by Hunger, The Story of the Donner Party.* New edition, 1960.

181

though he knows he will never come. . . . Eddy, failing, almost to safety, weakly bringing his rifle to bear on a chance-sent deer, as Mary Graves stands by, weeping. . . . Mrs. Reed, at Christmas, saying, "Children, eat slowly, there is plenty for all." . . . Patrick Breen, keeping his diary through everything: "Murphy's folks or Keseberg's say they can't eat hides. I wish we had enough of them." . . .

Those who first ate the human flesh "averting their faces from each other, and weeping." . . . The valiant seven of the first relief, whose names "ought to be recorded in letters of gold," grimly plodding in single file across the snow. . . . Matter-of-fact eight-year-old Patty Reed saying, "Well, ma, if you never see me again, do the best you can." . . . Reed, leading a relief party, meeting two of his own children on the snow trail . . . "Aunt Betsy" Donner, that kind and motherly soul, crying out in the hysteria of horror, "What do you think I cooked this morning?—Shoemaker's arm." . . . Tamsen Donner making the final choice, sending her three little girls away to promised safety, turning back to nurse her dying husband.

There is basic horror too in the tales of Keseberg. The storytellers would make him out to be as much ogre as man. Even so, we cannot echo Poe:

> And much of Madness, and more of Sin,
> And Horror the soul of the plot . . .

Instead I would rather write here again the words that I wrote—justly, I think—many years ago: "Through the story runs the scarlet thread of courage and the golden thread of heroism. . . . For though despair is often close at hand, it never triumphs, and through all the story runs, a sustaining bond, the primal force which humanity shares with all earthly creatures, the sheer will to live."

The summation may be brief: dead, forty; survived, forty-seven. The emigrants of that year attributed the disaster to Hastings. Eddy, his wife and children dead, set out one day to shoot Hastings, and was only with difficulty dissuaded. Although Keseburg has found defenders, no historian has attempted to whitewash Hastings. Returning to California, he found himself discredited among the emigrants and saw the American flag already flying. He had bungled at being Moses, and had missed his chance to be Joshua. During a few years he maintained himself as a man of some status. The historian, H. H. Bancroft, summed him up: "never without some grand scheme on hand, not over-burdened with conscientious scruples." Though born in Ohio, he chose the Southern side in the Civil War. In 1863 he went to Richmond with one of those grand schemes—to seize Arizona and southern California for the Confederacy. Nothing came of it. He died in 1870, still with a dream of empire, trying to establish a colony of ex-Confederates in Brazil.

"The notorious Lucinda," as Lienhard called her, reached California in high spirits. She at once married "a husky young fellow" who soon became ill and died. Edmund Bray, who had been with the Stevens Party, then became interested in her, but this "rather dried up Irishman" decided that he preferred a bachelor life. Lucinda then found her métier by marrying a sailor. She liked this so much that, according to Lienhard, "she repeated this experiment three times in six weeks." In consideration of the direction in which her career seems then to have been pointed, the present writer agrees with Lienhard, "It's a good thing I don't know any more stories about Lucinda." To conclude with a cliché: "It takes all kinds of people to make up a migration." . . .

The year is remembered as that of the Donner Party—and rightfully, since later emigrants were never free of the shadow of that disaster. The memory of death and cannibalism brooded over the yearly migration as the ultimate horror and the never-relaxed threat. The Donner name was fixed upon the creek, the lake, the mountain above the pass, and the pass itself. A bronze monument of heroic size and a state park identify the site. The whole emigrant route across the mountains has come to be known as the Donner Trail.

But '46 was also the year of a great and successful move-ment over the trail. It saw some important experiments at estab-lishing new routes. One of these, Hastings's Cutoff, was largely discredited at its very opening; because of its twistings it lost the distance that it theoretically saved. Besides being more difficult, it was also 125 miles *longer* than the route by the cutoff and Fort

Hall. Another experiment, the Applegate route, was at first only a trail for Oregon, but was later to exert its influence upon the California migration.

The really important trail to be opened in this year was the stretch of forty miles which the Donner Party cut through the thickets of the Wasatch Mountains, at their own great cost of time and energy. Once opened, this route proved to be a good one. Though rough and mountainous, it by-passed the dangerous Weber Canyon and opened a way to the fertile plain where Salt Lake City was to be founded. This trail was a godsend to the Mormons, who poured across it in '47. A considerable part of the later California migration used this route.

CHAPTER SEVEN

By '47 THE POLITICAL importance of the opening of the trail had become manifest. The Bear Flag revolt of June, 1846, had been the first in a series of events which ended with California becoming a part of the United States, and the participants in the revolt were largely men who had migrated by covered wagon. Among their leaders was William B. Ide of '45.

In November, 1846, Frémont enlisted a battalion, to ensure the conquest of southern California. It numbered 428; as Edwin Bryant stated, it was "composed of volunteers from the American settlers [chiefly the men of '45], and the emigrants which have arrived in the country within a few weeks [that is, the men of '46]." The list of officers included a number who have been mentioned in this history of the trail: Bidwell, Baldridge, Hensley, Myers, Reading, Russell, Bryant, Hastings, Grayson, and "Hell-roaring" Thompson. . . .

In '47 occurred the mass migration of the Mormons and the founding of Salt Lake City, and also the passage of some hundreds of wagons to Oregon. Among these multitudes, ninety wagons heading for California were almost curiosities.

Though this total was nearly twice that of '45, it was less than half that of '46. The obvious reason for the slump was the war with Mexico. In the preceding year, people had gone ahead

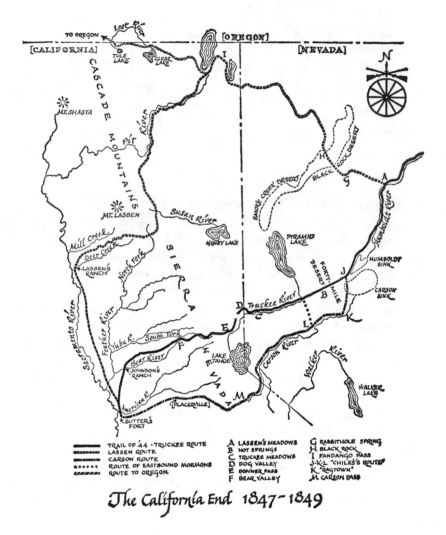

The California End 1847-1849

in spite of the news of open conflict, since by that time they could not turn back without disruption of plans and financial loss. But anyone starting in '47 must have so decided in the full realization that he did not know what was happening in California—that the whole country might be in the confusion of war, or that the Mexicans might be imprisoning every American who crossed the border. As so often before, we can only wonder that anyone at all started. Such action in the spring of '47 was an expression of sublime confidence that Americans could outfight Mexicans.

We may also think that the large emigration of '46 had exhausted the backlog of those interested in California, so that there was a natural shrinkage. A correspondent of the San Francisco *Star,* the only newspaper in California, had another idea—that certain returned emigrants "of the Genus Horse Thief" had declared California to be unsuitable for settlement, thus turning people to Oregon. (The image of a poor and weak California being slandered by a rich and powerful Oregon is a novel one in history.)

The emigrants, this year, seem to have been almost exclusively farming people. The scanty records indicate a prosperous journey, with only the ordinary run of incidents.

There were signs this year that things were developing, as civilization moved in. . . . West of Fort Laramie you had a split in the trail, offering the choice of whether you kept close to the river or farther back from it. Though the trail itself was not overcrowded, the establishment of such an alternate route doubled the possibilities for campsites and good grass.

A few days' journey farther west, at Deer Creek, you saw a billboard! Of course, it was a poor thing compared to those magnificent ones now lining our highways over the mountains and across the deserts, giving our city-dwelling drivers a feeling of comfort and security. Still, great oaks can only grow from little acorns, and this beginning at Deer Creek stood thus:

NOTICE

To the ferry 28 ms the ferry
good and safe, maned by experienced
men, black smithing, horse and ox
shoing done all so a wheel right

This was the Mormon Ferry, near the site of present Casper, Wyoming, established by order of Brigham Young on June 18, thus to turn an honest penny for the benefit of the Saints. The fee, significantly not given on the advertisement, varied greatly— seventy-five cents to four dollars for a wagon. Of course, the wagons differed in size and lading, but it was probably more a question of what kind of bargain could be struck and how prosperous a given company looked. The diarist at the ferry recorded for July 2, "11 wagons and 1 extra load for $12," and added, "ware agoing to Calafornia."

On the Sweetwater many emigrants met Bridger, and he told them of the Donners. But that news probably made no one decide for Oregon, because Bridger also had a tale that twenty wagons had been lost without trace on the way to Oregon. This latter story was not correct, but the emigrants would not have known it at the time.

Green River was low enough to be fordable, except for a narrow channel in the middle. To get across, some people doubled teams, so that either the lead team or the wheelers would have footing and could pull the wagon, when the other oxen were forced to swim.

This year no one turned off for Hastings's Cutoff. The news of the Donners had at least accomplished something!

Finally, at Raft River, the Californians pulled out to the left, leaving the Oregonians, and young Bill Trubody, accompanying twenty wagons turning off, always remembered how sad the people were, bidding good-by and calling, "If you ever come my way, come and see us."

The men of these twenty wagons, just after the separation, elected Charles Hopper as captain. He was a good man and a veteran of the trail—that same Hopper who had been the Bartlesons' best hunter in '41 and had ridden east with Chiles in '42.

Hopper's was the leading company, but others followed close behind. All the wagons must have formed a kind of long-strung-out caravan, so that the advance scouts of one party could sometimes see the dust column from the company ahead, and in the early darkness the cattle guards could make out the glow of distant campfires.

Along the Humboldt, at first, the Diggers came into camp

and were friendly. But inevitably those simple and unnoble savages, quite unschooled in the sanctity of private property, yielded to their natural instincts and made off with four oxen, a cow, and a horse. The emigrants then began to shoot at every Indian they saw. This system was probably as humane a one as could have been adopted. There is no evidence that any Indians were hurt, but they took the hint and stayed away from the camps.

How successful a journey it was may be shown by the small details that Bill Trubody remembered—for instance, that some people had a few hens along with them and were getting fresh eggs; then, when these people came to the hot springs in the Forty-mile Desert, they boiled some eggs in the springs, and had eggs for breakfast.

The party went up along the Truckee, where the crossings had been reduced to twenty-seven—a number often mentioned in the next year or two. In good time, about the middle of September, the wagons got to the lake under the pass. The cabins there had been burned by a party going east, but there were still some gruesome remains around.

Hopper's company decided, for some reason, not to go around by the route discovered in '46, but to reopen the original trail. They took their wagons along the north shore of the lake, then up the pass as far as they could go without too much trouble to a place that they called Timberline Camp. Fifty men, probably including some that were sent ahead from the parties following close behind, went to work with picks and shovels for a day. Their chief labor must have been to build ramps of stone to get the wagons up the granite ledges. Having done this work, they took the wagons across the pass with "little trouble." About October 1 the wagons began arriving at Johnson's, and within a few days about sixty were in. . . .

Only one party was still on the trail. Like those who had gone with Hastings in '46, these people had decided to follow their own particular piper. Again like those who followed Hastings, they were to supply most of the adventure for the year.

To understand what happened, we must shift back to '43. In that December, Frémont was making his way eastward and southward across what is now southern Oregon. About twenty miles west of the body of water that he called Summer Lake he came to a small stream which flowed east and then south. Instead of merely reporting what he saw, he committed the cardinal but common sin of explorers—making assumptions beyond the evidence. He jumped to the conclusion that he was on the headwaters of the Sacramento River. In reality this little run of water was the Sycan River, the waters of which eventually reach the ocean by way of the Klamath. But, in his great report, with all the authority of an official explorer, Frémont published, "we became immediately satisfied that this water formed the principal stream of the *Sacramento* River." Moreover, he also wrote of "subsequent information, which confirmed the opinion." One hardly cares to guess what this so-called confirmatory information may have been, since it was wrong.

The error was also enshrined on the magnificent map accompanying the report. Much better, if the mapmaker had placed, as the custom once was, a few elephants in place of towns! At least, such decorations would have deceived no one. But here, on the most authoritative map yet published of the West, the name Sacramento was bestowed upon this far-northern stream, which was then connected by a dotted line to the main river, eventually flowing past Sutter's Fort. What man in his right mind would doubt such authority? Certainly not the average emigrant, who was a simple farmer, barely able to read and write.

This year, instead of Hastings, it was William Wiggins. A New Yorker of no great ability or distinction, he had lived in California since '40. He had been at Sutter's Fort for a while, but there is no likelihood that he knew anything more about the mountainous northern area than he might have picked up in gossip with the few people who had traveled there. He went east on horseback in '46, and the next spring started back for California. With this experience behind him, he became either the captain of a company or its paid guide. Somewhere along the Humboldt, as Wiggins himself later told it, he and his men met "a company from California" who gave them a "waybill" from there to a river called Sacramento. Most likely this document was what has been preserved in another copy as Applegate's Waybill, an itinerary of the Applegate Route to Oregon, including the name, "Sacramento River."

Wiggins and his men need not have been merely naïve in

190

accepting this "information." Doubtless they had a copy of Frémont's report with them, and they would have found that it apparently checked with the waybill.

In reality, everything was doubly confused by now. The stream noted as Sacramento on the waybill was neither the Sacramento nor the Sycan, but what is now called Lost River.

Putting all the "information" together, Wiggins decided to avoid the Forty-mile Desert and the other difficulties of the California end by following the Applegate Route until he came to the "Sacramento." So far, we can commend him for basing himself on the best authorities. But his next idea was a bad one—that, having come to the Sacramento River, he would simply follow down along it to the Sacramento Valley. By so doing, indeed, he could be sure that he would not have to cross a high mountain divide. But anyone should have known, as the difficulties along the Truckee and the Weber had shown amply, that trying to follow a river could get you into trouble.

Nevertheless, Wiggins and his party so decided. They turned off the main trail—eighteen wagons, about twenty-five men, and twice that number of those hostages of fortune, women and children. Through the hard desert country they followed the trail of the emigrants who had headed that way for Oregon the year before. They must have been well equipped and efficient, for they took their wagons in good-enough time across three hundred miles of hard going. Eventually they came to the "Sacramento," which did, indeed, flow southward at that point.

Scouting a few miles downstream, however, they found that the river flowed into a lake. To the south of the lake were lava beds and high country, and no indication of an outlet. In addition, the lake water may have been brackish to the taste, and doubtless the evidence of different water levels indicated a lake without an overflow. Wiggins at once became convinced that the waybill was "entirely erroneous," and that the river was not the Sacramento.

He then acted with excellent judgment. He did not waste precious time in trying to force his way southward, pigheadedly, through almost unknown mountains. Instead, he brought the wagons back to the Applegate Trail, and followed it westward to the Oregon settlements, arriving there about November 1.

The disappearance of this party raised much to-do in California. People feared, with good reason, that another Donner disaster was occurring somewhere in the tangled northern mountains. Two expeditions pushed northward in attempts to find the vanished emigrants. On account of the snow neither expedition was able to get far, and their failures only renewed the strength of the rumors. As if in repetition of the Donner story, some men were said to have come in from the company and reported that the people were trapped in a canyon. The mystery was at last resolved in April, when Wiggins himself arrived at San Francisco by sea.

CHAPTER EIGHT

IN '48 THE MOST IMPORTANT EVENT to influence the history of
the California Trail occurred on January 24. "This day," wrote
a diarist at Sutter's mill, "some kind of metal that looks like gold
was found in the tail race."

But the significance of this discovery was not recognized for
a while, and then the news took time to spread. No one setting out
for California in the spring of '48 knew about the finding of gold.

The year was remarkable for boldness of enterprise. Doubtless the increasing geographical knowledge was making men con-
fident. By '48 an intelligent and experienced man could finally
begin to make a reasonable appraisal of the problem as a whole.
He would know that the trail from the Missouri River to California could be broken down into four main sections.

1. From the Missouri to South Pass everything was fine. The
route was direct enough and the going was good. You could
scarcely expect to find anything better. There were several points
of take-off from the Missouri, all of them satisfactory. Which one
you took merely depended upon what point was most convenient
for your start.

2. The second section twisted from South Pass to the head
of the Humboldt River. This was a hard one! Here you ran into
deserts, difficult mountains, and the Great Salt Lake. In '41 the

Bartlesons had come to grief by attempting a direct push westward. From '43 to '45 the California-bound wagons had gone circuitously through Fort Hall. In '46 Hastings had tried for something shorter, unsuccessfully. You still had to take your wagons clear around by Fort Hall, but you felt in your bones that there must be a better route somewhere.

3. From the head of the Humboldt to its sink, again, there seemed to be little chance of improvement. This route wound about a little, but it offered grass, water, and generally easy pulling.

4. From the sink to California—that was bad! Desert, canyon, difficult pass, rough mountains! Surely there must be an easier way! Wiggins had tried to find one in '47. His failure had not proved that failure was inevitable. . . .

In the spring the emigrants began to assemble at the frontier towns in what we may call the usual manner. The majority of them were Oregonians, but about a hundred ox-drawn wagons and four hundred people were bound for California.

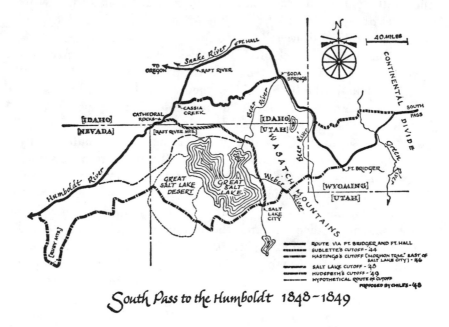

South Pass to the Humboldt 1848-1849

The suspicion of disturbed postwar conditions in California apparently held the numbers of the migration down almost to those of '47. Its constituency reflected this same uncertainty. The proportion of prosperous farmers and their families seems to have fallen off, though the McCombs clan formed a considerable part of one company. An observer gave as his opinion, "A more motley or heterogeneous transient population would be difficult to imagine: the canny Scot, frolicksome Irishman, sturdy John Bull, phlegmatic Teuton, besides representatives of every state of the Union from Maine to Georgia."

As was customary at the start, Oregon and California wagons mingled in the same companies. In one of the leading parties, California-bound again, was old James Clyman. With the rearward wagons—his record shows that he was not easily hurried—Joseph Chiles led a large company toward his habitual destination. This would be his fifth journey across, and this time, at last, he was bringing his children along.

We may consider that '48 established a "first." Some three hundred letters, addressed to people in Oregon, had piled up at Independence, but there was no mail service. The postmaster arranged with an emigrant named Bayley to transport these letters, with the understanding that he could collect forty cents apiece from each person to whom he delivered one. (This would seem to be part of the Oregon story, but it worked out differently.)

Let us also record romance. . . . Stephen Broadhurst was driving the oxen of Levi Hardman, whose unmarried sister-in-law, Martha McCombs, was caring for the Hardman children. Martha was to ride in the wagon driven by Stephen. This created what the pair considered to be "a difficult situation," or perhaps the propinquity was enough. "So they did the only wise thing possible—a few days before the take-off, they went to a preacher and were married, receiving a written certificate." They kept the marriage a secret, however, even from "the folks," until well out on the plains, when they confessed.

The year derived some color from three "stag" companies "on packs," as the saying went. . . . The Cornwall Party, which left from Council Bluffs two weeks ahead of anybody else, consisted of seven young men with a guide described as "woodsman, hunter, scout and freelance." Being so far in advance and thus isolated, they were all taken prisoner by the Pawnees. The young men managed to talk themselves out of it, glibly persuading the Indians that troops were following close behind and would take vengeance for any harm done. Eventually it came to shooting, and one emigrant was wounded and some Indians killed.

But be it known that this company, in addition to bullets, also carried books. Though packers must travel light, one man brought a Bible, a dictionary, *Irish Eloquence*, and volumes of Byron, Moore, and Burns.

Another company of packers included the much-initialed J. P. C. Allsopp, a youngster just out of the wartime navy, who was definitely adventure-bound, along with a group of other young Southerners—"fully armed and equipped; red shirts, pea jackets, rifles, revolvers, and the thousand and one incidentals which were considered indispensable." But these young men, also, may be considered carriers of culture. Halting along the Platte they indulged in amateur theatricals—thus, we may think, establishing a "first" for dramatic representations in Nebraska. Their plays, with men taking the female parts, were the then-popular farces *Box and Cox* and *How To Raise the Wind*.

A third party of ten packers left late, but traveled rapidly, and began passing the wagon trains along the Platte. The leader was that thoroughly experienced frontiersman, Samuel Hensley, who had been one of Chiles's horsemen in '43. He had gone east in '47, and was now returning.

Curiously, Hensley's was the only one of the pack trains to continue all the way through; the others, alarmed at rumors of hostile Indians, joined wagon trains. This is the opposite of what happened in other years, when people having wagons abandoned them somewhere and continued by pack train.

As usual, people also started eastward from California. . . . Peter Lassen was born a Dane, and had grown up to become a blacksmith. But wanderlust smote him. In '19, himself aged nineteen, he went to the United States; in '39, to Oregon, overland; in '40 to California, by sea. After knocking about for a while, he managed in '44 to get a land grant—one that might be described as "farthest north," about a hundred miles up the Sacramento Valley from Sutter's. There he lived, a Scandinavian island wholly surrounded by Indians, whom he gradually took into his

196

employ. Although he might be described as "colorful," Lassen seems to have possessed no outstanding abilities. (His main achievement has been to put his name on things. He has now become the eponymous hero of a high mountain, a national forest, a national park, and a county—this last, in a state which has named no county for either Washington or Lincoln. The name was pronounced "Lawson" by early Americans, and was often so spelled. It also appears as "Lasson" and "Lassin," carelessness in orthography being rather the rule in those days.)

Lassen had some ambition, and the greatness of Sutter must have been a spur to him. Could not a Dane do as well as a Swiss? And part of Sutter's prosperity resulted from his fort being the terminus of the emigrant road. Why should Lassen not bring emigrants to his own ranch?

An event of '46 may have moved him in that direction. Frémont had gone north, starting for Oregon, and then, at the word of the outbreak of the war, a courier had ridden after him to recall him. Lassen had been one of the courier's escort. In this expedition, if not before, he gained more acquaintance with the northern mountains.

In the spring of '48, like another Hastings, he rode eastward, presumably having some others in his party. To have explored the new route as he went along would have been the wise course, but the evidence suggests that he took the regular trail, probably going as far as Fort Hall.

The second company to start east was a very different one. ... At the outbreak of the war, the government had enlisted a battalion of Mormons. This battalion made a remarkable march through Santa Fe to California, but arrived too late for the party. Its members, having never fought a battle, were discharged in California, with the idea that they would rejoin the Mormon community and their own families. Meanwhile, they took whatever jobs they could find. Many of them worked for Sutter, and some of these were at the mill when gold was discovered. From then on, they amused themselves at digging nuggets out of rock crevices with their pocketknives, but the lure of gold never supplanted the lure of families and of religion.

On April 9—as Henry Bigler, a highly interesting diarist, recorded—"the boys" held a meeting, and decided to set out for

197

Salt Lake City by June 1. They also debated another question. Some of them had started east in '47, and had crossed Donner Pass. There the word from Brigham Young had reached them that they should go back to California to spend the winter. The bearer of these instructions, who may have had his own reasons for keeping these people in California, had apparently told them horrendous stories about the difficulties of the Truckee Canyon with its many river crossings—"very deep and rapid." At the meeting, therefore, a vote was taken "that we send out a few men as pioneers, . . . to pioneer out a route across the Sierra Nevada and if possible find a much nearer way than to go the truckey route and shun Crossing the Truckey river 27 times."

Delayed by late-melting snow and by the growing fascination of gold-mining, "the boys" did not get started by June 1. The wonder of it is that they ever got started at all. As Bigler wrote, "it seemed to me that all California was on the hunt of gold." Nevertheless—and it must be considered a high tribute to Mormon piety and discipline—they at last assembled near the site of present Placerville. On June 25 they sent three men ahead to scout and discover a possible route for wagons. Ten days later, nothing had been heard from these men, and everyone was growing uneasy. So ten more men were sent out to scout for the scouts, and the others, having moved their wagons about ten miles eastward, encamped in a pleasant little meadow which they called Sly's Park after one of their men who had found it.

On July 14 the ten men returned. They had not found the three original scouts nor, after passing a certain point, any signs of them. They also reported having discovered a pass which seemed practicable. But work would have to be done on a road for the wagons.

So, on the next day, working parties went ahead. On the two days after that, they took the wagons about twenty miles ahead, not at all bad going for an uphill road, and through country where, as Bigler averred, "a wagon never had been here before sence theese mountains were made—for aught I know not even a white man."

On July 18 they organized, electing Samuel Thompson to be captain. They also, Mormon-fashion, elected captains of ten.

They were forty-five men and one woman, William Cory's wife. There were seventeen wagons, 150 horses, about the same number of cattle, and two little brass cannon bought from Sutter.

On the next day, "the boys" moved ahead, making a few miles and camping at a spring. There they found evidence of a campsite of the three lost scouts, and also something that looked like a grave. Digging it up, they made a discovery. "We were shocked at the sight. There lay the three murdered men robbed of every stitch of clothing, lieing promiscuously in one hole about 2 feet deep." The many arrow wounds gave one more assurance that the California Indians were not always "acorn-eaters, harmless as deer," as a modern poet has seen fit to write. The men of the company then gave the apt and still-surviving name, Tragedy Springs.

They went ahead steadily, making road, until on July 28 they had worked a practicable way across the summit and had moved the wagons up almost through the pass.

This was remarkably good progress, and we must grant much to the energy and good judgment of these Mormon pioneers. On the other hand, they seem to have had no outstanding leader, and much of their success must be attributed, not indeed to luck, but to the advantages of the situation. Emigrants approaching from the east came to the Sierra Nevada with their animals worn down, and with their men tired out. In the Mormon company both animals and men were fresh and well fed.

Moreover, the geography was favorable. Though they were moving upslope, they had a curious advantage of which they themselves were doubtless ignorant. The west slope of these mountains is furrowed by deep and difficult canyons, converging downslope like the branches of a tree uniting to form the trunk. Travel must be generally along the ridges. Only by luck, however, would anyone starting from the top happen to get upon the proper ridge. The Bartlesons, the snowshoers of the Donner Party, and others were sometimes appalled to see the ridge upon which they were traveling come to an end, as two streams flowed together. They would then have to descend to the bottom, cross the stream, and climb again. Much of the difficulty of the Truckee Route on the western slope resulted from such situations. But for

199

anyone ascending the slope, from west to east, the ridges coalesce. The Mormons, therefore, having once got on a ridge, could follow it, by no virtue of their own, clear to the top.

On July 29 they took their wagons across the pass and down the steep slope on the eastern face, a mile and a half, to a pleasant opening that they named, and it still remains, Hope Valley—"as we began to have hope."

Ahead of them still lay a difficult canyon through which a small stream rushed over a rocky bed. They called it Pilot River, since it was taking them where they wished to go. This name did not survive—we may think, unfortunately, since the stream lacks a name of its own, being merely the West Fork of the Carson River.

Three crossings were required, and these were difficult, because of the boulders. The men here improvised bridges by felling trees.

On August 5 they emerged from the canyon into the broad sagebrush valley extending along the base of the mountains. Even though they were still breaking trail, they could then move rapidly, making about fifteen miles a day, following the river. They began to have the usual trouble with the desert tribes, and one man got an arrow wound in the chest muscles.

After several days of such travel they decided that they had gone far enough east to have avoided Truckee Canyon. In addition, an inviting gap in the mountains opened up toward the north. So, on August 12, they left the river, and after a long day's pull struck the emigrant road, about where the west-going wagons came to the Truckee River.

On this day the pioneering work of these Mormons ended for the time being. They had just performed one of the most successful feats of road-opening that the West was ever to see. In spite of the importance of their work, however, their contribution was scarcely recognized. Their road became "The Carson Route," so called from the river, but also as if Kit Carson had been responsible for its opening.

On August 14 the company started across the Forty-mile Desert from west to east. At the boiling springs, Bigler recorded, "Here we made our tea and coffee without fire to heat the water." He also recorded a not uncommon tragedy of the place. "A little dog walked up so near to one of these springs as to loose his balance and fell in, and was instantly scalled to death and boilt to peaces."

Marching on through the night, the company reached Humboldt Sink about sunrise, and encamped. Toward evening, eighteen wagons came from the east!

This vanguard of the migration was probably the company led by Clyman. Naturally there was an exchange of news. The Mormons had two dazzling items to report: the opening of the new route and the discovery of gold. Clyman's people had nothing comparable to tell. The westward journey, this year, had been humdrum—at least in the opinion of Clyman himself, who later dismissed it all in ten words, as being "without accident or interruption of any kind worthy of notice." Of course, that old-timer would scarcely bother to ink his pen for anything less than a full-scale battle with the Sioux.

One man, however, interested the Mormons exceedingly. This was Hazen Kimball, who had been in Salt Lake City until March 2. Though Kimball had apostatized, the Mormons probably did not mind learning something from him about the settlement and their families. Moreover, Kimball had done some trailmaking. With two wagons he had gone north from Salt Lake City to Fort Hall. Hearing his story, "the boys" probably decided to follow his trail. Up to this time they must have been intending to go around by Fort Bridger or else to break a trail for themselves.

A part of Kimball's route was later incorporated as a section of one of the branches of the California Trail. The willingness of a few men with only two wagons to travel through unknown country is of interest as showing that the Americans were beginning to feel much more at home in the mountains and deserts.

On the next day, August 16, the Mormons continued their march eastward, and on that same day they met twenty-five more wagons, probably Cornwall's company.

During ten days "the boys" continued up the valley of the Humboldt, without incident, except for the usual nagging troubles with the Indians. On August 26, having by now rounded the big bend, they met ten wagons, presumably those guided by Peter Lassen. Undoubtedly the Mormons told of their new route, but Lassen was not easily moved.

On the next day the company met "Captain S. Hensly and Company of ten on packs." Then "the boys" could receive important news as well as give it. In the first place, these men had come through Salt Lake City and might give some late information about families and friends. In addition, Hensley's company had had an exciting trip.

Moving rapidly, as packers did, they had reached Salt Lake City. Thoroughly schooled in western travel, Hensley decided, as Bryant had decided in '46, that Hastings's Cutoff offered the best route for packers. But when well out on the salt flats, the party was overwhelmed by a cloudburst such as occasionally strikes during the summer in that desert region. The abundant water softened the salt crust, and the whole plain became mere mush. The animals bogged down immediately. The equipment and provisions had to be sacrificed; pack saddles were cut loose in a desperate attempt to save the animals. During forty-eight hours without food or fresh water, the men labored, and finally managed to retrace their course and escape from the trap. There was nothing for it, then, but to return to Salt Lake City, and to reprovision.

Having done so, no one was in a mood to try the salt flats again. The safe-and-sane course would have been to follow the tracks of Kimball's wagons to Fort Hall. But this route was discouragingly long. By this time, moreover, the general lay of the land was fairly well known. Hensley and his companions therefore concluded to take another try at exploring—a bold decision for men who had just suffered so much loss.

They first went north about eighty miles, following Kimball's track. Then they prepared to swing off to the northwest and west; after a distance which they could feel certain was about a hundred miles, they would hit the emigrant road. They could feel moderately sure that they would encounter springs and grass. In any case, such an exploration on horseback offered no great hazard, since you could ordinarily expect to turn around and return to a place from which you had taken off. So they forded Bear River and set out boldly on their three- or four-day ride across the unknown.

Little is recorded of their journey, and probably there was little to tell. After crossing one range of low mountains, they had easy and dull country, sagebrush-covered, level, or gently rolling. One stream perhaps gave them difficulty in crossing, and their name for it, Deep Creek, still survives. When a mountain loomed up ahead, they had to decide whether to go north or south of it. The Bartleson Party, as Hensley may have known, had gone to the south without much luck. Hensley went to the north, skirting the base of the mountain through the sagebrush. At length he and his men rode through a gap between sharp-peaked mountains, and saw to the right and ahead the soaring twin spires of rock, like cathedral towers—a notable landmark of the trail— the southern outliers of the City of Rocks. At this point the packers had rejoined the main trail.

Hensley informed the Mormons of the new cutoff, which would, he thought, save them eight or ten days in getting to Salt Lake City. He prepared for them what was known as a "waybill."

Hensley went west. The Mormons continued east, and after two more days they met the largest company of all, the forty-eight wagons under Chiles's command.

That old-timer reacted vigorously to the news of a freshly discovered pass. Large regions of the West must have been imprinted on his mind with the clarity of a map. He even saw that he might make an improvement on the route by which the Mormons had come east, and he announced his intention of making the try.

In return he gave the Mormons some information—or perhaps it was merely advice. In any case, at this time occurred a curious incident and one which may even be entitled to rate as a mystery. . . . Chiles had come by Fort Hall. Since everyone in his company knew this, there cannot have been any concealment. Chiles, however, gave the Mormons a waybill for a route to Salt Lake City which he declared was even shorter than that traveled by Hensley. At some point a failure of communication must have occurred, for some of the Mormons came to believe that Chiles had traveled by that route himself. (And so he may have done, in part, but in '41, not in '48.)

Again the trains went west and east. The Mormons soon sent scouts ahead to locate Chiles's route. After nine days more, the main body arrived near the head of the Humboldt River, and there met their scouts. But these had found "no trace where

Capt. Childs had been," a statement which would indicate that the diarist thought Chiles actually to have traveled that way. Moreover the scouts had found no water.

Even so, the company sent out another detachment, and the rest of the men took the wagons ahead, presumably by directions that the waybill gave, to a spring five miles eastward. But again the scouts returned having found neither trail nor water. As Bigler declared, if they had found water, the company would have stuck to this route even without finding any wagon tracks. As it was, they held a meeting, and reached the inevitable decision, to return to the regular trail and go on to Hensley's cutoff.

What to make of it? Chiles was a Missourian, and Missourians hated Mormons. For this reason, one might suppose that Chiles was trying to deceive or to perpetrate a hoax. Such procedure would have been nothing short of criminal, and is not in accordance with what we know of Chiles's character. We must, on the contrary, remember that he was a man of great energy and of great curiosity about routes and possible routes. As captain of forty-eight wagons, he had manpower at his disposal. As he neared the head of the Humboldt, he would have realized that he was close to where he had been in '41. Possibly he sent scouts eastward, or went himself, and thus closed the small gap in his geographical knowledge. In '41 the Bartlesons had brought their wagons to a point which was, if they had known it, within striking distance of the Humboldt, not more than fifty miles away. Thus Chiles might well have been giving the Mormons good advice, based upon sound information.

The Mormons went ahead. On September 15, as Bigler reported, "near by on our left was 2 towering rocks near each other which Mr. A. Pratt named the Twin Sisters." They were the certain markers of Hensley's route. From there on, "the boys," skilled frontiersmen by now, could follow the traces of the pack train. Breaking trail for wagons across the sagebrush country offered no special difficulties. Hensley's waybill told them where to find water and grass. The diarists had little to record. On September 28 the train arrived at Salt Lake City, and the men were reunited with their families.

In being the first to take wagons from Cathedral Rocks (the Twin Sisters, as Pratt had called them) to Salt Lake City, the eastward-moving Mormons had pioneered an important route. Rather unfairly—but how often is history just?—Hensley was forgotten, and the new route came to be known as the Salt Lake Road, the Salt Lake Cutoff, and occasionally the Deep Creek Cutoff. Much of the later California migration went that way. . . .

The wagons which the Mormons had met along the Humboldt continued westward. Usually toward the end of the journey everyone was weary, and bored, and quarrelsome. In '48 things were different, largely because of the news of gold. On the day after meeting the Mormons a diarist with Chiles recorded that the stories of gold "really ran us all mad"; a week later, "All is good humor and high spirits."

He could so write, in spite of the usual Indian troubles. Two men, attempting to go it alone, were cut off and killed. Chiles's party, having had some animals wounded, took the offensive and shot several Indians.

The men of the Clyman and Cornwall companies, after considering the Mormons' story, followed the regular trail across the desert to the Truckee River, and then turned south, committing themselves to the new road, even though wagons had never gone over it from east to west. The third company on the road followed Lassen's directions—with results to be detailed later. Chiles's company did some pioneering.

From Humboldt Sink Chiles followed the established trail a few miles westward. Then, having made the crossing of the last salt-water slough, he turned southward, into the desert along the western edge of Carson Sink. His design was not altogether rash. He himself had gone that way in the rout of the Bartleson Party in '41: so had his own wagons with Walker in '43. Doubtless he at once began to look about, and even after five years he could probably find traces of the passage of wagons and oxen across that slow-to-change desert country. Skirting between the sink and the barren hills, he kept his leading team pointed south across waterless country—flat but in many places necessitating heavy pulling because of sand and ashlike dust. After a toilsome dry drive of thirty miles from the turnoff he brought the wagons to abundant water and grass along the Carson River.

This section of trail, sometimes known as Chiles's Route, was about equally as long, from water to water, as the Forty-mile

Desert on the old trail. Being absolutely flat, the new route may have been a little easier. On the other hand, it had no boiling springs in its middle to afford a resting place. Either way the going was hard, and there was not much to choose between the two. This region to the south of the sink also came to be known as the Forty-mile Desert, to the confusion of nomenclature.

After pausing to rest at the point where they struck the river, the emigrants turned upstream to the southwest. During about two days' journey they had to break trail, and then they came upon the tracks of the other wagons. Chiles's route to this point thereafter replaced the Mormon route, though it may be reckoned as actually a little longer and not noticeably easier. Here as elsewhere, the decision was determined more by accident and prejudice than by any survey or rational comparison of the two. No one traveled both ways, and so no one was really in a position to know which route was the better.

Chiles must thus be credited with reopening thirty miles of trail and opening another thirty miles. This section became an integral part of the Carson Route, which remained for some years the chief entry into California. This pioneering must thus be put down as another of Chiles's numerous achievements.

All three parties of emigrants, whether they struck the Carson River lower down or higher up, followed it upstream. The valley was broad, not a narrow canyon such as emigrants on the Truckee Route had to encounter. Instead of the twenty-seven dreaded fords, none at all of the Carson were required for a long distance.

At length the trail entered the canyon, which necessitated three crossings. But the stream here was small, and the Mormons' bridges still served. After ten miles of canyon Hope Valley offered a brief respite. Then came the steep front of the pass itself, much more difficult for the westbound emigrants to surmount than for the eastbound Mormons to descend.

By the amalgamation of the two leading companies probably sixty able-bodied men were available for roadwork. One of them wrote in an impressionistic retrospect:

Progress was very slow, and some days, cutting a way through virgin forests and skirting precipices, not more than half a mile would be covered. The men had often to take the wagons apart and they themselves pack both wagons and supplies up the steep ridges . . . hoping each would be the last.

Because of the formation of the mountains the emigrants had to cross a second summit, two miles west of the first one. Then things got easier.

Chiles's party, the last of the three to take the new trail, arrived at the site of Placerville on October 4, and could consider the journey finished. By this time about ninety wagons, and Hensley's packers as well, had entered California. Most of the men, and even some of the women and children, at once began a feverish search for gold. One of them, having thus unexpectedly arrived in El Dorado, wrote back deliriously on October 28, "Gold is nothing more thought of than dirt."

Also the mail had got through. Bayley had finally decided to come to California. He carefully kept the letters. Once arrived, he found that large numbers of men from Oregon had come to California after gold. They were so eager for letters that they gladly paid the postman two dollars apiece for their safe delivery.

The men of '48, eastbound and westbound, had thus succeeded in establishing the Carson Route, the second entry for wagons into California. It may be compared with the Truckee Route, which presented its fourfold barrier—desert, canyon, pass, and downslope. On the Carson Route, desert and pass remained equally arduous, but the difficult canyon was largely eliminated, its river crossings being cut to only three. The downslope, also, was easier. Since the distance to the California settlements was about the same either way, the Carson Route offered definite advantages. . . .

So all of this year's wagons were in, except those piloted by Peter Lassen. There were women and children, and ten ox-drawn wagons. So we may consider that it was a typical emigrant party.

Presumably, these were the wagons that the eastbound Mormons had met on August 26. Undoubtedly the Mormons told their story of the new route, and we can only assume that Lassen argued back, still maintaining the advantages of the route that led to his own ranch, especially the possibility of getting to California without having to surmount a high pass. After the Mormons had gone on eastward, Lassen was still there to talk.

The emigrants decided to take neither the old Truckee Route nor the new Carson Route, but to stick with their guide. So Lassen continued—with a few wagons instead of eighty, a kind of poor-man's Hastings.

About September 1 the party came to the far-stretching grasslands along the river, which were to be known as Lassen's Meadows. (Note again how his name stuck to things!) At this point the Applegate Trail split away from the main trail. It had been traveled by wagons bound for Oregon in '46 and by Wiggins in '47.

Over a considerable distance, therefore, Lassen would not be pioneering, but he was nevertheless about to take his wagons across a difficult desert country, which remains to this day one of the least known and most infrequently traversed parts of the United States.

Leaving the Humboldt, Lassen's party pushed out on a steady upgrade pull through the sagebrush. Toward the end of the day they came to the first water, where the Brown Party in '46 had become discouraged. (It is, indeed, about as miserable a little water hole as you are likely to encounter, especially since, in these days, it may be adorned with the body of a dead cow.)

Next day it was a steady pull of seventeen miles, mostly level, part of the way winding through a defile, and ending at Rabbithole Spring. The flow of water was sufficient for the cattle of a small party, and there was some grass.

Starting out from Rabbithole, the emigrants took their wagons a short distance down an easy ravine, and then came out to face a sight which was both spectacular and appalling. Looking out for many miles over the whole sweep around from west to north, they saw first the easy downslope, thinly covered with desert bushes, then an absolutely bare and level flat, whitish gray in color. Anyone could have guessed, especially by noting the lines of ancient beaches, that this was the bed of some now vanished inland sea. Splitting the expanse of the flats, right ahead to the northwest, rose some desert mountains, which had once extended as a headland into the water. At their end loomed a great rock, so dark in color that Black Rock was inevitably its name.

Ahead, across the salt flat, the emigrants could see, as far as their view reached, the track of Wiggins's wagons, pointing straight at the rock. From Rabbithole to Black Rock, in as direct a line as anyone could drive oxen, was twenty-one miles—without a blade of grass, or a drop of drinkable water, or a scrap of shade. Besides, in places, the pulling was heavy because of the sand and the porous and crusty surface of the flats. Few wagon trains finished that passage without leaving dead oxen along the trail.

Still, it could be made. Easy did it! If you took care not to rush the oxen and if you rested them occasionally, you could bring them at last—stumbling under the yokes, after the welcome sunset and perhaps long after nightfall—to the great and amazing spring.

By morning light you awoke, and wondered. To the east towered the huge black mass, and behind it the higher mountains of bare rock, bizarrely colored in red and white and black. A strange place for people who had grown up in the lush lands of the Mississippi Valley! At the foot of Black Rock the spring bubbled up, fifteen feet across in its cuplike basin, so circular that God's own compass might have drawn it. The water was not quite boiling. It was hot enough to make tea, if you had some tea, but it was not quite hot enough to boil eggs, if by an unlikely chance you had some eggs. Farther down, in other pools, the water cooled off so that the cattle could drink it. Still farther down, extending wedgelike into the desert, the seepage from the spring produced some acres of coarse grass. So, all in all, offering grass and water, the place was not as hostile as it at first seemed. You would be likely to take a day there to recuperate.

At this point Lassen showed his ignorance of geography. His own ranch lay almost directly west of Black Rock, across not too difficult terrain. Four years later this route would be traveled by wagons. But Lassen knew nothing better to do than to follow the Applegate Trail, far to the north.

The party therefore moved north, two days' journey, keeping the bare mountains on the right. They passed more springs, some boiling. (This is a country that breeds legends. So, in later days, they told of the silver bullets, of how an emigrant, lacking lead, picked up some heavy stuff, melted it into bullets to shoot at the Indians, and later discovered that his remaining bullets were pure silver—but no one found that mine, though many tried. Also, one of these who passed there in '48 may have shuddered as he walked over his own grave, and that was Lassen himself. In '59 he returned to that country, prospecting, and was killed there, close to the trail.)

Next they swung to the northwest, twisting about to cross a ridge with a sharp and dangerous descent. Beyond this, they passed through a narrow canyon, but flat-bottomed and smooth, as if miraculously made for the passage of wagons. On either hand the yellow cliffs rose up high and sheer, and it came to be called High Rock Canyon.

Two days brought them to a run of water still called Emigrant Springs. Then they went west across a dry lake bed, with mountains rising sharply beyond. They crossed these mountains, still following the Applegate Trail, with no great difficulty.

But by this time, as a few more days passed, they were probably arguing as to whether they should have taken this route. Anyone could tell that they were swinging a long way north.

But still they went north—two days' journey, skirting a lake for part of the way, and another day's journey to the northwest by a pass through some mountains.

There a large lake blocked progress to the west. The road swung to the south. That was better! After another day they came to the point where Lassen intended to strike out on his own. There he probably told them—if he did so, he was correct—that they were on the headwaters of a stream which flowed into the Sacramento River. Doubtless he had some idea of following the stream all the way down. He could have made this sound sensible to the emigrants, since they would not have to cross any more passes, and could consider themselves to the west of the Sierra Nevada. Also, they could expect to be moving steadily to lower levels, and thus to be free of the threat of snow.

By now it was the middle of September. In spite of the long detour to the north, the emigrants may still have had confidence in their guide. He could have assured them that they were not much more than a hundred miles from the Sacramento Valley, as the crow flies—though, of course, the emigrants with their ox-drawn wagons and their women and children were far from having the facility of crows. But even if you doubled the distance because of windings, and cut the daily average progress to ten miles because of the necessity of breaking trail, still you could figure to arrive in the valley after about three weeks, early in October.

High time, too! Like most emigrants near the end of the journey, they were running short on food.

So Lassen led his wagons southward. There was no trail. Thus began a journey which must have seemed to the emigrants to have about it a nightmare quality of uncertainty, vagueness, and terror. (The historian, too, feels about it this uncertain quality. The only detailed record is a reminiscence written years later—vague about time and place, as such reminiscences are. All that can be done is to compare this account with the actual topography. When the two fail to agree, as sometimes happens, one can only attempt to reconstruct a somewhat reasonable story.)

Lassen led them down along the stream, and everything went merrily. The stream became a fine little river, which Lassen might have known to be the Pit, flowing through a grassy valley between pine-covered mountains. It was, in short, a delightful country, especially to emigrants who had just come through the desert. Only a little road-making was required, and that was lucky, since only about twenty men were available. But all that would have been required in this country was to make dugways to ease off the banks of the little tributary streams, and to smooth out other small difficulties.

Then, after three or four days' journeying (though the record is too vague and uncertain to be trusted for exact time) the inevitable happened! The river flowed into a canyon too "tight" for wagons. Soon everyone must have come to realize that Lassen did not have much idea of where he was going. As a contemporary summed him up: "This route he had not previously explored. He only had a correct idea of the courses, and some general knowledge of the country through which they must pass."

So came the first suggestion of nightmare. They took the wagons south over some rather difficult country, and then worked west again to some pleasant open valleys, grassy and with scattered pine trees. They would have used up another week or more, scouting, making road, taking the wagons through. Still, it was not too bad. Moving circuitously, mostly through valleys, they managed to advance forty or fifty miles to the west and south. At last they followed a valley westward for eight miles. It was a dead end! Ahead of them rose what was later described as a steep mountain "which could not be ascended except by some creature that had either wings or claws."

They could not have come to that conclusion until they had spent a day or two at scouting. Then there was nothing for it but to loop around and almost retrace those weary eight miles, eastward. And every step of that way, they had the oppressive thought that even when they had escaped from this dead end, they did not know where to go and were surrounded by mountains. By this time, Lassen must have been getting plenty of hard looks, and hard words too, especially from the women, who would have been less restrained in such matters.

Blocked toward the west, they must attempt to move south. No more pleasant open valleys! They had to try taking the wagons up a steep and rough ascent, thickly grown with pines and firs, with many fallen trees. Either these tree trunks had to be cleared away, or else the wagons had to be taken around and about them. And a three-yoke team with a wagon is forty feet in length, and very awkward for twisting and turning.

The emigrants made the inevitable decision. They halted, and cut the wagons down to carts—at the same time probably reducing the teams to two yoke or a single yoke.

Even with the much more maneuverable carts the progress was snail-like. Two or three miles a day must have been all that they could make. The men were being worn down by constant work. All the flour had been used up. The only resource was to start eating the weakest of the cattle. And the worst of it was that they were not even going in the right direction! Forced by the lay of the land, Lassen was taking them south and even a little east. All they could do was to move in this direction until some gap opened up to the westward. But if a scout climbed to a high point for a view, all he could see to westward was a maze of sharp conical peaks, old volcanoes. And the emigrants would have already learned that close to volcanoes they might encounter rough lava beds, totally impassable for wagons. (Actually there was a good pass through that country, but they cannot be blamed for having missed it.)

So they went south, where they were lucky enough to find some little grassy valleys. But these lured them to the east until they were again on the headwaters of streams flowing out toward the desert!

By now it had come October. And in these northern mountains the snow would be flying even earlier than on the Truckee Route.

A generation later it had become legend, and old men of Lassen County were telling tales. But the stories have a ring of truth about them, at least of that legendary truth which sometimes comes closer to basic reality than mere history can. They told that in one day Lassen guided himself by Mount Shasta and the next day by Mount Lassen, not knowing the difference. They told also that when he finally got lost in the thick forest country, the men threatened to hang him. He said that if they would just let him climb to the top of a nearby mountain, he could find the way. They allowed him to go, under guard. After that he got back on some kind of right course.

At last the party began to go to pieces. Five men packed their gaunt oxen with what they had left and went ahead. The others continued to struggle with their carts. Lassen stayed with the second group.

Unable to break out toward the west, they found their course taking them to the east of Mount Lassen. Looking out from any open space, they could see the overwhelming mass of the great peak, blocking all possibility of progress in that direction. So they moved laboriously around the mountain, keeping it about twenty-five miles distant, in a kind of crude circular course— southeast, south, southwest. Then at last, with the peak well to their north, no barrier kept them from going west.

But the oxen, those that still had not been slaughtered for food, were exhausted with hard work and weak from scanty pasturage. The people, too, were tired, discouraged, and half starved. The men were worn down by weeks of hard labor with axes and shovels. And any day the snow might fall.

Relief came spectacularly and from an unforeseen quarter. ... Some settlers in Oregon, excited over the discovery of gold, had organized a strong party to go to California with wagons.

There was no established wagon road. They followed the Applegate Trail to Goose Lake and then turned south, breaking trail. They paralleled, for about three days' journey, without knowing it, the trail that Lassen had broken through a few miles farther to the east. Then, reaching Pit River, they were surprised to come upon the newly made trail. As they could tell by examining the traces, the wagons were making for California, and presumably their leader knew where he was going. So the Oregonians followed Lassen, being glad that they no longer had to pioneer the way. They were not so glad when they followed the tracks into the blind end, and then had to follow the loop around and come back. Traveling where the road had already been broken through and being a strong and fresh company, they made good time. About the middle of October, they overtook Lassen and five carts somewhere south of Mount Lassen.

The Oregonians had plenty of food, and gladly shared it with the starving emigrants. As one of them wrote in pity, "I never saw people so worn down and so emaciated as these poor emigrants." At one point, an Oregonian overtook an old woman on foot, driving a packed ox. Surprised at his approach, she called, "Who are you, and where did you come from?" Her next question was, "Have you got any flour?" And when she learned that they had, she cried out, "You are like an angel from Heaven!" So loud and so vibrant was her cry of thanksgiving that to the Oregonian it seemed that the primeval forest reechoed.

The newcomers numbered about seventy stout men: "We plied our axes with skill, vigor, and success, and opened the route about as fast as teams could well follow." Moreover, Lassen was getting close to home, and coming into country that he knew. He insisted that they keep to the top of a ridge, and not go down to the impassable canyons. Thus progressing, they came to a "strip of ground, about thirty feet wide, between the heads of two immense and impassible ravines, and connecting the ridge we were compelled to leave with another. It was like an isthmus connecting two continents." There they did some work on the road, and gingerly worked the wagons across what was later known as The Narrows.

They came to where the forest was thinner, and at last they could see, far ahead, the open valley. But even at this point they faced difficulty. "From the place where we stood, we could see three tall, narrow rocky ridges with deep ravines between, running toward the valley." Which ridge to choose? This was the necessary dilemma of the emigrant working his way down the west slope of the Sierra Nevada without certain knowledge! In the end these people merely "chose the middle one at a venture."

Eventually, after breaking a few wagons on the rocky ledges, both the Oregonians and the original emigrants got through to Lassen's ranch at the end of October, having taken about a month longer than if they had gone by either of the other routes, and having had to work hard and suffer much privation.

On October 31 a meeting was held—or, at least, Lassen issued the report of a meeting reputed to have been held. There is about this whole report a stench of what might be called false advertising. To begin with, it was dated at "Bentonville." But there was no such town, and this was merely the name which Lassen had given to the city which he was projecting at the site of his lonely ranch. Moreover, the report of this meeting, supposed to have been held by the emigrants, praised Lassen as a guide and advocated the use of his route. Obviously, they would have been unlikely to agree to either of these propositions. Possibly a few of them, well-liquored, held a "meeting," and subscribed to the resolutions. However that may be, the highly misleading document was sent east, was printed in newspapers, and exercised a dangerous influence.

The Lassen Route, or Lassen Cutoff, thus established a third covered-wagon entry into California, but one which compared badly with either of the others. True, it interposed no single barrier the equivalent of Donner Pass or Carson Pass. But its desert was equally formidable, and its distance of rough mountainous passage was much greater than on the other routes. Its chief disadvantage, however, was the mere distance resulting from the long swing to the north. From the turnoff at Lassen's Meadows to the Sacramento Valley, by either the Truckee or the Carson route, was about 135 miles shorter than by Lassen's route. If Sutter's Fort is considered the terminus, the margin increased to about 200 miles. . . .

The year was thus important, not for the number of emigrants, but for the opening of new branches to the trail. Both the Carson Route and the Salt Lake Cutoff were destined to be important. The Lassen Route, in many ways comparable to Hastings's Cutoff, was to have one big year. All these experiments, it is to be noted, were in the stretch between South Pass and the Humboldt or else at the California end. East of South Pass and along the Humboldt everyone let well-enough alone.

The year, moreover, demonstrated the importance of the establishment of Salt Lake City in '47. Hensley, having to turn back, could reprovision there. In earlier years he would have been forced to make for Fort Bridger or Fort Hall, and might well have had a hard time of it to come through alive. As it was, he and his men suffered a delay and some pecuniary loss, but did not incur much danger—or, at least, not nearly as much as they would have incurred if Salt Lake City had not yet been founded.

But '48 cannot be considered merely in terms of trails. Already the news of the gold discovery was reaching the world. Next year, the deluge! And if in '46 the trail had seemed crowded and the grass sometimes scanty, what would it be in '49?

Then, as the winter deepened, snow began to fall over the Rockies. Deeper and deeper it drifted, filling the ravines. Even the old mountain-men had not known such a winter. Those people favoring a religious interpretation of history might once more have said that God was taking care of his Americans.

CHAPTER NINE

BEFORE THE LAST of the tired emigrants of '48 had come stumbling into Lassen's ranch, the gold fever was raging in the East. An era had ended. In the early years of the trail a few wagons had moved westward, across the rolling prairie and among the desert sand hills, as lonely as men left swimming in mid-ocean from a sunken ship. But in '49 the diarists wrote of continuous trains six miles long. In a single year the numbers so increased that for *one* person who traveled the trail to California in '48 *fifty* traveled it in '49.

This sudden and appalling change was the direct result of the startling news of the discovery at Sutter's mill. This gold fever may have been unreasonable, imprudent, and incredible. But at least it was real. Under the influence of a mass hysteria, men decided to go to California, as they might get religion at a revival, or volunteer at the outbreak of a war. As one of them put it, the contagion became so universal that "the question now was, not who would go to California, but, rather, who would stay at home."

Behind it all lay, or seemed to lie, an irrefutable logic. To endure throughout a year some danger and hardship and thus to win a fortune! Young men left wives and little children, convinced that they were acting in the best interests of the family.

Doctors and lawyers abandoned good practices. Hundreds of farmers mortgaged their land.

But, we should not wholly forget, many men became forty-niners for reasons other than the expectation of finding wealth. Cooper, Irving, Frémont, and dozens of scribblers in newspapers and magazines had not written without effect. As in earlier years, to see the vast prairies and the massed herds of buffalo, to encounter Indians, to cross the mountains and the deserts—all this was romance!

Granted, the gold fever was the dominating factor. But it was not substituted for the older motives. Instead, it was added to them. Thus one man wrote that he had little confidence in the gold, but had read Irving and Cooper and had acquired "a strong passion for travel and adventure." Another stated that he went "wishing to regain my health," as well as for gold. William Johnston, preparing to leave Pittsburgh, was explicit: "Never having been far from home, the thought of an adventure of such magnitude as now seemed to loom up before me, possessed my mind more forcibly than any expectation of getting rich at gold digging."

Moreover, the country was somewhat depressed economically, and was in a disturbed and excitable state as an aftermath of the Mexican War. Thousands of young men had returned from the army and had not yet settled into jobs. Many of these had failed to see active service and were still eager for adventure. Thousands of others had been too young to enter the army, and now wished to emulate their older brothers and friends. . . .

Once these many thousands had made the decision to go, the next question was "By what route?"

In bar-room and in drawing-room, around the stove in a thousand village stores, as fall moved on into winter, men discussed routes. By aid of newspaper articles, occasionally by help of a book, or by authoritative information from someone's cousin who was said to have known a man who had been to California, the local pundits were soon able to discuss routes with some appearance of authority. First, you could go around Cape Horn by sailing vessel. Second, there were various land-and-sea routes, by which you took a steamer or sailing ship to the Isthmus of Panama (or some other place in Mexico or Central America), crossed by land, and then took a ship (*what* ship was a little uncertain) up the Pacific side. Third, there was the land route, which offered the alternatives of the trail through South Pass, or of a more southern trail, or trails, which took off from one of the southwestern states.

The Cape Horn route was comparatively sure and safe. It meant a six-month voyage which you could expect to be highly uncomfortable and very boring. The land-and-sea routes were theoretically fast and easy, but were dangerously uncertain. The southern trails had been little traveled and were not well known. So the trail across South Pass came in for full consideration.

Though certain figures cannot be established, about a third of the gold-seekers, it would seem, decided to follow where Walker, Chiles, and Stevens had led the way. This was a larger proportion than took any other single route. . . .

Until spring there could be no starting over the trail. The opportunity thus given for preparation was valuable. And of all kinds of preparation none is more important than the increase of knowledge.

People turned to their newspapers for information, and one article in particular may be cited. Appearing first in a tiny frontier paper of Arkansas, it was picked up and published all over the country. The article was unsigned. Its author, however, was obviously a man who had made the journey himself. He was eminently sensible, and he viewed the whole affair from a thoroughly Western point of view.

What in the world was there to get excited about? The route by way of South Pass was "the best." You took a light wagon, with three or four yoke of oxen or six mules. You took your family along if you wanted to. You should be at your take-off point by April 20. You could start when the grass was tall enough— about the first week of May. The trail was "plain and good," and the Indians were friendly. The conclusion was: "the emigrant by taking this route will certainly reach his destination in good season and without disaster."

By and large, all this was true. Perhaps more important, it carried the conviction of truth, for in no way did the man who wrote it seem to have any ulterior motive. Obviously it was all one to him whether you went to California or not, and how—

whether you swam, rode a camel, or sailed by way of Kamchatka. The very matter-of-factness must have been infinitely reassuring, and we can imagine in a thousand homes a husband or brother or son reading the words and saying, "Well, that's the way to go!" And one can imagine also a thousand wives concluding that having your man go to California might not be so bad after all, and few of them even saying, "Why don't I go too and take the children? Look, it says, 'carrying his family with him.' "

But the article was in some respects misleading. The author cannot be blamed. He was not a prophet. He was telling of how things had been in, say, '46—when he had most likely made the journey. He had no idea of how heavy the traffic would be in '49, and of whether, considering the problems of water and grass, such a heavy migration could possibly get through without a major disaster. Moreover, he had no idea of the kind of people who were to be the forty-niners.

Yes, we might call it "The Year of the Madness," for beyond doubt it was a madness that sometimes passed all understanding. But we might also call it "The Year of the Greenhorn."

Even in the earlier years, few of the emigrants had been mountain-men or skilled frontiersmen. But at least they were farming people and generally from the Western states. They knew one end of an ox from the other; when they spoke of a hound, they might mean a part of a wagon and not a long-eared dog. But a great number of the forty-niners were from towns and cities. They lacked even the knowledge of camping and woodcraft that is likely to be possessed by the average man of the mid-twentieth century from having been a Boy Scout or having taken a few fishing trips, to say nothing of the many thousands who have slept in foxholes. There were, of course, the veterans of Mexico, and a still large proportion of Western farmers. But the many city-dwellers were definitely men of a soft generation, far removed from the frontier and never having known war. They could learn, and did, but sometimes they paid heavily for that tutelage. . . .

Late March and time to be moving! In the barnyard they yoked up—two brothers, perhaps, or three or four young fellows gathered from the neighboring farms. They said their good-byes. Pistol-like, the whip cracked, and for the first time the six oxen set their weight against the yokes. At the crossroads this wagon would join with others from the same county. Ahead lay some weeks' journey before "the boys" would even arrive at one of the frontier towns. They might be a little saddened at the thought of leaving home, but ahead lay adventure and the dazzling expectation of a golden fortune. Thus, as a Detroit newspaper noted on March 26, "Almost every village in this state" had sent or was about to send its company "of young, active, enterprising men, embracing almost every variety of pursuit, but made up in chief of farmers." The article also mentioned that from three to five hundred dollars was required by each man, and that this cash had generally been raised by mortgages on farms.

Sometimes there was fanfare, especially for large organized parties leaving the cities. Thus there was the Sagamore and Sacramento Company of Lynn, Massachusetts, fifty-two young men, including one that was seven feet tall. The company took its departure from Boston by parading down State Street. A band led the march. Each member wore a gray uniform trimmed with silver braid, and was armed with rifle, revolver, sheath knife, and saber. Each made-to-order wagon (one for four men) moved behind four horses resplendent in silver-plated harness, and from the rear of each wagon, as the height of absurdity, projected a swivel gun. . . .

April was the great month for assembly at the frontier towns. Some came driving in, their teams already hardened to the road, the wagon tops weather-beaten. Many others poured ashore from the river steamers. Some of these had brought wagons and teams with them. The rest set about buying from the local dealers. Though everyone was in a consuming hurry to get going, so that they could begin shoveling up those bucketfuls of gold, all the old-timers agreed that you could not set out until the grass had had a chance to start growing. So, by dozens and soon by hundreds, they went into camp, to wait.

In early April a thousand emigrants were reported at Independence. By the middle of the month newspaper editors were expressing the fear that the excessive number of animals would eat up the grass along the trail. But even yet no one had any idea how large the migration would become. A man writing home thought that the whole number would be between three and four thousand! But on April 25 three thousand were reported at St. Jo alone.

This period of waiting was not necessarily dull. It was, for one thing, a time to study such books as might give you an idea of what you would encounter, though there was no book that really filled the bill. Many people had Frémont's report and Joel Palmer's *Journal of Travels*, but those were chiefly concerned with Oregon. William Clayton's *Latter-day Saints' Emigrants' Guide* was excellent, but it described the Council Bluffs road only, and stopped at Salt Lake City. T. H. Jefferson's remarkable *Map of the Emigrant Road* had been published so recently that hardly anyone had a copy of it; besides, it gave the route over Hastings's Cutoff. Probably the best book available, and it was vague and misleading in places, was a curious little volume by Joseph E. Ware, *The Emigrants' Guide to California*. The author had got this work together hastily, so that it could be published early in '49, in St. Louis. Ware had never been to California and did not so claim. He had compiled his data from Frémont and from talking with Solomon P. Sublette, one of the famous fur-trading family, who had captained one of the California parties of '45. The book included a fairly good map, showing Hastings's Cutoff as the South Trail. It also showed a trail marked Sublette's Cutoff, and the use of this name thus arose, for that route had generally been called Greenwood's Cutoff. All in all, however, the books were not very helpful.

During this period of waiting, many people had to buy mules or oxen, and nearly everyone had to make some last-minute purchases of supplies. Free enterprise met the challenge magnificently. In spite of all the hundreds that kept pouring off the steamers, the dealers were always able in some way to have a fresh supply of mules and oxen ready to sell, though often of poor quality. There were even fast-talking salesmen around, and the unwary emigrant was likely to find himself owning a goldometer and a gold-washer, a calico vest and some "boiled" shirts, and a case of jumping jacks and jew's-harps to be bartered to supposedly unsophisticated redskins.

There were amusements too, those kinds that flourish where large bodies of men are gathered. Whisky was cheap, and you could find a gambling game if you wanted it. One man reported the presence of what he called "magdalens." Instead of making a fortune on the trip, you had a chance of going broke before you even got started.

Just wandering around through the camps must have been fun. It was a time of good feeling, and you could expect a cup of coffee at almost any campfire. A youngster from some little Western farm could gape at the fine uniforms and dazzling equipment of the big companies from the Eastern cities.

But the Eastern boys could have learned a great deal, and some of them did, by looking at the Western companies and talking with the men. There were, for instance, some Missourians from Jackson County, where Independence was the county seat. They formed one of the biggest companies, having seventy wagons, about 250 people, with many women and children. At least two of their men had been over the trail before—the captain, Benoni Hudspeth, and the guide, J. J. Myers, who had been one of Chiles's horsemen in '43. Since that time he had spent five years trapping in California, and had crossed the Sierra Nevada at several places. That would be a train to watch, and Hudspeth and Myers did not mind giving advice.

Another Missouri company was from Ray County, just downriver from Independence. Its "pilot" was Milton McGee, who also had been one of Chiles's horsemen.

Other old-timers were there. Edwin Bryant, who had had a successful experience with a pack train in '46, was trying it again, this time with 150 men in his party. Bumbling "Colonel" Russell, of '46, was once more a captain. Young Billy Graves, who had been in the Donner Party, was acting as a guide for a party of Pittsburghers. Another party from that same city had the excellent good fortune to hire James Stewart, who had never been to California, but had years of experience on the Santa Fe Trail, and knew everything about handling mule teams. There were others of that sort too, and their backlog of experience was invaluable.

Brave days those! The April rain might be making the fine uniforms a bit sodden, and some cholera was reported, but the fires of hope burned hot within. You could read enthusiasm in the names painted on the wagons—"Live Hoosier," "Wild Yankee," "Rough and Ready," "Enterprise," "Gold-hunter." Many names of companies had a fine touch too—"Wolverine Rangers," "Ophir Company," "Boston and Newton Joint Stock Association," "Granite State and California Mining and Trading Company," "Washington City Company," "Colony Guard," "Helltown Greasers," "Spartan Band," "Banner Company."

Most of these companies took some time, while waiting, to have a committee compile a constitution and by-laws, many of which were about as long as the Constitution of the United States and resembled that document in wording. Laid end to end, their articles might have paved the way clear to Fort Laramie; their good intentions, an even longer road. . . .

Late in April a few companies began edging forward—not starting exactly, but jockeying into position. They moved westward a day's journey or two, not depending on the grass, but on grain that they carried along. One might suppose that those working into the lead so nervously were rash greenhorns, but they seem to have been companies that were excellently prepared to take care of themselves. Their leaders had figured out that the thing to do was to get ahead of the crowd and stay ahead of it all the way across. One of these companies was from St. Louis, captained by G. W. Paul. Another included William Kelly, an Irish journalist, who was out to get a story rather than to mine gold. Also in this advance guard were Russell's company, Bryant's pack train, and Stewart's Pittsburghers.

Finally, toward the end of the month, some of these parties took off. The gold rush was on!

On April 30 Paul and his St. Louisans were at the Big Blue, nearly two hundred miles along. They considered themselves to be in the lead, and were determined to stay there. They would not be easy to overtake. Behind Paul's company now came about five hundred wagons, in perhaps twenty-five companies. Most of them were mule-drawn, and they were pushing hard. But there was a course of two thousand miles to be covered, and those who led at the Big Blue might not be first across the Green. . . .

So it was May, and word was passing that the grass was tall enough! The camps sprang to activity as company after company made ready. Oxen bawled and men shouted, wagon chains clanked, half-broken mules squealed, whips cracked. And, as the days passed, the cry was "Ho for California!" and the wagons lurched forward.

At first, most of the emigrants left from Independence. Later, an outbreak of cholera made that town unpopular. Then St. Joseph took over, along with Savannah Landing a few miles farther north, really a part of the St. Joseph crossing. During the whole season a few more emigrants probably ferried over at St. Joseph than headed west from Independence toward the Kansas River ferries. Still farther north at Old Fort Kearny and Council Bluffs the ferries crossed a comparatively small number of the wagons, perhaps about 10 per cent each. Even some of the Iowans swung south to St. Joseph—one reason being that the road from Council Bluffs was now known as the Mormon Trail, so that others tended to keep away from it.

Because of the numbers of the migration, appalling bottlenecks developed at all the ferries. Early in May, the crowd at the St. Joseph landing was a dense mass. The scows and steamboats available, though running day and night, could not handle the traffic. As soon as one wagon was taken aboard, another moved down to take its place at the landing, and additional companies were falling in at the rear. There was no police regulation, and feelings ran high. Two teamsters shot each other to death with pistols in a quarrel over who should go first. And all this was just to get across the river and have an opportunity to start on a two-thousand-mile journey!

In one way, however, these bottlenecks of the ferries served a useful purpose. They spread the migration out, and prevented too great concentration at any one place on the trail.

Once started, the forty-niners had experiences during this first part of the journey that were much the same as those of emigrants in earlier years. Across the prairie country they followed the same four trails, converging from the same four points of take-off. They used much the same kind of wagons and teams, though in '49 mules were commoner than they had been earlier. As in '46, large companies not two weeks on the trail began to split into smaller ones, as constitutions became waste paper. As in all the previous years, the emigrants worried about Pawnees and rarely saw any, though at least one death was scored up against their record. In spite of the great number of wagons passing, the game was not wholly frightened off, so that many diarists reported shooting antelope and buffalo.

The difference between '49 and the preceding years, at least during the earlier part of the journey, can be considered largely quantitative. With fifty times as many people there would be a reasonable expectation of having so many times as many incidents. Where one wagon tongue was broken in '48, fifty were broken in '49. Moreover, the record in '49 is incomparably fuller, with 126 diaries known to have survived, and others still coming to light. This amounts to about one for every two hundred people. Such a remarkable number is in itself revelatory of the year. It shows a higher standard of education and literacy, and also indicates that the emigrants considered themselves to be participating in an important historical event. Only in '41 is the record proportionately fuller, and in that year, too, the sense of participating in history was strong.

The story of '49 can thus be told largely in terms of the differences between it and preceding years. It was, for instance, a wet season. This made the grass slow to start, but brought it along rapidly after it was once started. There was rich grazing for oxen and mules over all the prairie country. But the rains, which continued through May, made a muddy trail and heavy hauling. Every little stream crossing resulted in an hour or so of delay and frequently a broken wagon. Each company did just enough work to get its own wagons across, and the next company frequently had to do the work all over again.

Here was one of the breakdowns of free enterprise. With the expenditure of some man-hours of work, bridges could have been constructed across many of these streams, and the whole migration would have been speeded along. But there was no one to organize such work, and no single company could altruistically stop long enough to build a bridge. The only agency to do such work would have been the Federal government, but no one had thought so far ahead. As one of the emigrants pointed out, a few companies of troops under engineering officers, working for a few weeks, would have made a world of difference.

But the government had acted only to protect the emigrants against the Indians—a praiseworthy objective but not a very pressing one, since the Indians had never done the migration much harm. To this end the army had established, late in '48, a post called Fort Childs, a few miles above where the main trail struck the Platte. It was soon renamed and became Fort Kearny, sometimes called New Fort Kearny to distinguish it from the older post on the Missouri. In '49 it was garrisoned by a few companies of regulars. In addition, this summer, a regiment of mounted riflemen was moved west along with the migration. All that this regiment accomplished for the emigrants was to clutter up the trail a little more.

The wet weather culminated cataclysmically now and then in thunderstorms, which caused cattle to stampede in the night and greatly increased everyone's discomfort. Worst of all was the near-tornado that struck on the night of May 29, sweeping down the valley of the Platte, over the sprawling encampments of thousands of emigrants. Everywhere tents went down, and cattle started to run. The storm continued through most of the next day, while drenched and frightened emigrants hunted for their lost oxen. Many were never recovered.

The overcrowding can be easily exaggerated. Some have written of the whole trail as a solid line of wagons. Actually if all the wagons of '49 had been organized into a single close-spaced train, they would have extended for some sixty miles—a long distance, but only a small fraction of the whole.

The crowding was certainly bad enough, and continuous lines of five hundred wagons were noted. Sometimes the congestion was eased by two or more lines of wagons moving, and sometimes imprudently racing, on parallel trails. But this was really of little advantage, since there was sure to be before long a bottleneck through which only one wagon could pass at a time.

The chief problem of crowding was not on the trail, but at the campgrounds. "This evening," wrote one diarist, "we have somehow got into a perfect nest of emigrants. If I was to guess, I should say there was one thousand head of cattle within a mile of camp." But in the lush and well-watered plains country of the early days of the journey such crowding was a nuisance, not a peril.

More alarming and more dangerous was the cholera, though this too has been exaggerated. The disease was epidemic throughout most of the United States that year, and some had died on the steamers before they ever arrived at Independence or St. Joseph. Cholera was a mysterious and terrifying plague. A strong man might be taken suddenly and be dead within forty-eight hours. Rumor built up the number of deaths until the usually conservative historian H. H. Bancroft could write, "It is estimated that 5,000 thus perished."

"It is estimated" obviously means nothing more than "they say." The actual diaries make certain that some companies passed through with no deaths from cholera at all, and that many others suffered only one or two. The losses of a few unfortunate companies received much publicity. In a group of seven men from a Southern state, six were said to have died, though the report itself is scarcely better than a rumor. A party of Cherokees was reported to have lost nine out of fifteen. At least two companies, and individuals besides, returned east because of deaths from cholera.

On the other hand, the number of graves recorded—and several diarists were assiduous counters—indicates that not more than a few hundred could have died along the trail all the way from the border towns to Fort Laramie. One sober contemporary estimate put the loss from cholera, as of June 7, at "about 200." If this figure is doubled to include deaths occurring later, the total would amount to less than 2 per cent of the whole number of emigrants. This seems a reasonable figure, especially in view of the small amount of interest in the disease, which the diarists, on the whole, display.

The greenhorn quality of the forty-niners demonstrated itself in the overloading of wagons and the consequent dumping. Even in earlier years there had been the tendency to start out optimistically, with too much in the wagons. Parkman mentioned discarded furniture along the trail in '46. But in '49 overloading was almost universal. You seemed to be playing it safe by taking along everything that might possibly be useful. A few days on the muddy trail, some bad stream crossings, and a broken axle persuaded almost anyone to lighten the load.

The logistics of the journey, indeed, left little margin of safety. The weight of essential food and equipment was about five hundred pounds for the individual. With three men to a wagon, mated three and a half persons as an average. A compilation of figures given by various diarists indicates that 444 wagons were carrying 1,478 people, or just about three and a third apiece. We can therefore calculate that the number of people traveling to California by wagon was between 19,000 and 23,000, with 21,500 as a reasonable round number.

To be added are the packers. No count was taken of these, but Pawnee mentioned them as numerous. One emigrant estimated that the pack mules constituted about one-twentieth. Though it is hard to know exactly what he meant, he may have been trying to say that one-twentieth of the people were packing, and such a figure seems reasonable from the number of mentions that pack trains receive in the diaries. We may therefore suppose that a thousand people were so traveling.

The number 50,000 has often been given for the total South Pass migration in '49. But an overestimate in such matters is easy, and the data here presented seem reasonably authentic and accurate. From them an acceptable figure for the whole migration would be 22,500—certainly large enough!

Though Pawnee was careful to use the term "persons," the migration was so predominantly male that many observers merely wrote "men." Women and children were common enough to be mentioned by diarists without astonishment, but the great majority of the companies were composed exclusively of adult males. One diarist counted graves along the trail, with the result: men, 72; women, 2; children, 2. Of 112 diarists the summation is: men, 110; women, Sarah Royce; children, twelve-year-old Sallie Hester. The likelihood, therefore, is that men constituted at least 95 per cent of the migration.

Data are available for some analysis by states and regions. The most careful estimate is one for Iowa, which sets the number of Iowans at 1,200. If Missourians went in the same proportion, there would have been 4,200 of them. Certainly, people in Missouri and the Northwestern states, turned naturally to the South Pass trail, rather than to any of the other routes. After the Missourians, the Illinoisans and Ohioans would seem to have been most numerous. The states north of the Ohio River and west of Pennsylvania, including Iowa, probably accounted for as many as 11,000 emigrants, or approximately one half. Other estimates

the load could be handled by three yoke of oxen. But there was an inevitable desire to take extra supplies, and to put four men to a wagon, for the sake of economy. Thus the load, not counting the wagon, could easily reach 2,500 pounds, and this was too much.

The more efficient the company, the sooner it recognized the necessity. The Pittsburghers, under their experienced captain Jim Stewart, started on April 28 and dumped on the next day! They unloaded "a considerable amount of clothing, a fair-sized library, two bushels of beans, two pigs of lead, half a keg of nails, implements of husbandry (a plow among the number), and a lot of mechanical tools." Many companies struggled on during the first fortnight's journey to Fort Kearny, and there lightened their loads. That vicinity became a vast dump. "It makes a man's heart sick," wrote a frugal-souled son of New England, "to see the property scattered over the ground here." Since wood and buffalo chips were both scarce, campfires built of fat bacon sent up their smoky flames.

As the early abandonment of two pigs of lead by the Pittsburghers would indicate, most of the emigrants (too well read in the *Leather-Stocking Tales*) had overloaded themselves with arms and ammunition. Every man had a rifle and a revolver, or even two of them. One man had no fewer than three Bowie knives stuck in his belt. An Iowa company required each of its members to take thirty pounds of lead and five thousand percussion caps! Before long, stories were being told of rifles found along the trail, abandoned because of the weight, and smashed to prevent their use by the Indians.

Some interesting, though minor, differences of '49 may be considered the results of the Mexican War. For instance, big sombreros were popular for hats. In earlier years, there had been plucking of banjos and sawing at fiddles around the campfires, but in '49 there was strumming of guitars. A company might hold a "fandango" instead of a dance. Pinole, precooked corn meal with seasoning, was a well-liked item of diet. If the proportion of mule teams was much higher, we must remember that the mule has always been a favorite in Spanish-speaking countries and that the mule wagon provided the standard means of transport for the army. Moreover, the military organization of companies, which was common, must have owed something to the war experience. . . .

Fort Kearny, consisting of a few temporary buildings, was an unimpressive post. But for the emigrants it was the first punctuation point on the long pull. Having reached Fort Kearny, they could check that one off.

The commanding officer had ordered the guard to keep a count of the wagons, and many daily reports and the final summation were sent back to a St. Louis newspaper by a correspondent at the fort signing himself "Pawnee."

"The first specimen" of a gold-seeker was thus reported as arriving at the fort on May 6—"a large pick-axe over his shoulder, a long rifle in his hand, and two revolvers and a Bowie knife in his belt." Though the pickax must be taken as symbolic, the rest of the description may well have been realistic. Pawnee continued,

He had only time to ask for a drink of buttermilk, a piece of gingerbread, and how "fur" it was to "Caleforny" and then hallooing to his long-legged, slab-sided cattle, drawing a diminutive, yellow-topped Yankee wagon, he disappeared on the trail towards the gold "diggins."

Since a Mormon family had set up a boardinghouse at the fort, the buttermilk and gingerbread may be taken literally. As the first arrival he had, we can be sure, a hearty welcome.

Note that he had a "diminutive" wagon, so that he was not hauling much weight, and that the wagon was pulled by oxen, though mules were generally supposed to move faster.

This unknown and elsewhere unrecorded backwoodsman was apparently ahead even of Paul's company. But as he "disappeared" from Fort Kearny, so also he disappears from history. We can only hope that he got through prosperously and made his pile.

Pawnee's reports on the passing wagons are sufficiently complete to permit an analysis of what we may call the "structure" of the gold rush. . . . Pushing the leader hard came the advance guard—about five hundred wagons passing the fort in twelve days. Paul's company was probably in the lead of these. Two days behind came Kelly the Irish journalist. A few days farther back,

their wagons lightened, Stewart's Pittsburghers were beginning to hit their stride.

On May 18, the wave really struck the fort, as the count of wagons for the day jumped to 180. During a period of fifteen days three-quarters of the migration poured through. On May 22 the count broke the 300 mark; on May 28 it hit its maximum of 460. On the next day it had fallen only to 381, but after that it dropped swiftly.

By June 2 the main body had passed. The count was down to a hundred a day, and falling. From June 10 on, the passing wagons averaged only thirty. Finally, on June 23, the count seems to have been officially ended. On that day Pawnee wrote, "The great California caravan has at length swept past this point." Occasionally, he admitted, "a solitary wagon may be seen hurrying on like a buffalo on the outskirts of a band." But by this date, it would seem, even the rear guard had passed. Only the stragglers were still to come.

This count at Fort Kearny provides an excellent means of estimating the size of the whole migration. The fort, moreover, was a good point for such an estimate, because those who turned back before reaching it (and some did) can scarcely be said to have made a serious effort to reach California.

The count on June 23 was 5,516 wagons. To this figure must be added, perhaps, 200 for stragglers. The wagons traveling by the Council Bluffs road did not pass Fort Kearny. Pawnee estimated these at 600, but another correspondent gave them as 800, not counting Mormon wagons. Also on the trail were about 130 Oregon wagons, and 350 bound for Salt Lake City. There were, besides, the 150 wagons of the regiment of mounted riflemen, and these were not included in the count.

Putting all the figures together, we must conclude that the California wagons were more than 5,800 and fewer than 6,400, with 6,200 as a preferred figure.

The average number of persons to the wagon can be closely determined. An Iowa company laid down the regulation that there should be not fewer than three or more than four. This rule applied, doubtless, to adults, but there were not enough children in the '49 migration to affect the average greatly. Pawnee esti-

mated three and a half persons as an average. A compilation of figures given by various diarists indicates that 444 wagons were carrying 1,478 people, or just about three and a third apiece. We can therefore calculate that the number of people traveling to California by wagon was between 19,000 and 23,000, with 21,500 as a reasonable round number.

To be added are the packers. No count was taken of these, but Pawnee mentioned them as numerous. One emigrant estimated that the pack mules constituted about one-twentieth. Though it is hard to know exactly what he meant, he may have been trying to say that one-twentieth of the people were packing, and such a figure seems reasonable from the number of mentions that pack trains receive in the diaries. We may therefore suppose that a thousand people were so traveling.

The number 50,000 has often been given for the total South Pass migration in '49. But an overestimate in such matters is easy, and the data here presented seem reasonably authentic and accurate. From them an acceptable figure for the whole migration would be 22,500—certainly large enough!

Though Pawnee was careful to use the term "persons," the migration was so predominantly male that many observers merely wrote "men." Women and children were common enough to be mentioned by diarists without astonishment, but the great majority of the companies were composed exclusively of adult males. One diarist counted graves along the trail, with the result: men, 72; women, 2; children, 2. Of 112 diarists the summation is: men, 110; women, Sarah Royce; children, twelve-year-old Sallie Hester. The likelihood, therefore, is that men constituted at least 95 per cent of the migration.

Data are available for some analysis by states and regions. The most careful estimate is one for Iowa, which sets the number of Iowans at 1,200. If Missourians went in the same proportion, there would have been 4,200 of them. Certainly, people in Missouri and the Northwestern states, turned naturally to the South Pass trail, rather than to any of the other routes. After the Missourians, the Illinoisans and Ohioans would seem to have been most numerous. The states north of the Ohio River and west of Pennsylvania, including Iowa, probably accounted for as many as 11,000 emigrants, or approximately one half. Other estimates their wagons lightened, Stewart's Pittsburghers were beginning to hit their stride.

On May 18, the wave really struck the fort, as the count of wagons for the day jumped to 180. During a period of fifteen days three-quarters of the migration poured through. On May 22 the count broke the 300 mark; on May 28 it hit its maximum of 460. On the next day it had fallen only to 381, but after that it dropped swiftly.

By June 2 the main body had passed. The count was down to a hundred a day, and falling. From June 10 on, the passing wagons averaged only thirty. Finally, on June 23, the count seems to have been officially ended. On that day Pawnee wrote, "The great California caravan has at length swept past this point." Occasionally, he admitted, "a solitary wagon may be seen hurrying on like a buffalo on the outskirts of a band." But by this date, it would seem, even the rear guard had passed. Only the stragglers were still to come.

This count at Fort Kearny provides an excellent means of estimating the size of the whole migration. The fort, moreover, was a good point for such an estimate, because those who turned back before reaching it (and some did) can scarcely be said to have made a serious effort to reach California.

The count on June 23 was 5,516 wagons. To this figure must be added, perhaps, 200 for stragglers. The wagons traveling by the Council Bluffs road did not pass Fort Kearny. Pawnee estimated these at 600, but another correspondent gave them as 800, not counting Mormon wagons. Also on the trail were about 130 Oregon wagons, and 350 bound for Salt Lake City. There were, besides, the 150 wagons of the regiment of mounted riflemen, and these were not included in the count.

Putting all the figures together, we must conclude that the California wagons were more than 5,800 and fewer than 6,400, with 6,200 as a preferred figure.

The average number of persons to the wagon can be closely determined. An Iowa company laid down the regulation that there should be not fewer than three or more than four. This rule applied, doubtless, to adults, but there were not enough children in the '49 migration to affect the average greatly. Pawnee esti-

231

was common, must have owed something to the war experience. . . .

Fort Kearny, consisting of a few temporary buildings, was an unimpressive post. But for the emigrants it was the first punctuation point on the long pull. Having reached Fort Kearny, they could check that one off.

The commanding officer had ordered the guard to keep a count of the wagons, and many daily reports and the final summation were sent back to a St. Louis newspaper by a correspondent at the fort signing himself "Pawnee."

"The first specimen" of a gold-seeker was thus reported as arriving at the fort on May 6—"a large pick-axe over his shoulder, a long rifle in his hand, and two revolvers and a Bowie knife in his belt." Though the pickax must be taken as symbolic, the rest of the description may well have been realistic. Pawnee continued,

He had only time to ask for a drink of buttermilk, a piece of gingerbread, and how "fur" it was to "Caleforny" and then hallooing to his long-legged, slab-sided cattle, drawing a diminutive, yellow-topped Yankee wagon, he disappeared on the trail towards the gold "diggins."

Since a Mormon family had set up a boardinghouse at the fort, the buttermilk and gingerbread may be taken literally. As the first arrival he had, we can be sure, a hearty welcome.

Note that he had a "diminutive" wagon, so that he was not hauling much weight, and that the wagon was pulled by oxen, though mules were generally supposed to move faster.

This unknown and elsewhere unrecorded backwoodsman was apparently ahead even of Paul's company. But as he "disappeared" from Fort Kearny, so also he disappears from history. We can only hope that he got through prosperously and made his pile.

Pawnee's reports on the passing wagons are sufficiently complete to permit an analysis of what we may call the "structure" of the gold rush. . . . Pushing the leader hard came the advance guard—about five hundred wagons passing the fort in twelve days. Paul's company was probably in the lead of these. Two days behind came Kelly the Irish journalist. A few days farther back, the load could be handled by three yoke of oxen. But there was an inevitable desire to take extra supplies, and to put four men to a wagon, for the sake of economy. Thus the load, not counting the wagon, could easily reach 2,500 pounds, and this was too much.

The more efficient the company, the sooner it recognized the necessity. The Pittsburghers, under their experienced captain Jim Stewart, started on April 28 and dumped on the next day! They unloaded "a considerable amount of clothing, a fair-sized library, two bushels of beans, two pigs of lead, half a keg of nails, implements of husbandry (a plow among the number), and a lot of mechanical tools." Many companies struggled on during the first fortnight's journey to Fort Kearny, and there lightened their loads. That vicinity became a vast dump. "It makes a man's heart sick," wrote a frugal-souled son of New England, "to see the property scattered over the ground here." Since wood and buffalo chips were both scarce, campfires built of fat bacon sent up their smoky flames.

As the early abandonment of two pigs of lead by the Pittsburghers would indicate, most of the emigrants (too well read in the *Leather-Stocking Tales*) had overloaded themselves with arms and ammunition. Every man had a rifle and a revolver, or even two of them. One man had no fewer than three Bowie knives stuck in his belt. An Iowa company required each of its members to take thirty pounds of lead and five thousand percussion caps! Before long, stories were being told of rifles found along the trail, abandoned because of the weight, and smashed to prevent their use by the Indians.

Some interesting, though minor, differences of '49 may be considered the results of the Mexican War. For instance, big sombreros were popular for hats. In earlier years, there had been plucking of banjos and sawing at fiddles around the campfires, but in '49 there was strumming of guitars. A company might hold a "fandango" instead of a dance. Pinole, precooked corn meal with seasoning, was a well-liked item of diet. If the proportion of mule teams was much higher, we must remember that the mule has always been a favorite in Spanish-speaking countries and that the mule wagon provided the standard means of transport for the army. Moreover, the military organization of companies, which might run: Pennsylvania, New York, and New Jersey, 3,500; the slave states, except Missouri, with Kentucky most prominent, 2,000; New England, 1,500. The comparatively small number from the Southeastern states results partly from the fact that people from that region were more likely to take one of the southern trails. Similarly people from the Northeastern states were likely to go by sea. The foreign element was not large, but Germans (usually called "Dutch") are occasionally mentioned. A few Negroes, as slaves, accompanied their masters.

The number of draft animals hauling the wagons approximated 40,000. A few of these were horses. Six thousand, it may be roughly estimated, were mules. The rest were oxen, mingled with a few cows. Mules had almost been absent from the trail since Chiles's attempt in '43, and their increase in '49 is striking. In general, it would seem that Westerners and farmers still stuck by oxen.

Since Pawnee gave the total number of animals as 60,000, there must have been 20,000 riding horses, riding mules, pack mules, milch cows, and oxen driven along as spares or to be slaughtered for food.

As the wagons passed Fort Kearny, the organization by companies was still holding fairly well. Parties of ten, a dozen, or fifteen wagons were the commonest, as in earlier years. But the large number of people seemed to reduce the Indian threat and make nightly guard duty unnecessary. As a result very small companies became more common, and one man was reported traveling with a single wagon and looking upon the whole journey as a picnic.

Let no one imagine that Pawnee saw long trains of wagons all exactly alike. On the contrary, the variety was tremendous, including some buggies, carriages, and carts. There may even have been a few of the great Conestogas, now firmly fixed in the popular mind as the image of the prairie schooner. But most of the wagons were small, and the teams were rarely of more than four yoke. Three yoke, with a light wagon, was standard. Many wagons were of the "diminutive" size, mentioned as being that of the first comer. In fact, the smaller your wagon, the luckier you were.

The wagon tops, which were most conspicuous, differed

greatly. Some went straight up at the ends, and some were overhung; some were straight, and some were sway-back. They even differed in color. Pawnee mentioned the yellow-topped wagon of the first comer. The Washington City Company could be picked at a distance by its blue tops.

Even so, the migration at Fort Kearny presented in some ways much less variety than it had when leaving the frontier towns. Rain and mud and dust had tended to equalize the fine uniforms of the city companies and the nondescript clothes of the Western farmers. And there would be more rain, mud, and dust to come.

One day Pawnee witnessed a high point in variety—a solitary footman who said he had come all the way from Maine.

He is accompanied by a savage-looking bull-dog, has a long rifle over the shoulder, on the end of which he carries his baggage, in a small bundle about the size of your hat. He has no provision, but gets along fairly well by sponging on his fellow travelers. He says he wants but a hundred meals to carry him thro', and he rather guesses he'll find Christians on the road enough to supply him with that number.

On June 8 the arrival of the Pioneer Line gave Pawnee something special. . . . The idea had not been a bad one. Allan and Turner of St. Louis had advertised that for $200 apiece 120 passengers would be taken through in sixty days along with the mail. You would be one of a "mess" of six riding in a light spring wagon or "coach." The train would consist of twenty of these, plus baggage wagons. You would do your own driving, and would be issued army rations with which to do your own cooking. Teamsters and herdsmen would take care of the animals, even harnessing them.

This looked like a bargain, and the tickets quickly sold out. The resulting $24,000 must have looked large to Messrs. Allan and Turner, the value of money being what it was in those days. They seem generally to have done their best, but they had underestimated the difficulties, and everything rapidly went wrong. The partners skimped at the wrong places, though in all probability they were facing an impossible situation. But they assigned only two small mules to each coach, and that was simply not enough. Then the rains fell, and some blamed their troubles on the rains, though such difficulties could only have been expected. So there they were at Fort Kearny after a month of traveling, when they had expected to be halfway to the gold fields. Already the passengers were close to mutiny, though the manager, Pawnee considered, was a man of energy and was doing everything that could be reasonably expected.... But this was the beginning, not only of the road, but also of their tribulations.

The same, of course, might be said for the whole migration. Pawnee, summing up on June 23, was pessimistic. He questioned, "Can this vast crowd succeed in crossing the mountains in safety?" And he answered in two words, "It cannot." He added a brief explanation, "The leading trains will doubtless succeed, but those behind, will find the grass gone, and their heavy teams must then fail." He noted also that the jettisoning of provisions must result in shortages later on. His only hopeful note was that the rain, while it made the trail muddy, had produced luxurious grass.

So, at last, quiet settled down over Fort Kearny, and with that quiet a brooding sense of disaster to happen somewhere to the west....

By this date of June 23, when the rear guard was leaving Fort Kearny behind, the leading companies were already a long distance ahead. Some of them were approaching Fort Hall, and a few had probably even passed that post. Not even counting the stragglers, the migration stretched out over nearly a thousand miles of trail. Also, the line was lengthening—those with good luck, good equipment, and good leadership, gaining on those who did not know quite what they were doing, or were struggling along with second-rate teams, or were suffering from being delayed by cholera, or stampeded cattle, or for some other reason. Still the migration maintained its structure: an advance guard, a great central wave, a rear guard, and some stragglers. But just as the whole line was lengthening, so also the wave was not so sharp and so high as it had been. Its front, by June 23, was a little past South Pass, and its end was about at Fort Laramie, where you could say that the rear guard began.

Since there are so many diaries, besides reminiscences, mere details of the migration can be piled up almost to infinitude. Fortunately, there is no need to do so. Many of the diaries, though often interesting in themselves, greatly resemble diaries of the earlier years. Though people knew that they were traveling as part of a vast migration, they saw from day to day only the companies that happened to be near them.

Take Isaac Jones Wistar, for instance. He was twenty-two, the scion of a solid Philadelphia family, himself destined to fame as a Union general. The position of his company was such that about a third of the migration was ahead. The wagons behind concerned him not at all. Those ahead concerned him only in so far as the emigrants and their cattle cut up the road, ate the grass, burned up the buffalo chips, and otherwise caused him some inconvenience. He was also interested in what branches or cutoffs the wagons ahead were taking.

Wistar was young and healthy, got along splendidly, and enjoyed himself. Like most of the diarists he noted the crossing of the South Fork, the meeting with the friendly Sioux in their village just north of the crossing, the descent into Ash Hollow, the sighting of Chimney Rock, the arrival at Fort Laramie, the ferrying of the North Fork on a makeshift scow—all very much as a diarist of '46 might have done. He and his companions were excellent shots, and often lived high on fresh meat. On June 23 his party was safe across the North Platte and setting out for Independence Rock.

But the continuing interest of '49 lies in its differences from the preceding years. And at Fort Laramie and the North Platte crossing, as at Fort Kearny, the differences sprang from the greenhorn quality of the emigrants and from their fifty-fold increase in numbers.

Luck, indeed, still held. As one emigrant wrote, "there was more grass than had ever been known before." Even beyond Fort Laramie the pasturage sufficed, though there the trail developed two or even three branches by the efforts of the different companies to find ungrazed campgrounds.

This splitting of the trails was indeed only one of many evidences that something of the greenhorn quality was disappearing. Another evidence was that men no longer looked like arsenals. At first no one had thought of walking abroad without his rifle; Bowie knife and revolver were deemed mere articles of clothing. But with experience men abandoned all that useless and tiring weight. At Fort Laramie you could look around and see no one with anything more than a knife and occasionally a pistol.

During the same weeks, the emigrant's appearance had changed in other ways too. He was necessarily beginning to look like a man who has been camping out for two months, driving a team, and finding little chance to wash himself or his clothing. Already there had begun to appear that paradox between outer look and inner character of which Bret Harte was to make so much in his stories of these same forty-niners after they had become gold-miners. That likable young man from Illinois, the observant Alonzo Delano, who as "Old Block" was to precede even Bret Harte as a California man of letters, noted this paradox in his diary when his company was toiling through the hills west of Fort Laramie: "It is difficult to judge of the character of men on the road by external appearances." He explained:

A Mexican hat, a beard of twenty days' growth, an outer covering soiled with dirt and dust, a shirt which may have seen water in its youth, will disguise anyone so that he may look like a ferocious brigand, while at the same time his heart may be overflowing with the "milk of human kindness."

Among others thus changed in outward appearance must have been the fifty-two young men of the Sagamore and Sacramento Company who had paraded down State Street in all the bravery of gray uniforms trimmed with silver braid. They are known to have reached Fort Kearny, near the rear of the migration, in high spirits and going strong; beyond that point their record has not survived. But we can only suppose that they eventually sloughed off all the fancywork, and continued on to California looking about like anyone else.

West of Fort Laramie many were even yet paying the penalty of having been greenhorns, in that they were still being forced to lighten wagons. Naturally few people could bring themselves to face the whole necessity at once. First you abandoned some books and a pig of lead. Then, after an axle had snapped at a stream crossing, you pitched out, mournfully, a crowbar, some iron wedges, the goldometer, and a suit of winter clothing—though those were things, you would have to admit, that might come in handy. But before long you might be abandoning bacon, flour, and the extra blanket.

Like Fort Kearny, Fort Laramie was a punctuation point,

and its vicinity too was soon transformed into another wide-spreading dump. Name the article, and you could have found it lying about somewhere! There also occurred what might seem the ultimate act, though it was not quite that—the abandonment of the wagon itself.

You left the wagon because you had lost animals, and had to make do with one wagon instead of two. Or you left it because you decided to take to packing, as many did from Fort Laramie westward. These abandoned wagons did not altogether go to waste, for many were "cannibalized" by later comers who found themselves in need of parts. In fact, these wagons provided a kind of large insurance policy. The dangers inherent in a broken vehicle, which had faced all emigrants of earlier years, vanished when you could replace a part almost anywhere. The abandoned wagons also supplied wood for many a campfire.

The attitudes of people forced to leave goods and wagons differed considerably. Many merely dumped or abandoned. Some left notes, expressing the hope that others could make use of what was left, and stating that the food was edible. A few viciously poured turpentine into sugar, mixed flour with dirt, and burned clothes and wagons.

A certain remnant of the greenhorn quality also kept displaying itself in the continual readjustment of companies after the first few weeks. Many companies merely frayed around the edges, losing two or three men here and there, but maintaining the original identity, perhaps under the same captain. Others split in two, and often there was still further fragmentation. Sometimes the division was mutually approved with good feeling; sometimes there were quarrels. Israel Hale commented:

Hardly a day passes that a train does not split or a division take place. In a measure the like has occurred several times in our train. In starting we had more than twenty wagons. It is now reduced to eight.

But the greenhorn quality was thus fading out, and the most characteristic remaining feature of '49 was mere numbers. Delano summarized:

Our train did not travel for an hour without seeing many others, and hundreds of men. For days we would travel in company with other trains, which would stop to rest, when we would pass them; and then perhaps we would lay up, and they pass us. Some we would meet again after many days, and others, perhaps, never.

Many a proverb-loving forty-niner must have quoted, "There's safety in numbers!" though anyone might wonder whether it was the number of emigrants or something else that kept the Indians away. A well-planned and smartly executed raid upon the straggling line of wagons should not have been difficult, and would have been vastly amusing, from the point of view of a Sioux or Crow. But except for Kelly and some others of the advance guard few emigrants saw an Indian between the Sioux around Fort Laramie and the Snakes on Bear River.

Since grass was not yet a serious problem, the numbers became troublesome only at bottlenecks, of which the major stream crossings were the most notable. At the North Platte, always difficult and dangerous, some Mormons had a ferry working, but it could not handle the traffic. Besides, many parties preferred to get themselves across, instead of paying good money or bartering provisions—for, by this point, most people were down to the bare necessities that would take them through.

So along thirty miles of the river makeshift ferries were rigged up at every likely spot. Some people, having built a good raft and worked out a system, set up as ferrymen for a few days, made some money, and then sold out and went on. Israel Hale had his wagon towed across by oxen on a precarious raft of "four cottonwood logs with four binders strongly pinned to them." Oxen and mules had to swim. The stream was swift and deep, and there were many accidents which resulted in some twenty men being drowned—besides, one bad day in June, a woman and four children.

William Chamberlain, an Iowan, arriving on June 20 at the height of the wave, wrote:

The scene today is a very interesting one—hundreds of men at work, some preparing rafts—others up to their waists in the water, towing them up. Some taking wagons to pieces, some getting them together and reloading—about 80 wagons are now on the south side waiting to cross—5 rafts are making all haste in ferrying—cattle are swimming about in the river refusing to cross & constantly turning back—train after train going up the road to the ferry—all present an appearance of life & activity seldom exerted [?] in any civilized part of the world.

Numbers also produced, as in no preceding year, both social amenities and social problems. Several hundred people gathered on the same campground overnight, and by the standards of the time that was a town. Besides, even during the day's march people were in contact, especially at the nooning.

General good fellowship, charity, and hospitality abounded this season. A man off hunting cattle or merely sight-seeing could drop in at almost any camp and be welcomed to a meal and a night's shelter. As in earlier years there were dances, though lack of girls made such celebrations rarer. Musical instruments apparently survived even the lightening of the wagons, and Delano could write:

Around the camp-fires at night, the sound of a violin, clarionet, banjo, tambourine, or bugle would frequently be heard, merrily chasing off the weariness and toil.

In spite of altercations and splittings this good-fellowship seems to have been strong also within companies. Joseph Stuart, not without a touch of cynicism, declared:

One would suppose that such a close companionship would unite us as a band of brothers. This it did, and as brothers we quarreled, supported and assisted each other to the last.

Scattered along the trail were more than twenty thousand people, the equivalent of an important city by American standards of the time. They were totally severed from the effective authority of any government. In the vicinity of a military post, of which there were hardly any, the army officers exercised some power, and emigrants sometimes appealed to them. At Salt Lake City the Mormons had a government, but few emigrants recognized its jurisdiction. Both constitutionally and practically, the forty-niners were on their own.

As Americans they had a strong sense of government. The organization into companies and even the much-ridiculed constitutions and by-laws had the practical end in view of establishing a social order where none existed and where it might well be needed. The idea of natural law, familiar from the Declaration of Independence, was sometimes invoked. Thus the constitution of the "Green and Jersey County Company," of Illinois, based itself upon "the laws of order, right, and justice, which are evident to all men." It provided, if a trial should be necessary, for a jury, for witnesses under oath, and for punishment.

But what punishment? Death could not be considered except in the most extreme cases, if at all. Flogging in most persons' minds came under the heading of "cruel and unusual." One man, indeed, was reported "most cruelly beaten for stealing," but this might have been an informal beating with fists rather than a flogging. Fines and extra duty, if enforceable at all, would apply only to minor offenses. Banishment from the company, sometimes laid down as a maximum penalty, held no terrors when the banished man could probably attach himself to another company without difficulty. Besides, who wanted to turn a disgruntled man loose? If he did not take a shot at you from behind some bush, he might lame your cattle or do other mischief.

The joint-stock companies, organized as corporations, could theoretically dismiss a member for misconduct, and thus cause him to lose his investment. But such procedure was not ordinarily practical.

Fortunately, everything worked out a great deal better than would have been expected. There was very little crime, even in this city of more than twenty thousand. This probity need not be attributed to any special virtue of the forty-niners. Rather, we may ask, "What was the urge and opportunity for crime?"

Theft of goods? Why steal when you could pick up all sorts of things along the trail, and could not carry anything more yourself? Theft of money? That was not very tempting when you were in a place where money was not of much use, and when you expected within a few weeks to be digging up pounds of gold. Theft of animals was risky, since they had to be used along the trail, and could be easily identified there. This was, indeed, a crime often charged in a vague way, but ordinarily the oxen or mules had just strayed off.

The scarcity of women removed one of the traditional causes of crime. Even a Frenchman could hardly have suggested, "Cherchez la femme!" when he might have to ride twenty miles to find one. One rape was reported, and a "gross insult," which is doubtless a Victorian way of saying the same thing. In the one case the culprit was a deserter from a military post, not an emigrant. In the other case, the woman's husband shot the offender, thus presenting the emigrants with a case of homicide. The husband was taken back to Fort Kearny, a hearing was held, and he was acquitted.

Homicide was several times recorded. In many instances it sprang from sudden passion, as when two men, deciding to part company, got into a dispute about dividing the provisions, and the one shot the other. In such cases the killer could plead self-defense. The peaceable Delano once found himself close to taking life when an excitable fellow claimed the ownership of a horse, and threatened to take possession at rifle point:

I was armed with a revolver and a double-barreled gun, and had he made an assault, I should most surely have shot him down, unless he had been beforehand—a course in which I afterwards found I should have been upheld by the company.

On the Sweetwater a quiet and inoffensive man named Williams was several times threatened by another man. Believing himself to be in imminent peril, Williams made up his mind, approached his enemy under cover of darkness, and shot him down. Williams then offered himself up to several different companies, but was always freed on the grounds of self-defense, without formal trial.

Elijah Farnham, one of the Ohio diarists, recorded a grave on the North Platte with the headboard reading:

John Brown
found in the river June 19
shot in the head

Such a death might have been suicide. The possibility of self-destruction was ruled out by another headboard:

Saml A. Fitzzimmons, died from
effects of a wound received from a
bowie-knife in the hands of
Geo: Symington,
Aug: 25th 1849

242

On the whole, however, homicides were few. Men were likely to take it out in a fist fight, and then make it up. On such occasions, moreover, bystanders usually saw to it that there was fair play. In one instance a man was beating up a boy, when a woman dashed out of a tent, and delivered two solid slaps to the man's face. As he stood dazed, other men rushed up and stopped the row. It turned out that an older brother had been justly chastising a younger one, and the woman had never seen either of them before!

The most distressing incidents were the desertions of ailing comrades, though these might not be classifiable as crimes. When one man fell ill before reaching Fort Laramie, his companions deserted him "without water, provisions, covering or medicines." Suffering from thirst, he made the mistake of crawling away from the trail to reach some water. He lay there for two days. When found and relieved by some humane passers-by he was too far gone for recovery.

Pack-trains were probably responsible for most desertions, since packers had no means of transporting a sick man. There may have been extenuating circumstances. When companies were forming and dissolving rapidly, the man who was abandoned may have been with a particular company only a few days before being taken ill. In such a case the others can have felt little sense of responsibility, and may have considered that they should not endanger the lives of all by delaying to care for one whom they scarcely knew. The deserted were usually left with the means of sustenance. Some of them recovered sufficiently to be picked up by other companies and brought through. The exigencies of the trail sometimes made all men feel the threat of death, so that the abandonment of the sick, who would probably die in any case, might seem justified for the preservation of others.

What did *not* happen is really more surprising than what did. There was no mass violence, no breakdown of the general standards of decent conduct, no connivance with the Indians, no banditry. The men of a big Illinois company of sixty-four wagons, thinking that the owners of a ferry were charging extortionary rates (as they probably were), merely seized the ferry raft by force of numbers, used it, and went on, leaving a nominal fee. But no trouble developed between Mormons and Missourians. In spite of so many quarrels between individuals and between small groups, these disputes never set one whole company against another in open warfare. In spite of high spirits, universal possession of arms, and much sectional feeling, no Ohio company ever fought in battle against one from Kentucky, nor did Tennesseans organize a cattle raid against Pennsylvanian herds, and thus initiate a blood feud.

Such things might have happened, when twenty thousand men suddenly found themselves beyond the law. That disorder failed to develop on a large scale must be credited to the general decency of the emigrants, and an ingrained respect for law, order, and fair play. Perhaps also the golden dream with which they were all enamored kept their eyes fixed upon the goal ahead, and made them less likely to become involved in ephemeral bickerings. . . .

Nearing South Pass, the head of the column was approaching a point of decision, and the leading emigrants must have been discussing which route to take. They cannot have known much definitely, but the Mormon ferrymen at the North Platte would have spread the word that it was possible now to go to Salt Lake City and around the north side of the lake. As for Hastings's Cutoff, its reputation was bad. Almost certainly among the leading companies there were some men who had made the journey before, and had some knowledge of the trails.

As the first emigrants approached South Pass, they were surprised to see a cluster of tepees, which turned out to shelter Louis Vásquez, co-owner of Fort Bridger, along with a motley group of trappers and squaws. His object in camping there (one object, at least) was to trade with the emigrants, and he could offer buffalo robes, deerskins, buckskin clothing and moccasins, and three hundred horses and mules. But the emigrants must immediately have begun to question him about possible routes, and Vásquez was glad to comply with information that would send people through Fort Bridger. In fact, this may well have been his chief motive for locating his camp about two days' journey east of the split of the roads. It was as if the history of '46 were being repeated, with Vásquez in the place of Hastings. But he had something better than Hastings's Cutoff to offer. Even so, he was badly prejudiced in favor of the road by way of his own fort, and probably he knew very little that was accurate about the distances or comparative difficulties of the routes. In fact, it may be doubted whether anybody did. Yet, here were more than twenty thousand people, pushing westward, eager to get to the gold mines, many of them ready to accept any rumor that sounded favorable.

In reality, the choice you made at this point did not make a great deal of difference, if only you kept away from Hastings's Cutoff. Even with that possibility rejected, there were still three others.

First, you could go by Sublette's Cutoff and Fort Hall. From the turnoff at Big Sandy to Cathedral Rocks, where the two roads reunited, the distance was about 340 miles.

Second, you could go through Fort Bridger to Salt Lake City over what was now known as the Mormon Trail. Then from Salt Lake City you could follow Hensley's route, the so-called Salt Lake Cutoff, around to the north of the lake and thus to Cathedral Rocks. The distance, that way, was 420 miles—80 miles farther than by Sublette's Cutoff. The road was perhaps a trifle easier, though there was some heavy going across the Wasatch Mountains. An advantage was that you could expect to buy supplies and do some refitting either at Fort Bridger or at Salt Lake City.

Third, you could go to Fort Bridger and then swing back around by Fort Hall. The distance, that way, was about the same as the distance by way of Salt Lake City. There were no difficult stretches in this route, so that it was possibly the easiest of the three on teams.

Because of what Vásquez told, several of the leading companies, among them Kelly's party (packing since Fort Laramie) and Stewart's Pittsburghers (now nearly in the lead), turned to the left for Salt Lake City. Then, after a week or so, almost everyone began taking Sublette's Cutoff. Estimates ran that it was being used by three-fourths or even nine-tenths of the wagons. Some old-timer had undoubtedly come along, someone who knew the cutoff, and was not going to be lured away.

Then near the middle of the migration there was another change, and about half the wagons began going by Salt Lake City. Again we can suggest a reason. The ones in the second half of the migration were those who had lost animals, or had worn their animals down, or found themselves with wagons that were going to pieces. To these people such havens as Fort Bridger and Salt Lake City offered a great attraction.

The in-between route to Fort Bridger and back to Fort Hall appealed to only a few people, but the ones who went that way did not do badly. They had the advantages of an easy road and of an eighty-five-mile stretch of trail along which the grass had scarcely been grazed at all.

Those who took the Salt Lake Cutoff lost about five days by comparison with those who took Sublette's Cutoff, but the chance to recuperate at Salt Lake City may have been worth the time. Until August, when they harvested, the Mormons did not have much in the way of provisions to offer, except for dairy products and vegetables. But the emigrants enjoyed a little change in diet, and the chance of buying a new ox or two and of having some professional blacksmithing done on the wagon might be important.

The Mormons also had information to give about the route to California, and the Pittsburghers even picked up a guide. This was James Sly, who had come east with the Mormons in '48. He agreed to go to California again, with the curious proviso that his father-in-law should be allowed to go with him. (Though a Mormon, he had only one such kinsman.)

Thus reinforced, the Pittsburghers moved on triumphantly until they came back into the main trail and found that they had lost five days in the race by taking Vásquez's advice! Stewart was so wildly angry that he even thought of going back clear to Fort Bridger to take revenge on "the wily Spaniard." In the end he merely settled down to make the time up, handling his mules with the love and care that he might have bestowed on thoroughbred race horses, and moving ahead so fast that he overtook company after company.

In general, the Salt Lake Cutoff offered very dull going, and the diarists usually had little to report. In the history of '49 that route is of importance because about one-third of the emigrants used it, and thus removed themselves from the other trail. As a result, there was less crowding, and less difficulty in finding grass. People from Missouri, Iowa, and Illinois kept away from this branch of the trail because of their hostility to the Mormons, or fear of them.

The two-thirds of the emigrants who swarmed across Sublette's Cutoff had more adventures than those who went by Salt Lake City. First, they had to cross the desert from Big Sandy to Green River. From Ware's guide they believed the distance to be thirty-five miles, and when it turned out to be farther than that, the book and its author came in for a good deal of cursing. Some put the distance as high as fifty-five miles. One likelihood is that Solomon Sublette, who was Ware's informant, had not traveled the cutoff and was confusing it with an old trappers' trail that ran somewhat farther north. This trail would have required much work before wagons could have gone over it. One pack train tried it, got lost in rugged mountains, and had difficulties in getting out.

Green River was high that summer, because of the heavy winter snows. It did not become fordable until the end of July, so that nearly all the migration had to depend upon overworked, makeshift ferries. Many parties had to wait forty-eight hours to get their wagons across.

Alexander Ramsay, a Hoosier, arrived there on July 4, just about at the height of the migration. He wrote in some discouragement at the crowding:

We are much wearied by the toils & fatigues of the long journey, and the immense numbers of emigrants who are upon the road makes it doubly tiresome from the fact that they are constantly in each others' way and more particularly at the crossing of rivers and difficult places on the road; here at this time are two or three hundred wagons with their accompanying teams and men, and the ground is covered with a coat of light dust two inches in depth which the wind is constantly carrying to and from, whilst the sun is pouring down his hottest rays upon us, and the wonder is that some of us only and not all of us are sick.

Farnham, arriving five days later, pictured the scene:

There were emigrants here encamped some of whom had been here 2 days, and the place on both sides of the river had quite a city-like appearance, and when night set in, the numerous camp fires gave the place quite a cheerful appearance. And those that had been here

247

long enough to get rested were amusing [themselves] with music and dancing and the firing of guns and rockets and singing glee songs.

Adjusting their prices to the overcrowded situation, the Mormon ferrymen were charging $8 a wagon. Farnham added:

The Mormons made a good lot of money off the passing emigrants, not only by ferrying but by buying broken down oxen at cheap rates and clothing which the emigrants are glad to sell.

Beyond the river there was some hard work getting through the mountains, but it was pleasant to be in a country of flowing streams and pine trees. Then, following Bear River northward, you had good grazing, enjoyed seeing the colorful squaw-infested establishment of that old mountain-man, "Peg-leg" Smith, and marveled at the wonders of Steamboat Spring. Beyond that point everybody headed on north toward Fort Hall—until July 19. . . .

To explain the curious happening of that day, the story must shift back. California emigrants had always objected to the long swing northward to Fort Hall. As early as '45 Hastings had written that the road ought to go west from Soda Springs, but instead of opening that road, he had conceived the disastrously bad idea of going south of the lake. Jesse Applegate had argued, in a statement published in '48, that Sublette's Cutoff should keep on straight west, thus saving 125 miles. (So it would have, too, but you would have had to fit wings to your teams to take the wagons over many miles of precipitous mountains, and even the Greeks, who thought of Pegasus, never imagined flying oxen!) At least, anyone who knew that a straight line was the shortest distance between two points could tell that you ought to save distance by heading west from Soda Springs instead of following the great loop around by Fort Hall.

But, in this same connection, we must also consider some conditions of travel in '49. . . . The place that you held in the migration, how many wagons were ahead and how many behind, depended primarily upon when you had got started. If you were in the main body, you had little chance of bettering your position. On the trail passing was nearly impossible. As in '46, the previously most crowded year, you had to get started earlier in the morning, or get by during the nooning, or travel later in the evening, if you wanted to get ahead of another company. And

248

often, after all that work, you found yourself at the same campground with the people that you had passed, merely because there was no other campground near enough to be reached that day. On the other hand, you could fall *back* in the procession easily enough. No one objected to your pulling aside and letting him go by. More commonly you lost ground because you spent a day or two in camp while others kept on. Some people stopped more often to rest their teams. Not a few, for religious scruples, rested on Sundays, some of them reinforcing religion by maintaining that teams which were rested one day a week would make more distance than teams worked every day. (Whether this really was so or not must be left undetermined; no one ever ran a controlled test.) The other common reason for lying over in camp was serious illness in the company.

Many had supposed at first that the method of travel would considerably effect where you might be at a given time. There should be, they presumed, a natural arrangement—first, pack trains; second, mule wagons; third, ox wagons. On the trail it worked out in that way only to a very limited extent. Ansel McCall, when on the Salt Lake Cutoff, observed that pack trains had gained only a little, and concluded that oxen were best. Most of the advance guard—Paul's company, for instance, and Kelly's and the Pittsburghers—had mule teams. Also, however, they had all started early. But some ox teams, too, were well in the van. On the other hand, some pack trains and some mule teams, starting late, remained still in the rear guard.

Thus, to summarize, you could move ahead only as other parties fell behind you, but you could work your way toward the rear very easily by traveling slowly or halting often. In time, some results of all this began to show in the migration as a whole. Because of parties falling back, the concentration of wagons in the center became less notable. Three-quarters of the wagons had gone past Fort Kearny in about two weeks; the same number took about three weeks to pass Independence Rock.

This spreading had one good result. At Fort Kearny 460 wagons had passed in one day, and there must have been corresponding competition for campgrounds and grazing. But in the vicinity of Independence Rock not more than three hundred wagons would have been passing in one day—and that was important when the migration was getting into dry country. But the spreading also had a bad result, or was a bad symptom, because it meant that part of the migration was getting behind and might be too late to cross to the mountains.

Moreover, those who were falling to the rear were the companies who were the weakest and therefore the least able to endure the rigors of winter. They were particularly the ones with weak teams and poor equipment, the inexperienced and the foolish, those with women and children. Even at South Pass the so-called "family wagons" were beginning to concentrate in the rear.

But the tendency of family wagons to lose ground cannot have been noticeable with the big Missouri train that Benoni Hudspeth was captaining. These "Pikers," as Missourians were called, were a colorful lot. Wistar, at the North Platte, saw their skilled riflemen chagrined when they could not hit a swan that came swimming downstream, and then protesting that it must be a Rocky Mountain witch. According to Wistar, they then had forty-seven wagons, but Elijah Farnham, who traveled close to them, gave the number, farther along, as seventy. Perhaps, for a while, they had split into sections. They were like a pre-'49 company, with ox teams and many families. Again according to Farnham, "There were more women and children in it than in any other train."

The Pikers as they came down Bear River in the middle of July were in a crowded part of the migration. By this time they must have been tired of thronged campgrounds and gnawed-off grass and too many greenhorn Yankees and city folks. An idea was stirring in the minds of Hudspeth and Myers. Getting off the main trail might give better grazing and relief from crowds, and by taking a new route they might steal a march and put themselves days ahead.

Bear River, a few miles to the west of Soda Springs, bends sharply. Along it, southward, the Bartlesons had taken their wagons in '41. But that route offered little for California-bound wagons. At this same point, also, after following Bear River for many miles, the regular trail left the river and continued northward on its long loop around by Fort Hall. Here, on July 19, with Myers out ahead feeling the way, Hudspeth left the established trail, and took his wagons directly west!

On they went, breaking trail through the sagebrush, across a wide valley toward low mountains ten miles off. A cinder-cone crater, about a mile to the south, gave evidence that this was volcanic country, and the train had not gone far across the plain before it was halted by a broad crack in the ground, evidence of an ancient lava flow. Undaunted, the Missourians rolled big stones in, and then piled brush and earth on top and took the wagons over.

There is almost no record of the journey, the only anecdote being humorous not informative. According to Delano, the party met some friendly Indians who had learned a little English from passing emigrants. On Hudspeth's approach, they met him in the most cordial manner with " 'How de do—whoa haw! G–d D—n you!' It was in fact the most common language of the drivers."

What evidence exists would indicate that not even Myers knew where they were going. The country showed the typical arrangement of north-and-south mountain ranges. To cross them was difficult, and to go around them was unduly long. As would be expected, the result was a compromise. Here the route wound sinuously about, adding distance; here it went up and down steeply, adding difficulty. In addition, the country was dry, so that the finding of grass and water was a constant problem.

Nevertheless, Myers led the wagons on—without knowing whether he was getting them deeper into a disastrous dead end or taking them through to success. Moreover, though he cannot have realized it, the migration was blindly following after him, leaving the Fort Hall road deserted. If he should now have to turn and backtrack, he would create such confusion as the trail had never seen before.

Possibly Myers hedged his bets as he went along, looking up and down a north-south valley and realizing that in case of necessity he could either turn north, to the Fort Hall trail, or turn south, to the Salt Lake Cutoff. At one point, indeed, he was only thirty miles from the latter, and from a high point might have seen the columns of dust that rose from the passing wagons. Actually he would have done well to go south and join that road, thus saving distance. But he kept to the west, though forced to move sinuously.

His luck held. It must have been luck, for even the greatest skill cannot find a passageway for wagons if no passageway is there. But Myers found a way through the mountains, in many places along canyon bottoms just nicely wide enough for a wagon to pass. And when a spring was needed, there was a spring!

At last, on July 24, the Missourians crossed a dry plain, westward, and came again to the main road. As an emigrant who met them there described it, "They were almost thunderstruck, when upon emerging they found they were only 70 miles from Fort Hall." Actually, they were a little farther than that, but a small point of distance need not be argued.

The fact is that Myers and Hudspeth were bad at geography. They worked by wishful thinking and not by consulting the best maps. So they did not, as they had expected, come out of their cutoff at the head of the Humboldt, but hit the main trail a good 120 miles farther east, only about 25 miles from where the Salt Lake Cutoff came in.

But as an example of handling a wagon train, the work of Hudspeth must be placed clear at the top. Though breaking trail, he lost no time, and came into the main stream of wagons in just about the same position that he had held before. Such a feat would indicate that wagons following behind, not having to break trail, should save time by taking the cutoff.

The emigrants themselves, seeing the new trail, at once jumped to the conclusion that that was the proper way to go. Farnham, arriving at the turnoff a day after Hudspeth, noted that the cutoff was already worn down "so it now looks like an old road of a good deal of travel." Like ants in a stream, each party followed after the one ahead. From this time on, the Californians took the cutoff, and Fort Hall got only an occasional wagon!

Farnham wrote that his company "beat by two days" those that went by Fort Hall. Such a statement sounds conclusive, but means very little. His own company may have hurried, and those others may have rested a while at Fort Hall. As a contrary opinion, J. Goldsborough Bruff gave the distance, by the cutoff, as measured by an odometer, as 132¾ miles, and stated that the distance by Fort Hall had been computed as 134 miles. Measurements on a modern map show Bruff as very close to being correct. The cutoff eliminated the major loop, but introduced many minor loops and twistings to get through the mountains.

Only Bruff seems to have made a careful attempt to compare the two routes, and he came to the conclusion, "the 'cutoff' was no cutoff at all." Unfortunately, sufficient records are not available to make possible a wholly valid comparison of the two routes. There was probably not much difference.

Planned in ignorance but executed with consummate skill, much traveled but of questionable value, Hudspeth's Cutoff—or Myers's or Emigrants' Cutoff—stands as the only new route, aside from minor splits and detours, accomplished by the forty-niners who used the trail through South Pass.

On July 24, when Hudspeth brought his wagons back into the main road, some emigrants had already been in California for as long as a week! The exact day need not be too precisely inquired. California is a large place, so that an entry into it might be variously dated. But the evidence indicates that the first party could have arrived at Sacramento on July 16. (More likely, they never went to Sacramento, but stopped somewhere to work in the mines.) This first company consisted of packers, and they may have been Paul's St. Louisans. In fact, the first companies to arrive were all packers, though most of them, like Paul's company, had not packed for the whole distance.

One of Stewart's Pittsburghers claimed that they brought the first wagon in; another of them was content to have it the tenth wagon. Certainly they had done well, and their expended time totaled only 93 days. In spite of being lured into taking the Salt Lake Cutoff, Stewart's unexcelled skill in mulecraft had enabled him to overtake and pass the companies who had got ahead. As one of the party could write, "Stewart's concern is always for the mules—he wastes no thought on the men." That journey must certainly go down as one of the most outstanding, and it was fortunate to have an able chronicler in William G. Johnston.

From this point on, the story of the year must be conceived in terms of one of those children's games in which "men" are moved around a course and through certain obstacles until at last they are "home." Well before the end of July, then, some of them were thus "home"—a term which many, indeed, would eventually apply to California. But what we have called the beginning of the wave (now so flattened as not to be much of a wave) had not yet reached the head of the Humboldt, and the end of the wave was about at Green River. Then, more scattered along the trail but still numerous enough to keep anyone from feeling lonely, came the rear guard. Finally—from about the North Platte crossing eastward—came the stragglers.

Thus, at the middle of July, you would have found wagons on the trail all the way across. Some people, indeed, even left the settlements after this time. Such late starters, however, can hardly have expected to get all the way through to California that season—if, indeed, they had any clarity in their minds at all in this Year of the Madness. But, whether they knew it or not, the best they could expect to do now would be to make Salt Lake City and either winter there or head southwestward for Los Angeles.

Just below the soaring twin spires, twenty-five miles beyond where Hudspeth's Cutoff rejoined the old trail, the Salt Lake Cutoff came in.

Approaching the junction by way of the cutoff, John Benson wrote:

We are in sight of the Fort Hall road, that is, we are in sight of the dust. We can count the passing teams as the dust is rising from them, like the smoke from so many steamboats.

From the point of junction for four hundred miles all the emigrants—except for a very few who had been lured into Hastings's Cutoff—moved along a single road.

Still, the crowding now was not so pronounced as it had once been. No one was there to count and set the record down, as at Fort Kearny. But if there had been, we should guess that rarely would he have noted as many as 200 wagons passing in one day. For one thing there were fewer wagons. All along the line, from Fort Laramie westward, they had been abandoned.

Mile by mile, also, horses and mules and oxen had died, or had failed and been abandoned, or had been slaughtered for food, or had not been recovered after a stampede, or had simply disappeared in some mysterious way. A few had been bought at Fort Bridger and at Salt Lake City, but not enough to replace the deficit.

If 6,200 wagons set out for California, did 5,500 ever reach

254

Cathedral Rocks? If 60,000 animals passed at Fort Kearny, did 40,000 ever go over the Goose Creek Divide?

Among the people there had been no such shrinkage. Cholera had been the worst killer. Others had died of that vague disease called "mountain fever," which seems to have meant any fever you had when you were in the mountains. Others had dropped with heart failure, or succumbed to tuberculosis or some other chronic disease that they were carrying with them. Accidents, chiefly shootings and drownings, might have taken fifty or a hundred. One could add a few homicides.

To offset a few of these losses, you could add some births, and some recruits at Salt Lake City or from the mountain-men. Besides, at least one party with ox teams had come up from Arkansas by a northwest route across the plains and had not joined the main trail until after crossing Green River. They thus established what later came to be known as the Cherokee Trail, since many members of the party were of that tribe.

By this time the look of the individual emigrant had altered considerably from what it had been even at Fort Kearny. Ansel McCall, an upstate New Yorker, could indulge in *O tempora*—

How times change and men change with them! I look in vain among the ragged, grave and bronzed codgers, dragging themselves wearily along, for those dashing, sprightly and gay young fellows, full of song and laughter, whom I saw in the valley of the Blue, on the banks of the Platte, two months ago.

Certainly, the greenhorns had vanished. A man might reach Goose Creek and still be a natural-born fool, but after two months on the trail he was scarcely a greenhorn.

There had been some change in manners also. Card-playing had taken a tremendous upsurge, and many men thus spent nearly all their spare time, though they can hardly have had any stakes for gambling. Some men still kept the Sabbath and gathered then to hear a preacher, but profanity had become distressingly common for strait-laced William Chamberlain, who had apparently never heard of how the army swore in Flanders:

I do not think there ever was as many men together or on any road so shockingly blesphemiss [sic] as the emigrants ... they hardly use any expression to horse, mule, or ox except G'd D'n your Soul (or heart) to H'll, or to damnation.

As the French of Joan of Arc's time knew the English soldiers as *godons*, so the friendly Snakes knew the emigrants from that same common oath. Just as one Indian had addressed Hudspeth, so another gave information about a campground, "Plenty of grass for the *whoa haws*, but no water for the G—d D—ns!"

But even Chamberlain, though swearing shocked him, had lapsed from civilized standards in some ways. On July 22 he took a bath, reporting,

Changed my undercloths & think the first time since I took my bath in William Creek— Got out my glass & looked at myself. But for certainly unmistakable evidences of identity would have as soon believed myself almost anybody else.

Chamberlain's previous bath—and that, an involuntary ducking! —had been more than three weeks back.

But the diaries record no sense of the offensiveness of fellow emigrants. These men were living much as front-line infantry, with only two ideals—to stay alive and to advance toward the objective. Besides, who was there to complain of smells? Generally speaking, the pot does not even know that the kettle is black. And by this time the noisomeness of rotting carcasses of mules and oxen filled the air at every campground.

Under the conditions of the migration, privacy was difficult to attain. Yet there were still people who sought it, and it could be found only a little distance from the trail, if you were not afraid of being lost or encountering Indians. Dr. Henry Austin, physician for the Washington City Company, wandered off one day with Captain Bruff, ostensibly to shoot grouse. In the quiet afternoon Bruff lay down and went to sleep under some sage bushes; Austin found himself a place with a good view, and sat there, reading Cowper's *Task*. But Austin had really sloughed off the conventions very successfully. "Dined off badger," he wrote one day, "and excellent meat it is."

Sarah Royce also enjoyed withdrawal:

I have found a quiet spot at a little distance from the wagons, where I am seated on a stone, with book and pencil in hand, the babbling

256

brook just at my feet, and close beside me, my little Mary who is picking up the colored pebbles and throwing them, with exclamations of delight, into the sparkling waters.

The children also had their fun, as Sallie Hester wrote self-consciously:

Several of us climbed this mountain [Devil's Gate]—somewhat perilous for youngsters not over fourteen. . . . We were amply repaid for our tramp, for the scenery was grand, gloomy, wild, and picturesque. We were gone so long that the train was stopped and men sent out in search of us. We made all sorts of promises to remain in sight in the future.

Even aside from the individual, the whole look of the migration had changed and was changing. Many wagons had been shortened for greater lightness and maneuverability, and some had even been reduced to carts. Fewer people were riding on horseback or in wagons, and correspondingly more people were walking; even women were walking, because animals had died or grown too weak. The loose cattle had almost disappeared. The number of people and animals to a wagon was larger.

Pawnee, at Fort Kearny, had put the average per wagon at three and a half people and six oxen or mules. But Major Osborne Cross of the Mounted Riflemen, probably giving his impression of the migration during the middle part of the journey, declared "it was a small average" to estimate four people to each wagon. He set the number of oxen as very seldom fewer than ten to the wagon and "more frequently twelve."

What had been happening is clear enough. The abandonment of each wagon required some readjustment. Sometimes people left all their wagons, and took to packing. If they already had mule teams, the shift was easy. They used the same mules, manufactured pack saddles from the wood of the abandoned wagons, packed up, mounted themselves on the extra mules, and took to the road. With six mules and three men to a wagon, a company could shift and have a pack mule and a riding mule to each man. One mule could pack about 200 pounds, and it could pull at least three times that. But by the time people abandoned wagons, they had also abandoned all idea of taking anything to California except themselves, and so they loaded the mule with food, and made a dash for it, knowing that the mule's load would grow lighter every day, and hoping to reach California before the load disappeared completely and they would have to eat the mule.

Though oxen could be packed in an emergency, no one set out on a long journey in that fashion if he could help it. People with oxen shifted when they could trade them in on mules or horses, as some of them did at Fort Bridger and Salt Lake City.

But an ox-team party often abandoned a single wagon. Perhaps they had suffered a loss of oxen or found the oxen growing too weak, or perhaps the wagon had met with an accident. Often the party had been forced to throw out almost everything but food, and then, week by week, they ate the food up. In the end they could distribute the contents of one wagon among the others, get rid of the dead weight of the wagon, and put its oxen to work at helping to haul the remaining wagons.

Inevitably more and more people had to walk. At last only the sick and injured were riding in wagons all the time, along with the very few young children and old people. Women and the older children walked at least part of the time.

Moreover, you would have seen some people who were walking with packs on their backs. Probably they were few, though they get a fair number of mentions in the diaries—because rarity gets mentioned while the commonplace thing does not. "Walker's Train," as it was called, had begun to appear suddenly about halfway across. Farnham, passing Independence Rock on July 2, recorded in surprise, "saw a man today packing his effects on his back." But only five days later, at Big Sandy, McCall wrote, "The great army of tramps . . . seems to be gaining numbers daily."

Some were eccentrics. Such must have been that first one to be mentioned—the down-easter who passed Fort Kearny with his ferocious bulldog. Such also must have been the man whom Delano saw on Bear River. He carried a bow, and shot prairie dogs with arrows as he went along. He lived chiefly on these, but also accepted handouts. But among twenty thousand some mental troubles would be expected, and one man seems clearly insane. People could gather nothing from him as to who he was. A diarist reported him wearing only pants and a shirt, both badly torn. He had some provisions given him by emigrants, and he sat by a fire over which he performed strange gestures.

258

Another type had joined **Walker's Train** because of bad luck coupled with self-reliance. If the bad luck happened east of Fort Laramie, or even east of South Pass, you might head back to the states, and diarists reported a trickle eastward. But west of South Pass it was as practical physically to reach California as to return to Missouri, and psychologically you could find it easier to continue than to take the road back, where the miles are always twice as long and the dust deeper. So some men kept on. They could not carry enough on their backs to get them through, but they might attach themselves to some company to drive oxen, or might have some luck, or at worst could beg their way. Delano met such a poor fellow whose cattle had died. He had bought a horse, and it too had died. Now, with a lame leg and a running sore on one hand, he was limping along, his only property a small bag of flour on his back.

But some men were in Walker's Train because they liked such a life, and even felt that they made better time being thus unencumbered. McCall had a low opinion of them, thinking them "churlish, querulous fellows, who cannot well agree with associates." Many of them were doubtless professional tramps, taking naturally to a hand-to-mouth life. As long as people were lightening wagons by throwing good food out, there was no problem of sustenance. But after a while there was no more food being thrown away, and scavenging became impossible. Then you asked for a handout, and at first found people easygoing and charitably minded. But as time passed, people began to worry about having enough for themselves, and they were slow to feed a good-for-nothing who came hungrily to the campfire at suppertime.

With the midpoint of the journey now well behind, a contemplative strain began to appear in those diaries kept by more thoughtful men. Israel Hale commented upon unfavorable circumstances—wind, dust, poor water, and scanty grass. He added:

But the worst is still to come. Grass, when we strike the Humboldt, we are told, will be very scarce and the water not so good as this and in many places none at all.

Then, as if frightened by his own catalog of present discomforts and of terrors to be, he put a brave front on:

But this is borrowing trouble and I will stop and take a view of the other side. Our cattle are in fair order, our men are mostly in good health and we have a plenty to eat at present and are about two weeks ahead of the time that emigrants generally pass this place, and if no bad luck happens we will, in thirty-five or forty days, reach the land that is said to abound in gold.

We should note his words—"*is said* to abound in gold." There had been time now for sobering second thoughts.

John Benson was one of the few to make an occasional entry sound like a letter to the folks, and to generalize a little:

Aside from the thoughts of home (on which we do not dare to dwell too much for fear of that dread distemper homesickness) and what may wait us at the end of the road—our thoughts, our hopes, our fears and our anxieties are all centered about the train—the health and spirits of the company, grass and water for the oxen, and in a limited way, fuel with which to cook our meals. . . . Rumors of hostile Indians are floating in the air most of the time, and while we pay little attention to them, we cannot altogether dismiss them from our minds, so that you can see that the world in which we actually live scarcely extends beyond the dust of the train by day and the smoke of the camp fires at night.

On the monotonous Salt Lake Cutoff, he generalized about the passage of time:

Nor does the time seem long as one would suppose. The days as they pass frequently seem very long, and the nights when there is sickness in camp and when we are anxious about the oxen, but the week ends and the month ends come around surprisingly fast.

Also, you might have seen pass the remnants of the Pioneer Line. "How different is the figure now cut," wrote its diarist, Niles Searls, a lawyer from upstate New York. Almost everything possible had gone wrong. Cholera had ravaged the company, and from that and other illness Searls's own mess had been reduced from six to three. Though Captain Turner was still staunchly standing by his contract, the luxurious transportation promised for $200 had vanished into bare subsistence. Tents had been abandoned; baggage allotments, cut; "coaches," reduced to twelve. The passengers themselves were alternating between mutiny and despair. On August 19, Searls wrote:

Our men are becoming emaciated and querulous. . . . Rancid bacon with the grease fried out by the hot sun, musty flour, a little pinoles and some sacks of pilot bread, broken and crushed to dust and well coated with alkali, a little coffee without sugar—now constitutes our diet. The men need more and must have it or perish. . . . A deep gloom prevails in camp. The men know we must all inevitably starve unless relieved and yet feel like cutting the throat of him who reminds them of it.

They were much worse off than most of the emigrants, and were unable to do much about it because of having committed themselves.

(And now, finally to end this lugubrious story of the first public transportation to California, let us merely record that the bedraggled and exhausted remnant finally got through over the Carson Route in October. A second detachment of the Pioneer Line, having left some weeks after the first one, had better luck, and arrived only three or four days later.)

So the great migration pressed ahead, up Goose Creek, down Thousand Springs Creek, and on to the Humboldt—except for the few who had involved themselves with an old booby trap. . . .

Little record is available of what happened on Hastings's Cutoff, and who took it, or why. Yet we need not be surprised that some made that choice. Given so many Americans, many of them hysterical with the lust for gold, will not some of them be sure to go against all reason? After all, it was known, wagons had gone that way in '46 and had got through. That the Mormons in Salt Lake City were warning against the route might only make some suspicious people think that the Mormons had their own reasons for so doing.

So a few set out, some with packs and some with wagons. Among those to make the attempt, with mule-drawn wagons, were some of the Colony Guards. Since they were from New York and had started late, they may well have had a copy of Jefferson's map, and have been depending upon it. Other companies were from Boston and Milwaukee. Thus, as so often, the city people rather than the farmers seem to have been more gullible.

As in '48, there had been rain. Though the animals did not bog down, as Hensley's had, the surface of the salt flat was mushy, and the wagon wheels sank deep. Again, property was thrown out to lighten the loads. In spite of everything, five wagons and a cart stuck so deeply that they had to be abandoned. Animals were dropping from thirst and exhaustion.

Before long, the crossing degenerated into a rout, worse

even than that of the Donner Party during the same passage. The Boston party lost all their animals except four mules. Some "Dutchmen" lost all of their twenty-five oxen, but managed to get across with three horses and eight mules. Men struggled on afoot until they too dropped by the trail. Some in the desperation of thirst drank the urine of their mules. The Germans were reported to have been three days without water. Black-tongued and bleeding from the mouth, others staggered in to the springs beneath Pilot Peak.

There they revived, and after a while were able to go back along the trail with water for their failing comrades. According to one account, many men died, but this may be mere rumor. Captain Howard Stansbury, who passed that way in November with a government expedition, reported the jettisoned property, abandoned wagons, and dead animals, but neither human bodies nor graves. . . .

Even those few who took the cutoff returned to the main trail part-way down the Humboldt, so that for 150 miles, around the Big Bend, the whole migration—wagons, carts, packers, and Walker's Train—followed the same route. Gradually that summer, new passageways were punched through the sagebrush, so that eventually there was a north-bank trail and a south-bank trail all the way, with some consequent relief of congestion. In some places there were additional branches, and along with many crossovers these produced a sometimes complicated road pattern.

Still, as long as the main wave was passing, there was no lack of company. "In sight of hundreds of wagons," wrote Delano, "we reached the celebrated Humboldt."

That was a long drag down along the river—day after day the desert sun ablaze, the earth light and powdery, the wind strong and steady from the west, blowing the dust stirred up by the long trains of wagons. The dust was always with them. As Delano wrote, they ate, drank, and breathed it.

To escape the heat and some of the dust, a few emigrants took to resting by day and traveling at night. Gradually more and more of them did so, until the trail was almost as busy in the darkness as in the light.

The look of the migration was still changing, as some parties cut wagons down to smaller size, others shifted to pack mules, and still others abandoned everything and took to walking. Benson noted, "I saw today for the first time a woman foot packer."

Loads were still being lightened, but people noted that no food was now being thrown away. The typical American tendency to make a "deal" was still observable. One emigrant arranged for six hundred pounds of freight to be carried in another man's wagon. Even food could still be bought for cash, though you could not always expect the accompaniment recorded by Joseph Stuart:

I was fortunate enough to see a pretty woman who told me I could buy some provisions a quarter-mile farther on. I bought 42 lbs. at 16 cts. We camped near the beautiful lady.

This sight for tired eyes along the Humboldt cannot have been the Boston lady encountered by McCall, though she sounds even more interesting. He politely recorded her age as "somewhat uncertain, or rendered so, by the exposure to fervid suns and rude winds." To his inquiries she said that she enjoyed the trip very much and borrowed no trouble for the future. She was "out of all patience" with the men of her company who complained about the tolls and hazards and were frightened of Indians.

She said she had been in the habit of walking miles ahead of the train in search of plants and flowers, and other curious things, and had met, alone, numbers of Indians. They had never offered to molest her, and she had no fears of them. Her companions were very apprehensive that their teams would give out. She said, "I do not share in that apprehension, for if they do, I know the distance is only four hundred miles, and I am satisfied I could walk that without any difficulty."

To do them justice not all the men were of that timorous state of mind which marked those accompanying this indomitable lady from Boston. Samuel Dundass from Ohio, that staunch Presbyterian, knew that his God, if not the law, ruled even along the Humboldt:

We have laid up here in our usual observance of the Lord's day. It is a dreary barren spot, but the Lord Jehovah is here. The universe is his great Temple—and the devout worshipper can everywhere look up to his Father in Heaven and be in fellowship with him.

The wolves, however, not recognizing the Lord, were trouble-some that night. Dundass and his companion tried unsuccessfully to get a shot at them. He thereupon noted with Biblical wording, though in a somewhat confusing metaphor: "they deprived us of an opportunity of stretching their uncircumcised carcasses upon the sandy plain."

There were many religious meetings, and we may thank Elisha Lewis of Wisconsin for giving some details, even though his spelling broke down. He wrote:

preaching by Elder Smith of Missoury state—the meeting was opened by reading the 8 Chap. Deuderon—his remarks were founded upon the 5 Chap of 2 Kings.

The reading was well chosen for a group of meagerly fed men in the dry valley of the Humboldt—that eulogy of the long-sought Canaan, "a land of brooks of water . . . a land wherein thou shalt eat bread without scarceness." The applicability, in the sermon, of the curing of Naaman's leprosy is less obvious, though there was already some scurvy. In any case, "had a very good discourse," was the diarist's conclusion. . . .

But now, ahead, was looming up for each party the necessity of a major decision as to route. That decision must be made with the benefit of little exact information. At the same time, an incredible amount of rumor was circulating—naturally enough, since so many people were involved and since few of them were in a position to speak authoritatively. Stories were even being told that wagons had never been taken to California and that it was impossible to do so! One man, giving heed, left his wagon and took to pack mules.

When leaving the frontier settlements, few people knew that there was a choice in how to get across the mountains into California. Books and old-timers alike told only of the trail that followed the Truckee River. There was, however, a faint report of a trail that took off toward the northwest, and avoided the difficult crossing of the mountains. No less an experienced moun-taineer than Myers had written a letter to the War Department about it, and at least one emigrant had a copy of that letter along. Myers cannot have heard of Lassen's almost disastrous journey in '48, and he may not even have heard about Wiggins's in '47. He knew, however, about the Applegate Trail to Oregon, and in his letter he had favored it as a good route leading to an entry into California. Therefore, favorable rumors of this route must have circulated among some of the emigrants.

Moreover, all those who went through Salt Lake City could have heard of the new Carson Route. You could actually talk with the Mormons who had brought their wagons east.

Others of the leading companies, besides Stewart's, may have picked up Mormon guides. In addition, Chiles in '48 had turned south from Humboldt Sink to take the Carson Route. The freshest wagon tracks would therefore run in that direction. Once a few had gone that way in '49, others would be the more likely to follow.

The first emigrants to reach Humboldt Sink had got there about July 4. The first diarist to arrive, on July 14, was David Cosad, an upstate New Yorker, whose record was generally little more than a logbook. By that time some hundreds of emigrants had already crossed the desert on the Carson Route. Cosad went that way too, and so also did Stewart's Pittsburghers, who arrived a day after Cosad. In fact, throughout July, everyone seems to have headed south, to a total of about three thousand people.

There is no information fully to explain this popularity of the Carson Route during the first month. Certainly, the emigrants did not find it an easy passage. Cosad's usually dull account becomes a tale that seems more fitting to Hastings's Cutoff —thirty hours on the desert, with abandoned wagons and dying oxen and men crazed by thirst.

When he came to the ox-team one of the men had got crazy and took most of the cover off the waggon—they had to hold him & pour water in his mouth twice before he knew enough to drink. Capt. Sealy rode about ten miles & met Samuel Cosad with his hand twisted in the mules tail a-whipping them through with a ramrod of my gun. He gave him water & passed on about half a mile & found Mr. [?] He had pulled the hot sand off & lain down under a sage bush & the old Frenchman was a-going back. Capt. Sealy gave him water and he fainted twice before he could get him on his mule. He brought him about half a mile and then Sealy returned for more water and he carried water for three days.

Even the efficient Pittsburghers had a hard time of it, especially when it was discovered that the last cask of water had been given to the mules. Johnston, suffering from thirst and wondering if he could ever reach the river, described this as "a terrible blunder." But one is inclined to question that. May it not have been, unknown to Johnston, only another indication of Captain Stewart's policy of caring for the mules, no matter what happened to the men?

All of Stewart's mules—and his men too, incidentally—got through safely. But many emigrants lost animals, and at least one company was so completely stripped that the men had to walk the rest of the way to California.

One trouble, apparently, was that the weather was exceptionally hot, even for the desert. The extremity was such that another usually dull diarist became, like Cosad, suddenly vivid. This was Delos Ashley, of Michigan. As he was approaching the sink, his entries assumed a staccato eloquence:

Tues. July 17   Very warm—sand roads. Toilsome as hell.
Wednes J 18   Sand!!! Hot!!! Grass parched & dry—
     P.M. 10 ms of R[iver] Camp 8 P.M.
Thurs July 19   Camped 10 P.M. No grass (wheugh!!!)
Fri. July 20, 10 o'c   Hot!!! No halt at noon.
     Camped 6 o'c P.M. Grass 3 ms. Spring at slough.
Sat. July 21   Staid at slough
Sun. July 22   From slew to Sink (O barrenness)

In the desert Ashley's party had great difficulties, but his record lapsed into almost unintelligible memoranda, "Extreme thirst. Wagons & animals abandoned—Came back with 8 horses & took in 1 wagon at night—Pi Utah indians—Stumps [sic] fight." Similarly tantalizing is the entry, "Slept in the Sun & was near killed." Was it sunstroke or something else? From such memoranda Ashley might have told a fascinating story to his grandchildren, but he was no literary artist.

All these emigrants, having reached the Carson River, were only about 150 miles from the gold diggings. They got across the mountains by Carson Pass, and ended the journey with the usual difficulties, but without noteworthy hardships. Those who had been forced to abandon their wagons now had an advantage of rapid movement to compensate to some extent for their loss of property. The walkers were reported to be making better than thirty miles a day, two or three times as much as those with wagons could make across the mountains. . . .

While they were going ahead, word had worked back of the troubles in the desert. William Chamberlain, at the sink on August 3, noted, "hear very bad account from Emigrants." Presumably those telling the story were people who had tried to get across, had gone far enough to see the abandoned wagons and dead animals, and then had been forced to come back. Naturally, then, people turned to the old Truckee Route.

The shift came just about at the end of July, and from then on, through the first half of August, at the very height of the migration, the great majority took that trail. During this time, we may estimate five thousand people went that way, and a thousand others by way of the Carson.

The crossing to the Truckee was difficult enough. Wagons had to be abandoned, as oxen failed and dropped at the trailside by dozens. "It was hard for us," wrote Charles Tinker of Ohio, "to part with animals to die with hunger & thirst which had served us so long and faithful. . . . The road sides were strewed with dead cattle, horses, & mules." Well-adjusted Ansel McCall took the crossing philosophically, and enjoyed his midnight snack at the boiling springs:

While our animals were resting, we selected an overturned wagon wheel, built a fire in the tarred hub, and boiled thereon a pot of coffee, and then squatted around it on the ground, like merry knights of the round table, and partook of our midnight meal of coffee and hard tack, the only refreshment we had taken for twelve hours.

Continuing, he wrote a passage that almost suggests *Moby Dick:*

Others had arrived here before us. Their baleful camp fires gleamed here and there, and in their pale and misty light, tall gaunt figures, with long disheveled locks, long beards, and tattered garments, perfectly white from the fine impalpable dust which covered them, flitted about in moody silence.

So McCall and his merry men sat, as it were, within a charmed circle, surrounded by wrecks and horrors:

The ground was covered with bleached and whitened bones of horses and cattle, the wrecks of other years, and the dried and decaying carcasses of innumerable animals of this, broken carts and wagons, and all imaginable debris.

Finally arrived at the shady bottomland and flowing water of the Truckee, Tinker enjoyed his day of luxurious rest, as did everyone else too:

It seemed the most like home to me that it had in any place since I left the States. Here was the first feed to speak of that we had had for the last 150 miles. Here we were contented. It seemed as though we had passed over the scorching valley of death to life. Tongue cannot express the joy that we felt when we see that we was safe over these deserts of America.

On the whole, the desert crossing to the Truckee seems to have been accomplished with less loss than that to the Carson. But the Truckee Route was more difficult farther on.

There were, at first, the twenty-seven troublesome crossings of the river. Later the road was relocated so that some crossings were eliminated. Young Sallie Hester mentioned only ten, and she had good reason to remember, since at one of them she fell into the river and almost drowned.

The pass, too, was more difficult on the Truckee Route. Sterling Clark, crossing the summit on August 17, counted twenty-six broken and abandoned wagons. Most of the emigrants took the route by Coldstream Canyon, but some went over the pass at the head of the lake.

Isaac Wistar, as would be expected, came through everything undaunted and even enjoying himself. Once in the mountains, he and his comrades found wonderful hunting, and bagged geese, deer, bighorn, and a mountain lion to boot. . . .

August 11 was destined to be an important date. . . . On that day, the advance guard—about two thousand people, who had nearly all traveled the Carson Route—were already in California. Also on that route, two thousand more were still advancing. Another five thousand were on the Truckee Route, some just leaving the sink, some arriving in the gold-mining region. About fifteen hundred people had passed Lassen's Meadows, but had not yet arrived at the sink, where the Truckee and Carson routes divided. But about eleven thousand people, half the migration, had not yet arrived at Lassen's Meadows, where the Lassen Route split off.

So far, no one seems to have paid any attention to that

branch of the trail. The numerous diarists who passed the meadows before August 11 did not even note that a road turned off.

Why should they have noticed it? It was not mentioned in the books. Only a few wagons had ever gone that way, either for Oregon or for California. An experienced man, looking for it, could have seen last year's wheelmarks and the broken sagebrush. But the ordinary person passing there would merely have thought that this was some minor branch of the main trail.

During the first days of August, however, Milton McGee was guiding his wagons down along the Humboldt, getting close to the turnoff. He had it fixed in his mind. Moreover, a few days' journey behind McGee, came Hudspeth and Myers with their big Missouri company. Having pioneered one cutoff, Myers had gained such a reputation that some emigrants called him "the great desert god." No three men that season had greater reputations for knowing what they were doing than had McGee, Myers, and Hudspeth.

So the whole course of the migration was changed, when McGee turned off on Lassen's track with eleven wagons. Once more, automatically, other emigrants followed.

The fact is that McGee on August 11, like Hudspeth and Myers on July 19, had only the very slightest idea of what he was doing. To give him his due, he did not attempt to get others to follow him. He was only trying to get his own party through, and was doubtless disgusted at first, then horrified, to discover that he was being followed by hundreds of wagons and thousands of people.

His embarrassment must have been the greater when he realized that the trail was not going where he had thought. As he had apparently believed, from the turnoff to some point in California where you might expect to find the gold mines, the distance could not be very great—150 miles or 200 at the most. This was correct. But his incorrect supposition was that the road went directly there.

It started out well enough—even, you might say, deceptively. From the turnoff clear to Rabbithole Spring, a very long day's journey, the trail headed generally west. But from the spring it turned sharply north, and went across the desert to Black Rock.

There McGee undoubtedly climbed to the top of the rock,

as many emigrants did. From that vantage point several hundred feet up, he could see the trail continuing north, and from the trend of the mountain ranges he would have known that the road would have to go north a long way. Apparently this was not what he had counted on at all. He must have realized immediately that this road was heading for Oregon, and that if it ever reached California, it would only be at the end of a long detour. And at that very moment, probably swinging his gaze to the south, he saw the dust rising from whole strings of wagons that were crossing the desert on his trail. Doubtless he cursed them for fools, but he himself had lured them on. Like the sorcerer's ap· prentice, and many another man, he had started something that he could not stop.

McGee must have looked longingly westward toward a broad gap between mountains. But the country in that direction looked like an absolute desert. (Not until two years later was anyone to work out a route in that direction.) So McGee continued to the north with most of the wagons of his company, though for some reason he left his own wagons near Black Rock.

His leaving the wagons seemed to the emigrants now arriving at the spring to be an evidence that he had gone ahead to explore, and would return to guide them through. They halted, waiting to see what he would come back to report, and more wagons came in to the spring.

But what McGee may have discovered about the road cannot have improved his peace of mind. He never returned to Black Rock, and he may never, indeed, have intended to do so. But neither did he altogether forget his responsibility to the emigrants who were following him.

Back at Lassen's Meadows there was much confusion for a few days. Most of the emigrants were following after McGee; others continued down the main trail; still others encamped, uncertain.

People were telling the usual tales about the main trail—dangerous desert crossings and impassable mountains. A special rumor was circulating that the grass on the lower Humboldt had been exhausted. As to the new road, so many rumors were buzzing about that you could end up believing what you wanted to believe. Some said that everything was bad—the road did not even go to California, but to Oregon; the Indians were hostile; pasture and water were lacking. Others replied that McGee was an experienced man, and that after passing Rabbithole Spring, only thirty-five miles, all trouble about grass and water would be ended. A few men, properly skeptical, went out on horseback to take a look before committing their teams and wagons. But the reports, even of these people, were conflicting.

One man rode out for what he claimed to be sixty miles, a distance that would have taken him to Black Rock. By the time he got back he had decided that he wanted nothing more of the cutoff. He yoked up his now well-rested team, and went off down the main trail. His example may have had its influence, and for a few days fewer people took the cutoff.

In this time of confusion, on August 15, Delano arrived at the turnoff, and took the Lassen Route. During the next few days, soon regretting his decision, he struggled ahead, finding little water or grass at Rabbithole, and discovering that far from ending there, the desert really began. The cattle of his own party, prudently and carefully driven, struggled in to the big hot spring at Black Rock after almost forty hours without food or water. Other trains were not so fortunate, and on that twenty-mile stretch of desert many animals stumbled and fell, and could not be pushed farther.

Delano himself, walking, came upon a wagon without oxen. In it a woman and small boy sat, both weeping. The husband had gone ahead, driving the oxen to water, in the hope that he could then return and bring the wagon in. All Delano could do was to give them a little water, and go ahead.

At the springs and meadow two miles north of the rock— "the second oasis," as he called it—Delano halted during the day of August 18. There McGee's wagons were standing, and the emigrants of about fifty other wagons were encamped.

Everything was still uncertain. No one was sure that the road, now swinging so far to the north, would even take them to California. Delano, studying what maps were available, concluded that his company should try to follow Frémont's trail of '43, south by Pyramid Lake, thus to rejoin the main trail on the Truckee River. Most of the men ridiculed this idea: "the word was 'Drive ahead; if McGee can go it, we can,' and the man who hesitated was set down as a coward." Possibly Delano's idea was a good one, but it was never put to the test.

Back at the turnoff, the consensus of opinion had again shifted, and almost all the wagons were abandoning the old trail. One reason certainly was that by this time Hudspeth had taken the cutoff. From the point of view of the ordinary emigrant, what more assurance could you have? He himself was ill-informed, and was even beginning to feel a touch of panic. What better could he do than follow after the Pikers' wagons. Surely Hudspeth, who had taken his train by the cutoff to avoid Fort Hall so successfully, did not commit all those women and children to a new trail without knowing what he was doing. And his guide was Myers—"the great desert god!"

Myers and Hudspeth made no effort to get anyone else to take that trail, but their example was eloquent. So, after about August 20, nearly all the emigrants turned off on the Lassen Route.

These people got definite information only when they met a small train of government wagons, going to Fort Hall. "When they came to our camp," wrote Farnham, "we drank down their talk with gaping wonder." Though this expedition had set out from Oregon, its members knew that Lassen's trail could be followed into California.

The men of this expedition made an attempt of their own to explore a cutoff across to the Humboldt. But two scouts, after going only a few miles, met some Indians and got into a fight. One was killed, and the other wounded. Their personal disaster made no difference in the history of the trail. Even yet no road crosses that stretch of rugged and waterless country.

The thousands of emigrants thus lured into taking a "cutoff" were not in nearly such a bad situation as the few had been who had followed Lassen the year before. Now, because of the work of Lassen's party and the Oregonians, there was a passable trail for wagons all the way. Its comparison with the two other routes was not altogether adverse. Its desert crossing was no more difficult. Moreover, the route, as was claimed, had no bad pass, and more or less managed to go around the northern end of the Sierra Nevada, as Chiles had done with his horsemen in '43. But the Lassen Route, as if in expiation for having avoided a difficult summit, had to go through many miles of difficult mountainous country lacking in grass.

Its greatest disadvantage, however, was in mere distance. Theoretically the greater mileage should have meant only ten or twelve days' travel, and so should not have been of great importance. The trouble was that this distance must be added at the end, when food was low and oxen thin and winter approaching, and when some emigrants were already too far behind.

Those who had first turned into the Lassen Route had been just about the mid-part of the migration. Those who soon followed them along that trail therefore had been in the rearward half of the main body and in the rear guard. These people showed little that was suggestive of rout, or disaster, or even of great emergency. The oxen might be showing some ribs, but most of them were tough and trail-hardened. The men might be thin, but they were not starving. The wagons might have some loose spokes in the wheels, but they were scarcely to be called rickety. Nevertheless, because of the distance to be traversed and because of the lateness of the season, there was a major disaster in the making, one that could have dwarfed that little affair of the Donner Party. In all probability it would have happened, except for a remarkable intervention. . . .

In August the people of California had begun to grow alarmed at the stories of thousands of emigrants, still far back on the trail, many women and children among them. At the same time, to write of "the people of California" is an anomaly. Human beings were, indeed, living there, but everything was in wild confusion because of the gold rush. These people scarcely formed a community, had no social organization, lacked the ordinary means of mobilizing public opinion, and were under a military government. That anyone even stopped to think of the plight of the emigrants is somewhat remarkable.

Yet the idea of sending out relief was not new in California. Dennis Martin had rescued Schallenberger in February of '45. Sutter had sent supplies in '45 and '46. The Donner relief parties in early '47 had represented a considerable effort for a sparsely populated region.

The head of the military government in California was General Persifor F. Smith, a man of decision and high character.

Realizing the emergency, he appropriated $100,000 as a relief fund, and private donations supplemented this somewhat—the citizens of San Francisco contributing $12,000. On August 27 the command was assigned to Major D. H. Rucker and he at once set about organizing the work, using both military personnel and hired civilians. . . .

And still, a hundred wagons a day, or two hundred—though the height of the wave had passed—filed along the dusty Humboldt trail and paused at the turnoff. It came, now, as no surprise to the emigrants. The government train and an eastward-bound company of Mormons had told of the new route, but even yet little was known about it certainly. Some emigrants saw a sign there, "Only 110 miles to diggings." One man, on September 18, reported a piece of paper stuck into the top of a split stick, announcing simply, "This is the turn off road." By then, many hundreds of teams had gone over the cutoff. So, nearly all the late-comers continued to take it. Some people, trusting to the signpost and still feeling the need to lighten wagons, threw away more food, retaining only enough to take them the promised 110 miles.

By September 1 so many emigrants had taken or passed the turnoff that we may begin to use the term "rear guard" for the remaining four thousand who were still plugging down along the Humboldt. These later emigrants were suffering and would suffer greater hardships than those who had passed through earlier.

Grass was harder to get. People complained that places where there had once been grass looked now as if they had been mowed, or eaten down by sheep. The only thing to do was to hunt for smaller and less attractive places, as yet ungrazed, or else to drive the animals several miles off the trail.

Moreover, as had happened in other years, the late-comers were harassed by the Indians. Early in the season, the leaders had passed along the Humboldt, having little trouble and scarcely even seeing an Indian. But the passage of this horde of emigrants was a devastating experience to the desert tribes, and threatened them with starvation. The killing of antelopes and rabbits was one thing. But also, these Indians had to live through the winter largely on supplies of seeds, laboriously gathered by their women

274

during the summer. Not only did the oxen and mules eat the vegetation off before it could bear seed, but also the continuous passing of emigrants made it impossible for the women to gather seeds anywhere along the river.

The Shoshones, along the upper Humboldt, scarcely organized above the family level, shot or stole an occasional ox, but were not warlike enough to cause much trouble. Near the sink the Paiutes were friendly, probably because of the policy of their chief Truckee, who had got along well with the whites, ever since he had helped the Stevens Party in '44.

But the Paiutes of the middle Humboldt grew more and more troublesome as the season advanced. Curiously, the passage of thousands of men armed with rifles was not sufficient to drive the Indians away from the trail, or even to kill any appreciable number of them. These Paiutes had a lifelong familiarity with the desert, and they also had behind them five years' experience at outwitting emigrants. They were able to deal just about as they wished with these comparative greenhorns of '49. It was not a question of killing and taking scalps. The Paiute had no sense of glory. But he liked both beef and mule-meat, and that year oxen and mules were easier to get than were antelopes or rabbits, or even rats. He must have looked upon it as easy work—profitable, rather exciting, not very dangerous.

What saved the emigrants was that there were really very few Indians. Besides, when a Paiute had run an ox off into the hills and slaughtered it, he doubtless sat down there with his family and friends, and they all gorged, until the meat spoiled, and it was time to go back and get another ox.

From the emigrants' point of view, the situation was maddening. It meant constant work at guarding the animals and constant anxiety. You could profitably have traded off a single ox, to gain immunity of passage. But there was no such arrangement possible. The Paiutes took only a small percentage of the animals of the whole migration. But this would have been no comfort to the individual emigrant, even if he had known it, because that small percentage, if concentrated upon him alone, might deprive him of all his team in a single night.

Contrary to what the emigrants had been given to expect, these lowly Diggers were not frightened of firearms. Instead, as

Delano wrote, "They would often stand and fight man to man with the most desperate courage." In fact, a tough, desert-hardened Paiute could shoot many arrows while an emigrant was reloading his rifle, and at close quarters was not too badly outmatched even by a man with a revolver.

On one occasion four emigrants, following the trail of stolen cattle, came upon four Paiutes, and a Homeric combat ensued, man against man. Though two Paiutes were badly wounded at the first fire, they continued to fight, and struggled with the whites hand to hand. Three Paiutes were killed, and two of the emigrants were left badly wounded.

Even after entering the cutoff, the emigrants found no peace. Here the Indians were Paiutes too, and may have learned from their kinfolk along the river how to deal with wagon trains. Still farther along, the so-called Pit River Indians were even more truculent, and had a certain interest in killing emigrants as well as cattle. Along that stream late-comers read the inscription over a grave:

Mr. Eastman;—
The deceased was killed by
an Indian arrow;
Octr 4th, 1849.

In the dirt of the grave an arrow was sticking upright, on it a card with the note:

This is the fatal arrow.

Some miles farther on, a note set in a cleft stick gave the information:

Beware of Indians,
they have shot several
animals & wounded a
man just below this

These harassed people of the rear guard may be put into two classes. Some of them were there merely because they had started late. This did not mean that they were any less efficient than parties which had started earlier, and it did not mean that they had become demoralized by the long weeks of travel. But many of the rear guard had not been particularly late in starting, and had slowly lost ground because they had had sickness, or had not handled their animals properly, or had been dogged by bad luck. Many of these parties had women and children with them, and there was, as the weeks progressed, an increasing concentration of the women and children in the rear guard.

Well back in the line was the Washington City Company, which deserves comment, if for no other reason than because we happen to know so much about it. With seventeen mule-drawn wagons and sixty-six men, under the command of J. Goldsborough Bruff, it had made a late start on May 16. The company was well equipped, and had met with no bad luck. Still it did not better its position in the migration. Not until September 19 did the wagons come to the Lassen turnoff, and by that time they had been 107 days on the trail.

Perhaps the company did not get along faster because of something in the temperament of their captain. This is not to criticize Bruff adversely. On the contrary, he was one of the very best captains of that whole year. But his solidity and inability to worry made him a man who was not inclined to hurry.

Besides, for Bruff, the whole experience of the migration was so interesting that he can have seen no need in getting it over with too soon. Trained at West Point, he had become a civilian cartographer. Something of the army officer remained about him, and he stood for no nonsense. But he was an officer of the type who holds his men because he takes good care of them, and not because he is backed by army regulations. (Besides, there were no army regulations on the trail.) So Bruff held his company together well, only losing a few malcontents.

He was a man of unflagging energy. Besides acting as captain, he wandered about everywhere, observing everything topographically, geologically, zoologically, anthropologically. He filled his sketchbook with dozens of pictures. He kept the fullest journal of any forty-niner. He even, though perhaps unfortunately, wrote poetry—achieving such a distich as:

> Our banner flutters in the breeze,
> In spite of Sioux and black Pawnees....

On September 14 Major Rucker was in Sacramento—as people now called the new town that had grown up near Sutter's

Fort. He had organized his relief parties, and was about to send them out on the Truckee and Carson routes. On this day, however, he was approached by an emigrant who had arrived from the north, and was informed that conditions would be worse on the Lassen Route than on either of the others. A few days later Rucker received a letter from McGee himself, to the same effect.

These first emigrants over the Lassen Route had done well enough, taking just a full month over the 430 miles. McGee and the others, however, had learned of the great numbers following them, and must have realized that pasturage would be scanty. Besides, there was always the threat of early snow.

As the result of this surprising information, Rucker readjusted his plans, and decided that he himself would go north. He was, however, tied to Sacramento for the present, since he must direct the relief work upon all three routes. Accordingly, he assigned John H. Peoples to take immediate charge in the north.

Peoples was a civilian, a newspaperman from New Orleans, who had come to California that year by the southern trail. No better choice could have been made for the arduous work to which he was assigned.

Equal praise, indeed, must be given to Rucker, who appears to have been a very model of conscientiousness and efficiency, though forced to work under very trying conditions. His plans were simple. Send out a well-equipped party on each of the three routes. Have each party pass clear through the migration, since those in the rear would be most in need of help. Then, distribute supplies of food as needed, and aid the emigrants, particularly the women and children, to get across the mountains. . . .

But if Rucker had known the situation fully, he might well have been appalled. In the middle of September, when he was just getting his work organized, the number of emigrants still on the trail cannot have been fewer than ten thousand! Many of these were close to California, and could get through on their own. But many had not yet even reached the Lassen turnoff, and a few were only approaching the Humboldt. Bruff's Washington City Company was at this time just leaving the main trail at Lassen's Meadows.

That passage from the meadows to Black Rock, as described

by Delano in the middle of August, was bad enough. On September 17 Delano, who had been among the first to follow McGee, had arrived at Lassen's ranch, tired but still in good-enough condition. In the meantime the Black Rock passage had shifted into something that was close to sheer horror.

On September 19, at two P.M., meticulously posting a notice to that effect, Bruff turned his wagons off on the trail of the thousands who had already taken the Lassen Route, happy thus to be avoiding "the pestilential marshes and alkali pools of the 'sink.'" Just at the turnoff he noted the recent grave of a three-year-old girl.

The first pull was not too bad. Bruff, a methodical man with an interest in statistics, counted dead animals and ran up a score of twenty-two oxen and two horses for the afternoon. Beyond counting, were the scattered wheels, hubs, tires, and fragments of wagons. After dark, having done thirteen and a half miles by the odometer, the Washington City boys came to the first spring and camped.

Next morning they went on, winding along a ravine between mountains. There was even a little grass to be had for the mules, if they were driven away from the road, up the gulches. Toward noon came a sinister touch. On the hillside, to the left of the road—as the always meticulous Bruff noted—lay part of an axle, and written on it, "This is the place of destruction to team."

Nearby, illustrating the point, lay several dead oxen and a broken wagon. Bruff's count for the morning was fourteen oxen dead, and one dying. In the afternoon the score was thirty, and then the company arrived at Rabbithole.

There the water supply was better than when Delano had passed a month earlier. Emigrants had dug a number of wells— as Bruff carefully recorded, three to six feet deep and four or five feet across. Water had oozed in, clear and cool, but a little brackish, about half filling the holes. Unfortunately, half-dead oxen had a habit of wandering around, trying to drink at the wells, falling in head first, and drowning. Bruff saw four of the wells thus choked up, the carcasses swelled so as to fit the holes tightly, only the hindquarters and tails showing above the ground. All the ground in the vicinity was littered with carcasses. Though the stench was almost unbearable, Bruff conscientiously counted a dead mule, two dead horses, and eighty-two dead oxen. In addition, there were several lame and abandoned oxen, the wreck of one wagon, fragments of others, and the grave of a fifty-year-old man from Ohio. Bruff himself abandoned an exhausted mule, to add soon to the collection of carcasses.

His company had carried grass in the wagons for the mules. In a nearby company a woman was busily baking large loaves of bread to feed the horses and oxen. Asked if he would eat horse rations, Bruff agreed enthusiastically, and found the bread excellent, particularly when his hostess supplemented it with a slice of fried pork fat and a cup of coffee.

Friendly hospitality thus continued to be typical of '49 even when the going was hard. It was illustrated again that afternoon, when one man voluntarily rode back several miles along the trail with canteens of water, to relieve and encourage thirsty people struggling toward the springs.

On the other hand, next morning, a rarer quality was illustrated, when several "scoundrels" tried to make away with Bruff's horse. The undauntable captain, quickly drawing a revolver, was about to shoot them down, as "a bloody example," but relented in pity.

Leaving Rabbithole on September 21, the company set out for Black Rock. As the odometer clicked off five and a half miles, Bruff counted forty oxen and a horse.

Going five miles more, the company nooned at a place where others had done the same. One may wonder why, in a country thus lacking in water and shade, people should customarily pass the noon hour at the same spot. Possibly it is merely another illustration of the gregariousness of man. This particular place was noisome. Around and about it lay the carcasses of sixty-six oxen and a mule. The oxen, Bruff noted, often lay in groups close to an abandoned wagon, as if still in hope that men would care for them.

In the afternoon Bruff's wagons moved out upon the vast and level surface of the desert. To the northeast it stretched away out of sight, and to the west almost as far, ending against desert mountains. The surface was white, shining, and crusty, devoid of growth. Far ahead to the north, desert mountains loomed up—

at their left, the mass of the great black rock that was almost a mountain.

During the afternoon the inevitable mirage appeared, and some of Bruff's men were convinced that they looked at a lagoon fringed by tall trees. Their captain learnedly explained the phenomenon. He thought, however, that even cattle had been deceived, and had stampeded toward the "water." Carcasses lay scattered about in that direction, as far as could be seen. Close at hand, where he could count accurately, Bruff ran up the total of 103 oxen, two horses and a mule. To these might be added three abandoned oxen, which—according to Bruff—were looking up and down the road for help. One of these he mercifully shot.

Continuing steadily on, passing many abandoned wagons and fragments of wagons, Bruff reached the big hot spring under Black Rock a little after sunset. Along the last miles of the road and at the spring itself, he counted 150 oxen, three horses, five mules, and a cow and calf. He checked his odometer to show that he had come 21 miles from Rabbithole, and 51¾ from the turnoff.

Bruff and his company had made the passage without extreme hardship. At least, his journal makes little of it, though we should remember that he was a man of great endurance, abounding energy, and unflagging interest in everything that he saw, even if it was only a dead ox to be counted. Except for the mule abandoned at Rabbithole his company suffered no loss. But it had been well equipped at the start, had had the advantage of his excellent supervision, and had become trail-hardened without becoming exhausted. The dead animals and abandoned wagons demonstrated the agonies that others had suffered on this passage.

Bruff's total for the fifty miles was: oxen, 511; horses, 10; mules, 9; a cow and a calf. Naturally, the concentration was upon the latter part of the journey. About nine-tenths of these animals had died at Rabbithole and between there and Black Rock.

In addition, as Bruff noted, many animals had wandered away from the trail, and had died where they could not be seen, or where they were too far off to be counted individually. The total of dead animals might well have been as high as a thousand. At this time, the cutoff had been used for a little more than five weeks.

Many of the emigrants were now close to exhaustion, and to

panic—especially when they learned, as they did sooner or later, that the distance to the first California settlement was four times what they had supposed it to be. Many of them were short of food. Fortunately their health was generally good, and in contrast to the vast number of dead animals Bruff enumerated only two graves in the fifty-mile desert passage. In sinister fashion, however, scurvy was appearing in some of the companies which were depending too exclusively upon flour and salt pork. . . .

In the myth of the trail, the wagon train is beleaguered by Indians, and the cavalry comes galloping to its relief. In '49 the Indians were not greatly involved, and the cavalry figured only in that Major Rucker was an officer of the First Dragoons and used some of his men in the relief parties. But the situation was no less dramatic. Certainly it was vaster, since not one wagon train but a hundred or more were involved, and not twenty or fifty people but thousands, including hundreds of women and children. If these unfortunates were not threatened with the rigors of scalping and captivity, over them hung the no less ominous threats of starvation and freezing.

The relief party on the Truckee met with a surprise. As late as September 25 the emigrants had been reported coming in over that route at the rate of a hundred wagons a day. But the relief party, pressing on over the pass in early October, found only a few pack trains. Again, as a result of some rumor or of some accident, the fickle migration had shifted. Cut off as with a knife, migration over the Truckee Route had stopped. No relief needed!

Therefore, following orders, the commander of the party swung to the south, and joined others who were working on the Carson Route. Here a few wagons were still coming along, and the emigrants in them, though themselves enduring considerable hardship, told stories of others who were farther behind and in critical condition. But the number of emigrants on the Carson Route was comparatively small. . . .

The real crisis, with all the elements of disaster, was building up on the Lassen Route. Curiously, among the tail-enders on that route were a surprising number of people keeping diaries, so that many details are preserved of the experiences of those companies.

For instance, there were the Wolverine Rangers, so far back that they did not get to the turnoff until September 21. This large and well-equipped company of men from Michigan had started late and never made up distance. It is in some ways the best-known company of the year in that no fewer than four of its members kept records which have survived.

Though they were nearly the last company on the trail, the Wolverines plugged along from day to day, and their diarists seem surprisingly unconcerned about snow on the mountains. For instance, on October 14, when they had not yet got to Goose Lake, you would have thought they might have been holding prayer meetings.

But no, that evening they had a fandango with the three attractive daughters of an emigrant. This occasion was a notable one, and lasted until the very late hour of ten P.M. The memory of it is preserved on the California map by Fandango Valley. . . .

During late September and early October, Peoples had advanced his relief party along the Lassen Route as far as Pit River, and had done some good work at helping people along. Rucker himself, detained at Sacramento until the end of the month, finally left from Lassen's ranch. He made his first contact with needy emigrants on October 2, noting:

Loaned Mr. John Scroggins a mule to bring his wife to Lassen's. He said that she was sick, and nearly out of provisions, but his teams were broken down, and that he had come ahead to get assistance. I issued him some coffee, hard bread, rice, etc.

Continuing to advance, Rucker met many wagons daily, and also many people afoot. The condition of the emigrants varied greatly. Some, though travel-worn, were still moving steadily ahead. Others were discouraged, destitute, and half starving. Many were ill with scurvy and dysentery. Rucker issued rations frugally to those who seemed most in need, but continued to move along, realizing that the last companies would be in the worst condition.

On October 8 he had the satisfaction of meeting Mr. Scroggins once more:

He had his wife who was sick with the scurvy riding the mule, with a child in his arms, and leading the animal by the bridle, with her little boy by her side: they seemed in a fair way to reach the settlement.

On October 16 the notation was:

Passed 106 wagons, many with families, and a Boston pack company, number 70 men and 125 pack mules, and a few beef cattle; also met 75 footmen, some destitute of provisions; issued bread and beef to a few.

On the night of October 10, rain fell, turning to snow before morning. When daylight came, the emigrants could see the mountains an unbroken white. Rucker recorded:

40 wagons, 35 pack mules, and some footmen, passed my camp today, all the emigrants were considerably alarmed in consequence of the snow last night.

Fortunately, a period of thawing weather followed. Rucker continued to advance along the loop of the trail that swung around Mount Lassen to the south and east.

On October 12 he met eighty-three wagons. He was forced to become parsimonious in his doles. The men of a large pack train from Arkansas thronged around him, demanding provisions. He refused, since the men seemed well enough mounted to get through.

On October 14, Rucker fell ill. On this day, also, Peoples came into camp. Having fallen ill with fever, he had been forced to return from Pit River. Now his fever left him, and he was ready, valiantly, to take up his labors again.

On October 15 Rucker recorded that he met Captain Bruff and gave him some provisions. Bruff's own account, as we should expect, was more detailed. By this time, even the well-organized and efficiently commanded Washington City Company was going to pieces, and its morale had broken. On this day Bruff had been forced to abandon two wagons. The men demanded that he should solicit supplies from Rucker. He replied indignantly that the company could get through, though on short allowance, and that Rucker's supplies were designed for starving women and children who were still farther back along the trail. But the men clamored, as if, Bruff thought indignantly, they would take the biscuit out of a woman's mouth. He then made application, and in his always careful way recorded that Rucker gave them thirty-one pounds of pork, and fourteen pounds of crackers. The men of the company ate up all the crackers while Bruff was busy about various matters, and reserved no share for him.

On October 19 Rucker found himself too ill to go farther. On this day, only twenty-one wagons passed, and reports came in that not more than fifty or a hundred were still to come. The rear guard, then, had passed this point; only the stragglers were left.

Rucker, prostrated by his fever, could only return. Peoples, with a few men, remained. Though winter was at hand, and he was deep in the mountains, he continued at his task. . . .

But there was work of that kind on the Carson Route too. On October 6 following Rucker's instructions, a party had crossed over from the Truckee to the Carson. This party consisted of some thirty men and more than a hundred mules laden with provisions. But on October 10 only a family with two children came along the trail. These people said that there were still other families behind on the desert. The relief party gave two mules and a horse to help these people along, and some men with pack mules went eastward to look for other families, among whom were the Royces.

In the history of the year the brief rewritten diary left by Sarah Royce is in many respects unique, and certainly stands as second to none in interest. It is the only contemporary record of one who, in the full sense of the word, may be called a straggler. It is the only record left by a woman, unless twelve-year-old Sallie Hester can be granted that status. Moreover, Mrs. Royce was destined to become the mother of Josiah Royce, the notable American philosopher, and she revised her diary for his especial use.

The Royces—Josiah the elder, Sarah, and two-year-old Mary—did not really get started from Council Bluffs until June 10, much too late for anyone to be setting out. They had an Indian scare and the usual trouble at stream crossings, but went along not too badly. Their company, being so far behind, found the grass eaten up, and beyond Fort Laramie once had to go fifteen miles away from the trail before they could find enough grass to recruit the animals with two days of rest.

Some of these stragglers were beginning to be greatly discouraged. Among them was a young teamster, William Lewis Manly, and his desperation led him to an act of extreme temerity. . . . Coming to Green River about the middle of August, he learned that its water reached the Pacific, and he and a few others decided to reach California by floating downstream—ignorant that they would thus have to pass through all the canyons of the Colorado River, and would end at the Gulf of California, no closer to the gold mines than when starting the voyage. They floated down the river for a considerable distance, but then made for Salt Lake City on foot. There they joined a party setting out for Los Angeles, suffered great hardships in Death Valley, and eventually won through. In his *Death Valley in '49* Manly wrote one of the classics of the West.

John Hale, one of the diarists with the stragglers, commented lugubriously on another "floater." The man's companions, he said, did not attempt to dissuade him from the attempt. After he had started, however, they said that they believed him to be going to his death. This carelessness for others, Hale concluded, was the spirit of the trail. And so it may well have been—among these last and desperate few.

Shortly after Manly had committed himself to the current of the Green, the Royces arrived in Salt Lake City, on August 18. There they spent eleven days, resting and uncertain just what to do. Since it was now generally considered too late to start from Salt Lake City with the intention of crossing the Sierra Nevada, a party was being organized to take a southern route through Los Angeles. But the elder Josiah Royce—as the younger one also was destined to be—was a man of great determination and individualism. He decided not to join this large party. (In so deciding, he may have done well. Many of these people, Manly being one of them, wandered off, and became the unwilling discoverers of Death Valley, and some of them died there.)

The Royces, however, started over the Salt Lake Cutoff on August 30—the family triad, one other man, one wagon, three yoke of oxen. They were shortly joined by two rather shiftless young men, mounted, but with almost no food. The odds against any of them reaching California were high.

In the first place, they had to pass along hundreds of miles of trail where the Indians had been troublesome all summer. Even if the Indians were not interested in taking scalps, they might make away with the six oxen, and that would be equally disastrous. Then there was the other threatening problem of snow on the mountains. The Royces were even farther back than the Donner Party had been. On August 30, when the Royces were just leaving Salt Lake City, the Donners had been across the desert, at Pilot Peak.

The Royces had one bad fright from Indians, but kept on steadily and reached the vicinity of Humboldt Sink on October 2. Fortunately, their hand-written guidebook, purchased in Salt Lake City, had advised the Carson Route and kept them from taking the Lassen turnoff. Even so, they were so late that their situation was desperate. Moreover, at the sink they made an understandable but almost disastrous mistake.

Setting out before daylight to avoid the heat, they took the wrong branch of the trail in the darkness, and entered the desert crossing when they had intended to take a side road and stop at the sink to cut grass and fill their water containers. After proceeding a considerable distance, they had to return, thus exhausting their oxen even before they could attempt the crossing. While returning, they met another little wagon train of stragglers, including one woman, who pitied them but was unable to offer aid.

Setting out again on October 8, the Royces managed to struggle across to the Carson River, though losing two oxen. On October 12 they prepared to move again, following the trail along the Carson, with the long pull up the canyon and over the mountains still ahead of them. Mrs. Royce had little hope but some faith. She prayed. Moving slowly through heavy sand, the pitiable little group had made only a few miles, and it was noon. Then, looking up at some hills ahead, they were surprised to see dust rising. Suddenly, out of the dust, high up on the hill, rode two horsemen, each leading a pack mule. Their loose garments flapped at their sides like wings. Thus seeing them appear, winged and high in the air, Mrs. Royce thought of angels, and the words came to her, "They look heaven-sent!"

As if to make it all the more miracle-like, the first word of the approaching stranger was, "Well, sir, you are the man we are after!"

The two men were those sent ahead from the relief party. The emigrants who had been relieved on October 10 had apparently been those whom the Royces had seen in the desert, and they had described the family and its plight.

287

Some hardships still lay ahead, but danger of death was now over. Mounted on a well-trained mule, holding her baby, Mrs. Royce rode on toward the mountains.

In one respect, actually, the Royces had had a bit of luck of which they were ignorant. If they had been a few days' journey farther ahead, they might have been caught in the vicious storm which swept across the mountains on the night of October 10—the same storm that Rucker had reported near Mount Lassen.

Near the summit on the Carson Route, the altitude was over eight thousand feet, and the storm was severe. One party was caught just as its wagons had started the last ascent. Hard-blown hail and snow flew so thickly that no one could proceed. The party encamped and built fires. During the night several people were frostbitten. Two mules, which kept close to the fire, were saved. All the other stock, mules and oxen, froze to death. Fortunately, the storm was of short duration.

During the next week the relief parties worked hard. Many stragglers were coming across, most of them on foot. One of the relief parties reported an old man with his wife and daughter, who had nothing in the world but a few blankets which they were packing on their backs. "We let them have two mules and some provisions."

In Carson Valley this same relief party met two Germans on foot. Their only sustenance for a week had been the flesh cut from dead mules. They were trudging along, each with some pounds of decaying mule-meat strung around his neck. Their smell was so high that the relief party refused to do anything for them until they had gone to the river and washed.

The last train proved to be that of Captain Sackett. The relief party met this company in Carson Valley. Except for being so late, these people were not too badly off. They had several wagons and included a number of women and children. Apparently the leaders had difficulty in realizing the critical danger that arose from being east of the mountains so late in the year. Like many others, they would not abandon their property until faced with an emergency. The men of the relief party persuaded them that the emergency had arrived. They themselves supplied the women and children with mules, and started back, escorting them. The men followed.

288

Some snow fell on October 27, but by this time the people of the Sackett Party were across the summit, and well down on the western slope. On the Carson trail, everybody was "home" by November 1. . . .

Far to the north the situation was still critical. The stalwart Peoples, scarcely recovered from his bout with fever, had advanced again, and on October 22 was a day's march along Pit River. He was expecting, from news brought in by his scouts, to meet the St. Louis Company, last on the trail. Instead, some packers came in bearing word of disaster.

The St. Louis Company comprised thirty-two men and twenty-five women and children, with ox teams. Like many companies at the end of the journey, they had become demoralized and careless. On the night of October 19 the Indians made a descent and drove most of the oxen off. Peoples's note to Rucker was succinct, "The Indians swept the cattle off the rear, and the emigrants are in a devil of a fix."

Finally, on October 26, these emigrants came into Peoples's camp, struggling along as best they could with what animals they had remaining. Even after they arrived, the men still quarreled about what they should abandon and what they should attempt still to take with them.

But winter was at hand, and a storm was threatening. Still to be traversed before reaching the valley, was a distance of 150 miles, across rugged mountainous terrain, most of it at an altitude of about five thousand feet, subject to fierce storms with heavy snowfall.

Peoples found his patience exhausted. As he reported, "I *ordered* the women, children, and sick men to get into my wagons." At two o'clock he started, and the able men finally followed him.

To add to the difficulties, Indian fires blazed at many places on the mountains that evening. Since the loss of more cattle might mean final disaster, Peoples forestalled trouble by attacking. Surprising a camp, his men killed six Indians, and drove the others off.

After two days more, progress had been so slow that Peoples urged the men still further to lighten wagons. They refused, and he wrote in disgust that they seemed determined to bring their mining tools, beds, and cooking utensils in—or die with their wagons.

Snow fell on the night of October 30, and the emigrants for the first time became alarmed. On the next day there was a furious storm. November 1 was warmer, and Peoples moved his train ahead through melting snow. But there was a still harder storm on November 2.

By this time Peoples had reached the point where the trail was southeast of Mount Lassen, and he overtook other emigrants. These also were in a bad way, having lost many of their animals in the storm.

It became a fight for life. During four days of alternate snow and thaw, Peoples struggled on with his charges, losing many of his mules. Finally, on November 6 he could move the wagons no farther. He established a camp, and left the wagons and most of the people in it. He himself rode on for help, taking with him some of his own men and six young women from the emigrant parties.

Luck was with him. He had struggled ahead with the wagons far enough to get definitely on the downslope, and after riding ahead for only three hours he got out of the snow.

Once in the valley, he reorganized, and a week later was able to start some men back in, driving cattle before them. He himself followed on November 20, through a heavy storm. Arrived at camp, he prepared for the final push, and at last was able to move.

A few emigrants, however, chose to spend the winter in the foothill country, where game was plentiful. Bruff, also, unable to get the wagons through, established a camp in that region, and guarded the company's property through the winter—a final demonstration of his responsibility as captain. His demoralized company, however, may even be said to have deserted him.

The stragglers under Peoples's guidance gave little suggestion of the gallant companies which had left the frontier towns, seven months before. As Peoples wrote:

A more pitiable sight I had never before beheld. There were cripples from scurvy, and other diseases; women, prostrated by weakness, and children, who could not move a limb. In advance of the wagons were men mounted on mules, who had to be lifted on or off their animals, so entirely disabled had they become from the effect of scurvy.

This story of relief on the Lassen Trail ranks as one of the heroic stories of the West. Peoples and his men, civilians working without military discipline, ran greater risks and endured more than money could repay. A good leader, Peoples commended his men in his report, writing that "not one of the party had a dry blanket, or dry clothes, for half a month." He further commended them:

At every river and slough, they stood ready to wade over, with the women and children in their arms; and even after reaching the settlements, many of them took the money out of their purses, and gave to the destitute.

Thus, on November 26, with the arrival of the last of the stragglers at Lassen's ranch, the story can be brought to an end. We may let Samuel McCoy of Ohio, writing in his diary at Lassen's, pronounce the benediction.

Praise the Lord for all His benefits. I have been preserved in all my wanderings. May I evermore be grateful. Many have been stricken down at my right hand or my left, but I have been spared. . . .

This overland migration of '49 by the trail through South Pass is a historical incident which is almost without parallel. Certain ones of the later years saw more people cross by the trail than crossed in '49, but these years were mere echoes of the first great one.

The most remarkable feature of the whole movement was its success against all reasonable expectation. A trail which had been developed for the use of a few hundred people was suddenly required to accommodate many thousands. And, in general, these people were not well qualified by experience or training to survive such a test. This success may be attributed to many factors. The heavy rains of the preceding winter and spring had produced grass along the trail such as had never been known before. The equipment and techniques of travel which had been developed in the years from '41 to '48 were sound, and proved workable under the greatly changed conditions.

In spite of everything, a major disaster, costing the lives of hundreds of people, might well have occurred if General Smith had not realized the emergency at an early date and taken decisive action, and if such men as Rucker and Peoples had not been at hand to undertake the work.

Finally, much of the success must be credited to the American character of those years. Emerson's *Self-Reliance*, itself dating from the year of the Bartleson Party, might well have supplied the motto of the covered-wagon emigrants. So strongly were they oriented toward taking care of themselves and expecting nothing from the government or from anyone else that many of them were genuinely surprised to learn that General Smith had thought of their predicament; they derived a kind of personal pleasure from learning of it.

But the year cannot be termed very creative. The Hudspeth Cutoff was the only important new route opened for wagons, though the Carson and Lassen routes were greatly developed. The Cherokee Trail and the route from Salt Lake City to Los Angeles cannot be considered parts of the California Trail as here conceived.

The three routes into California were about equally traveled, though almost the only evidence is supplied by the number of diarists using each of the three. On this slight basis, we may calculate: by the Lassen, 8,000; by the Truckee, 7,000; by the Carson, 6,000. The figure for the Lassen checks with the estimate of seven to nine thousand, made by Peoples.

The year saw little new development in equipment and methods of travel, although the return of the mule team may be noted. A few emigrants used sheet-iron wagon boxes, which were waterproof and so could be used as boats.

Of the approximately 22,500 people who had started over this trail, we may estimate that at least 21,000 reached California this season by the Truckee, Carson, and Lassen routes. Some of the rear guard and the stragglers turned off at Salt Lake City, and took the route to Los Angeles, and others wintered in Salt Lake City. About 750 may be considered to have died—chiefly from cholera, but also from other diseases and from accidents. Probably not even a dozen were killed by the Indians. The loss of people may be therefore considered negligible. The death rate of those times being what it was, many of these people would have died even if they had not started west. Especially, we must remember, cholera was prevalent throughout most of the country that summer, and quite possibly the death rate from that disease was no higher on the trail than it was elsewhere.

The wastage of property, however, was tremendous. Of the wagons that started probably half were abandoned along the trail, and at best served for firewood. About the same estimate may be made for the animals. A comparatively small number of the cattle even served to supply beef. Most of the thousands that perished were merely left to rot by the trail, or to desiccate beneath the desert sun. They lay in too great numbers for the wolves and ravens to devour. In many places, as Searls wrote, "a blind man might find his way by the odor of dead oxen."

Even the animals that got through were so travel-worn as to be of little value. The milch cows, however, could be sold at a high profit, since dairying was not yet established in California.

The property which was being carried in the wagons, even much of the food, was either thrown away or abandoned with the wagons.

The most important result of the movement was to bring so many thousands of people to California. Nearly all of them were men. Many returned to the East, but many others eventually brought wives from the East, established families, and contributed largely to the later population of the state.

A curious by-product of '49 was the development of Salt Lake City. Not only did the Mormons make money by selling supplies to the emigrants, but also they acquired large amounts of much-needed goods. Late in the season, scavenging parties moved out from Salt Lake City, collecting useful materials of all kinds.

The trail itself—as John D. Lee, one of these Mormons, described it—presented a strange sight. Where a year before there had only been a double line of wheel tracks, now one saw a beaten roadway forty feet wide. A traveler was scarcely ever out of sight of an abandoned wagon:

Dust very disagreeable, but not to compare with the stench from dead carcasses which lie along the road, having died from fatigue and hunger. Destruction of property along the road was beyond description, consisting of wagons, harness, tools of every

293

description, provisions, clothing, stoves, cooking vessels, powder, lead, and almost everything, etc., that could be mentioned.

Lee also mentioned that there was some difficulty in keeping to the road, in spite of the many wagons that had passed. This was because so many spurs had been developed by the rear guard, whose wagons had to be driven away from the main trail for distances often of ten miles, in order to find grass. "Every camp ground" he concluded, "presented one continued scene of destruction."

One should not leave '49 without another mention of the remarkable good feeling which generally prevailed among these emigrants. The "accursed hunger for gold" is supposed to lead men into all kinds of infamy. But these gold-seekers seem to have been less quarrelsome and more cooperative than the emigrants of '46.

One party, indeed, having made and used a ferryboat, destroyed it when leaving, with the idea (probably ill-founded) that they could thus gain on the parties behind and get better campsites. Charges were also made that people sometimes, from the same motive, set fire to the dry grass when leaving a campsite. These stories, however, are recorded only as rumors. Such fires started all too easily by accident, and at the end of the season many black scars marked the course of the trail. Tales of purposeful incendiarism could thus easily arise.

In general, as would be expected from the numbers of people involved, the keynote of the year is confusion. One seeks in vain for an analogy. The migration cannot be compared to the march of an army, for an army possesses, as its very essence, its chain of command and its organization. One might think of a demoralized army, as in a retreat from Moscow. But the migration was not disorganized; it was merely unorganized—and there is a great difference. Moreover, the migration was advancing, not retreating, and it thought in terms of victory, not in terms of disaster.

We must think then of a folk movement, essentially without leaders. In '49 even the family unit was not common. Each man commanded only himself, and sometimes even traveled alone. The so-called captains exercised little authority and their companies seldom numbered more than fifty people. To take refuge in military analogy—we have a body of men large enough to call for the command of a lieutenant general, but with no officer above the rank of captain, and even these exercising no real command.

This is not to say that '49 did not have its interesting characters and able leaders. Many can be named—Stewart, Bruff, Delano, McGee, Hudspeth, Myers, Wistar, Mrs. Royce. Nor should we fail to remember Rucker and Peoples. But to emphasize any one of these or even a half-dozen of them, would be to falsify the story, and to present in terms of personality what was essentially a folk movement.

Thus, as in some great battle, in contrast to a skirmish of guerrillas, the individual was blotted out. Bayard Taylor, professional traveler and writer, was in Sacramento that fall. He sensed this anonymity:

The experience of any single man, which a few years ago would have made him a hero for life, becomes mere commonplace, when it is but one of many thousands.

Yet, in another sense, the very opposite may be maintained. Where else in the long annals of history can we discover a movement of this scope, essentially conducted by individual initiative, without a larger organization of any kind—military, corporate, national, or tribal? And in a world which seems to move steadily toward greater suppression of the individual, when shall we look upon its like again?

CHAPTER TEN

AFTER '49 THE STORY can be brief. The next decade, indeed, was not lacking in colorful and even heroic episodes. Inevitably, however, the events of succeeding years became repetitive. Moreover the trail itself—as it was more heavily traveled, more firmly beaten down, and more improved by planned work—was ceasing to be a trail and becoming what we may better term a road. When, as often happened, some old-timer set out westward, he scarcely recognized things. . . .

The gold rush continued into '50 and intensified. The numbers approximately doubled, so that a reasonable figure for the California migration of that year is 45,000. The women and children were better reported than in '49, and the proportion of these can be set at between one and two per cent of each.

The character of the migration was somewhat different. By this time a regular route of travel had been established by way of Panama, so that fewer people from the Eastern states set out across the plains. There were also some forty-niners, who had gone east by Panama and were now returning to California with their families. On the whole, '50 was less of a greenhorn year than '49 had been.

The routes were much the same, though there was some of the inevitable shifting. The Council Bluffs road took heavier traffic. Beyond South Pass the route by Sublette's and Hudspeth's cutoffs remained the main line, though many people went by Salt Lake City and some by Fort Hall. Hastings's Cutoff, for some unknown reason, was more traveled than in '49; conditions on the desert seem to have resembled those of '46, so that the emigrants suffered much hardship, but escaped disaster. At the California end only a few used Lassen's Route, about which plenty of information was now available. The emigrants of '50 called it the Greenhorn Cutoff, or else Lassen's Horn Route, with the implication that it was as bad as going around by Cape Horn. In addition, the Truckee Route was little used, with the result that almost all the people crowded across the desert to the Carson River.

No new branches of major importance were opened this year. At Scott's Bluff, a new trail through Mitchell Pass saved a little distance. Some emigrants on the Council Bluffs road, instead of crossing the Platte at Fort Laramie, continued up the north bank across some rough country and eventually got through, thus establishing a route that was regularly traveled later. Through the difficult Wasatch Mountains, Golden Pass was opened as a toll road, but did not manage to replace the original trail, as cut through by the hard-pressed Donner Party.

As the result of heavy travel in two successive years the number of minor branches and "camping roads" became so numerous as to be troublesome. At Lassen's Meadows the trails developed into a maze, and the place was sometimes called Fool's Meadow. One man described seeing two hundred wagons going every which way at the same time, as each driver tried to work his way through the labyrinth.

Important in speeding the migration were numerous local improvements. Not only were there ferries across the North Platte and the Green, but also there were ferries and even some bridges elsewhere. A diarist, three days out of Old Fort Kearny, mentioned that he had been able to pass all the bad streams on bridges. There was even a bridge of two split logs across Smith's Fork, one of the tributaries of the Bear. Trading posts sprang up at various places, particularly at Ragtown—so called, it would seem, because of its appearance—where the trail came to the Carson River after crossing the desert. There was even a post office at South Pass, established by the army, with the flag gallantly flying above it, and the postmaster charging one dollar for a letter.

Yes, civilization was moving in, and as parts of American civilization we must always include free enterprise and capitalism. Gone was the time when an emigrant could start out with twenty-five cents in his pocket and get to California without having had any need or any particular temptation to spend it.

There were changes in techniques of travel too. Horses had suddenly become popular. In the first third of the migration the estimated proportions were: horse teams, 55 per cent; mule teams, 25 per cent; ox teams, 20 per cent. Farther back, the proportions altered strikingly, and one man stated that four-fifths of the wagons were hauled by "the faithful ox." Oxen may have been rarer because the experience of '49 had apparently shown that the thing to do was to get ahead and stay there. A technique of doing this had been developed. Buy good horses; load your wagons partially with grain; start early; feed your horses on the grain for three or four weeks.

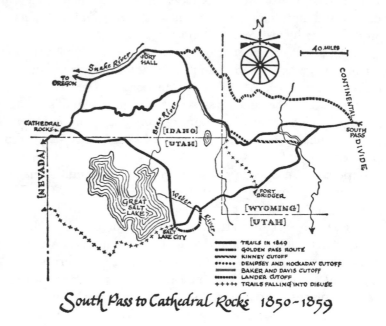

South Pass to Cathedral Rocks 1850-1859

In '50, also, there was a trend toward heavier wagons, requiring four yoke of oxen or even longer teams. The use of such teams shows, for one thing, that the trail had been improved. The sharp turns must have been eliminated to make the use of five yoke or six yoke practical.

Because of an improved trail and new techniques and more places to buy supplies, people made better time. Lorenzo Sawyer, with mule teams, got through in seventy-six days, and did not even claim a record.

By and large, '50 was much like '49—so much so, indeed, that there has been a tendency among historians to amalgamate the two. In '50 there was again a prosperous advance guard (Sawyer, for instance) racing ahead and rather enjoying the whole journey. Then came the great wave in the middle, crowding the campgrounds. Behind, followed the rear guard, suffering from lack of grass and taking punishment. At the end trailed the frightened and harassed stragglers.

Once more, there were hailstorms and buffalo-hunting and cholera on the Platte. Again, there were shiftings from wagons to packs. Again, the diarists noted the eccentrics—men with wheelbarrows making twenty-five miles a day; a Negro woman, walking and carrying all her possessions on her head. Again, there was public transportation, supplied this year by McPike and Strether.

There was again the harassment by the Paiutes and the terrifying shortage of grass and the even more terrifying approach of starvation. One trouble was that the stories of the dumping of supplies in '49 had worked back, and people had become even too much impressed with the necessity of traveling light. In '50 many of them set out with scanty supplies of food. One special difficulty arose from the flooding of the Humboldt early in the season. Water covered some sections of trail, and forced the emigrants to break new trails across the hills. Later on, after the flood had receded, the growth of grass was doubtless better because of the ample moisture.

Perhaps we should revise the judgment, and put it that '50 was like '49 but worse—largely because more people were involved. In '49 there was always a touch of the heroic, but in '50 there was more than a touch of the sordid. Men were reported cutting the flesh from dead animals, subsisting on the haws of wild

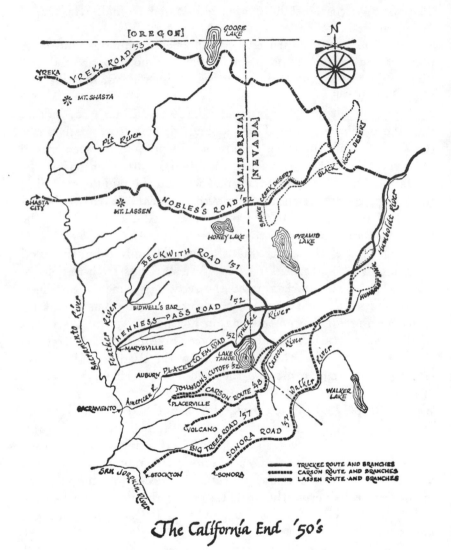

The California End '50's

roses and on frogs, and eating rats like the Diggers themselves. Many did not despise "bush-trout," as they euphemistically called rattlesnakes.

On the lower Humboldt half the people were reported to be destitute and starving. Thousands were on foot. Cholera was prevalent. The price of flour reached $2.50 a pound. Desperate and starving people sometimes took food, or appropriated cattle for slaughter, by what was the equivalent of highway robbery. On one occasion the apparent hopelessness of the situation produced mass suicide, and three men and two women drowned themselves in the Humboldt. The women had had families, but the long-continued suffering of their children had driven them past the point of endurance.

The horrors of the desert crossing to the Carson River were worse than ever. A count recorded the bodies of 9,771 dead animals. Abandoned wagons were estimated at 3,000. Traders, exploiting the emergency, went out with water, and sold it, according to an eyewitness, at fifteen dollars a glassful. This same man reported talking with people who had paid a hundred dollars for a pint of water.

Again, relief parties pushed out from California, but one can scarcely maintain that the catastrophe was averted. The majority of the emigrants arrived on foot, and three wagons out of four had been abandoned.

Many emigrants died of cholera and other diseases, to which hardships and near starvation had made them more susceptible. One count arrived at a total of 963 graves. . . .

The year after '50 offered a contrast almost as great, though in reverse, as that between '48 and '49. In '51 a contemporary estimate put the migration as such that it would "scarcely exceed a thousand souls." The explanation for this slump, as given at the time, was that the reports of the hardships of '50 had discouraged migration.

Other reasons are not far to seek. Obviously, the hysteria of the gold rush could not be maintained. By this time the returned Californian—back from the mines, and stony broke—was a well-known figure in every village. Besides, liberalized laws for the acquisition of land in Oregon had diverted most of the migration.

In addition to the many who started for Oregon, no fewer than two thousand people were said to have set out for California and then shifted.

The California emigrants of this year had an easy time of it, as might be expected with so few wagons on the trail. One man reported the journey as being "without obstacle or difficulty, other than is inseparable from so tedious a travel." Another described the trip as "delightful—good grass and an abundance of game upon the whole route." Good health was reported. As usual, some parties lost cattle to the Indians, but others did not.

The spanning of the North Platte with a bridge, described as fine and substantial, should have been the big news of the year. There was, however, continued use of the ferries, which by this time were well organized.

Little is recorded as to methods of travel, but the explicit advice left by an emigrant of the preceding year may be taken to show what was being done in '51. He specified oxen (though he himself had used horses) and four yoke. Even with four yoke there should be only three men to a wagon, and no more than that under any circumstances. Each man should have four hundred pounds of provisions. There should be one riding horse to a wagon. You should start in mid-April (never mind about the grass), and carry grain along to feed for the first few weeks. Though each man should have a revolver, there was need of only one rifle to a wagon. Each man, however, should have $200 in money.

In spite of the small number of emigrants, the year saw the opening of an important new route at the California end. . . . In the spring Jim Beckwith, an old mountain-man, had found an easy pass. That summer, he intercepted some emigrants at Truckee Meadows, and persuaded them to try his new route. This in itself was something of an achievement, for emigrants had become very skeptical indeed about trying cutoffs, and were even known to have threatened violence against anyone thus attempting to persuade them.

In this wagon train was William Pickett with his family, including a ten-year-old stepdaughter who would be known as Ina Coolbrith. In later life she was to be the friend of Bret Harte and Mark Twain, and to bear proudly the title Poet Laureate of

California. In '51, to judge from her later appearance, she was a beautiful child.*

So old Jim Beckwith—mulatto trapper, most unrestrained of Western storytellers—put the pretty little girl on the horse in front of him, and thus they led the first wagon train across Beckwith Pass.

It has everything! All that the picture needs is a calendar below it. What more can Hollywood or TV even ask? Here, if anywhere, must be the Old West.

Yet we must remember that this was '51, not '41. This was really the New West—of the businessman, and the chamber of commerce, and the subdivider. For, as he himself tells the story, Beckwith was developing this route for the commercial benefit of Bidwell Bar and Marysville, and he was as much interested as anyone in making money out of it. . . .

In '52 the migration surged to a new height of 52,000. The year was also notable for a sharp increase in the numbers of women and children. Of people passing Fort Kearny, women comprised 13 per cent; children, 17 per cent.

There was no simple reason for this huge migration, and even contemporaries could not explain it. It was not a gold rush. By this time, however, California was known as a rapidly developing state, with much good land and many jobs at high wages. The return of many forty-niners with their families also helped to swell the total.

One diarist, remarkably class-conscious, divided the emigrants of this year into five groups. At the top were the proprietors or the partners who were the owners of the wagons. A second group was composed of men who were traveling with these wagons, working their way as teamsters or in other capacities. Third, there were men who owned a single pack animal, which they were driving before them, as they themselves walked. Fourth, there were men who were pushing handcarts or wheelbarrows. Fifth, there

* More than thirty years ago and more than seventy years after her entry into California, when I was working on a biography of Bret Harte, I interviewed Ina Coolbrith—a very handsome and vigorous-looking old lady, strikingly dressed in a purple dressing gown. On a small table beside her was an array of well-used tobacco pipes. Because of this interview I have had at least one contact with a covered-wagon emigrant.

was the occasional man with knapsack and canteen; these last, the diarist declared, "would just walk away from everybody." With sufficient pocket money, they could renew their supplies at any of the numerous trading posts. One man was traveling with his pack on a donkey so small that it seemed no bigger than a sheep.

Some of the covered-wagon ladies of this year were proving themselves up-to-date by wearing the highly controversial "bloomers," which the feminist Amelia Bloomer had begun to advocate publicly in '49. One fifty-year-old matron used her own imagination by appearing in short skirt and pantalettes.

The year saw many developments of route. . . . Kinney's Cutoff solved the problem of the desert crossing on Sublette's Cutoff, which had been troublesome since '44. To take the new cutoff you followed the trail toward Fort Bridger down along Big Sandy to within a few miles of where that stream joined the Green. Then you cut across the angle between the two streams, a distance of about ten miles, and came to the Green at a spot where a ferry was operated at times of high water, and where there was a ford at times of low water. Then you went on west, along Slate Creek, until you rejoined the main cutoff. Kinney's Cutoff was not only easier, but was probably shorter also. Moreover, it was so obvious that it could almost have been worked out by sheer deduction, and one is surprised that it was so long in being discovered. A rival cutoff, known as the Baker and Davis Road, later paralleled it a few miles northward.

The other developments of route were at the California end, but these might be considered roads rather than trails. Each was opened for the purpose of steering the migration toward a particular town. Money was raised locally, and enough work was done to make the route passable. Then fast-talking agents were sent east along the trail to persuade people to go that way.

The development of these roads shows the free enterprise of the time, and the tendency of local governments to be more active than either state or Federal governments. The total result was bad. What was needed was one *good* road across the Sierra Nevada. Such a road could have been built under either state or Federal auspices. But before either of these got around to considering the matter seriously, the counties and towns and private individuals had preempted the field.

No fewer than six competing roads were opened in '52—all of them passable and not one of them good. There was the Placer County Emigrant Road, built for the benefit of Auburn, crossing the summit at the head of Squaw Valley. There was the road by Henness Pass, which took you to Downieville or Nevada City or Marysville. There was a spur road branching off the Carson Route to enable wagons to reach Volcano.

More important was Johnson's Cutoff, which split from the Carson Route, skirted the southern shore of Lake Tahoe, and came into Placerville, on the direct route to Sacramento. It soon became the main road, held that distinction for a decade, and still remains essentially as U.S. 50.

Nobles's Road, often recorded as Noble's Road, was developed for the benefit of Shasta City, after extensive and bold explorations by William H. Nobles in '51. He accomplished the task at which Wiggins, Lassen, and McGee had failed—the establishment of a short cut from the big bend of the Humboldt into California. His road followed the Lassen Route as far as Black Rock, and then headed west, skirting the Smoke Creek Desert, and depending upon springs. It got over the mountains by an easy pass, and went on westward across not too difficult country. Over a distance of about twenty miles, east of Mount Lassen, it made use of Lassen's Route in reverse. Along that stretch a wagon going south over Lassen's to California might have met a wagon going north over Nobles's to California!

Special interest attaches to the opening of the Sonora Road —which, as anyone might guess, led to the town of Sonora. . . . In July the citizens of that region subscribed money for a relief train to be sent out to the aid of the emigrants, and also to lead them to Sonora. Joseph C. Morehead was selected to head it. Morehead, a flamboyant character, had once been Quartermaster General of the California militia, and had just returned from an unsuccessful filibustering expedition into Mexico.

He crossed the mountains, and on August 5 Thomas Turnbull, an emigrant then on the Carson River, reported, "some men come here last night that has run a road through to Sonora."

These agents made the usual claims "a nearer & better route for grass & not so mountainous [!]" Turnbull, however, added skeptically: "but deception in people here can not be fathomed." In the end, a party totaling thirteen four-mule wagons and three ox-drawn wagons was "induced' to try. Morehead had presumably explored this route on his way east, but little or no work had been done on it.

The party went southward to the Walker River, and up its West Fork. In so guiding the wagons, Morehead was following closely, though he can scarcely have known it, the route of the Bartleson Party in '41. At the head of the West Fork the pass was about ten thousand feet above sea level, and the terrain was thoroughly alpine. At one point, it was later related, a small lake blocked the way, so that the emigrants were forced to dig a ditch and lower the water level, before they could proceed.

Soon it was the old story. Mules and oxen were dying from starvation and overwork, and wagons were being smashed on the rocks. Thus delayed, the emigrants ran short of food, and themselves faced starvation.

Morehead left the company and went ahead for supplies. He returned with a pack train, met the emigrants somewhat west of the summit, and managed to bring them through. The names Emigrant Meadow and Relief Valley commemorate this adventure.*

Thus in '52 which way you went had come to depend largely upon what part of California you wanted to reach. Because of these newer developments the California end of Lassen's Route was hardly traveled at all any longer. Similarly, the original Truckee Route, which had been the only trail until '48, fell into disuse. Few people used it in '50, and after '52 it was practically abandoned, until the opening of the Dutch Flat–Donner Lake Road in '64.

The vast migration of '52 naturally brought about a great flourishing of ferries, toll bridges, and trading posts. Two traders were reported at Independence Rock, one at Devil's Gate, another at South Pass, and several along Green River. That point

---

* Various accounts have dated the opening of the road as of 1853. The 1852 date, however, is established by the article in *Alta California,* Aug. 23, 1852, and by Turnbull's diary of 1852 (*Wisconsin Historical Society Proceedings,* 1913).

also furnished a gambling joint. From California the traders worked out a hundred miles to the north of Humboldt Sink.

Little change occurred in the technique of travel. Just as the migration of this year resembled the earlier migrations by having more women and children, so did it also by a greatly reduced proportion of horse teams and a correspondingly increased proportion of ox teams.

The most striking difference in the appearance of the migration was supplied by the great herds of cattle and sheep, totaling about 100,000 head. In the old days the idea of driving cattle to California would have been a coals-to-Newcastle notion. But the demands of the greatly increased population had depleted the herds of the ranchos. Besides, the American farmers wanted something better than the Mexican longhorns. Similarly, better breeds of sheep were needed. So a great business of droving suddenly developed—highly speculative, since a single stampede might ruin all your prospects. Though the losses on the road were considerable, the venture as a whole was successful.

Also listed at Fort Kearny were 150 turkeys, two guinea fowls, four ducks, and one hog.

Improved conditions still further speeded up the migration. One party with a single ox-drawn wagon left St. Joseph on April 25. Traveling rapidly, as a small party was often able to do, they arrived at an unspecified point in California on July 18, their eighty-fifth day, thus establishing what was thought to be a record for ox teams. (Larkin and Stanley in '46 had taken 136 days.) Another party with mule-drawn wagons left St. Joseph on April 20 and arrived in Sacramento on July 3—seventy-two days.

Being a crowded year, '52 somewhat resembled '49 and '50. Again, there was some cholera. In August a California newspaper reported, "the same old melancholy story of privation and suffering." Again, a relief expedition was sent out as far as Humboldt Sink, where its leader recorded "great suffering." He sent back a request for more supplies—especially, *pickles!* He declared, "the women and children are all anxious to have them."

Yet, everything considered, the migration of '52 was comparatively prosperous. Once more the weather had been favorable, and a returning forty-niner reported the grazing as better even than it had been in '49. Although some diarists noted short-age of grass, the hordes of animals were got through in some fashion. Probably by this time people had learned better where additional pasturage might be found in places back from the trail. The sheep would not have caused so much difficulty, since they could eat certain desert plants that the cattle would not use.

Indian troubles reached a new stage of intensity. Near Gravelly Ford on the middle Humboldt the Paiutes were reported to have massacred the men and women of a train, carrying off six children. This year the government at last took steps, by sending an Indian agent. He distributed gifts, urged the tribesmen to be kind to emigrants, and advocated the establishment of a military post. His most significant comment was that the worst problem was with "white men who are more desperate and commit more depredations, it is thought, than the Indians, and who keep the Indians in a state of excitement."

The year also supplies the classical story of wagon-train justice. To place the incident in a larger setting, however, we should remember that by '52 many isolated mining camps had already faced the problem of law enforcement in the absence of functioning government, so that the emigrants of this year were somewhat accustomed to the idea. And, we may say, they had even learned a technique.

After crossing Green River on Sublette's Cutoff two partners, Balsley and Beel, separated without hard words and apparently without hard feelings. Beel went on, joining a small party. Balsley, brooding over real or fancied wrongs, waited a while, then rode ahead, overtook Beel, and with a single pistol shot killed him.

The party halted and waited until a larger party of thirty men had come up. They then buried Beel and took Balsley into custody.

On the next day, uncertain what to do with him, they traveled on, and in the early afternoon came to Ham's Fork, where three companies, totaling a hundred men, were encamped. The combined companies at once chose a jury of twelve, with an elderly man to act as foreman and presiding officer. Witnesses were sworn in and gave testimony, none of which the prisoner denied. The jury then gave the unanimous verdict of guilty. Seven of them, however, were for immediate punishment, and five were for taking

Balsley to California. (To do the latter would have been to acquit him, since a California court could not have accepted jurisdiction for a crime occurring a thousand miles from its borders.)

The question was then referred to the whole company, and its vote was for immediate action. The jury agreed, and the sentence was formally read: "Leanadas Balsley, arise and receive your sentence. . . . We the jury find you guilty of willful murder and sentence you to death by shooting tomorrow morning at six o'clock."

The next morning twelve men were drawn by lot. Six rifles were loaded with powder and ball; six with powder only. The squad was put under the orders of the elderly foreman. Balsley, by his own choice, knelt on a blanket by the side of the trail with his back to the firing squad. No minister was present, but the prisoner had already conversed about "future destiny" with one man, who had afterward been drawn as a member of the firing squad. Balsley requested a prayer, and this man laid down his rifle, knelt, and prayed. He then took his rifle, and stepped back into his place. Balsley, a Kentuckian with a touchy sense of honor, had asked, in the tradition of Marshal Ney, that he should be allowed to give the final order.

The foreman commanded the men to take aim. Balsley gave the signal by raising his right hand.

The body was buried by the trail, with an inscription stating the facts. The emigrants continued westward, and their diarist noted that they made, that day, twenty miles. . . .

Though the numbers of '52 could not be maintained, the migration of '53 was considerable. A detailed count at Fort Kearny listed 15,219 people as heading for California. If, as seems likely, this total did not include people leaving from Council Bluffs, the count for the year probably reached 20,000 and may have equaled that of '49. The numbers of livestock were the highest yet. The Fort Kearny count was: 5,577 horses, 2,190 mules, 105,792 cattle, and 48,495 sheep. Again, these figures should probably be considerably increased to make allowance for livestock on the Council Bluffs trail.

The number of wagons counted at Fort Kearny was 3,708, so that the average number of persons to a wagon was 4.1, as opposed to 3.3 in '49. The average size of wagons had increased a little, but also there were more children. This year it was: men, 65 per cent; women, 15 per cent; children, 20 per cent.

A new bridge across the North Platte was described as "a very strong one built of hewn timbers," and was reported to have cost $14,000. From this time on, the emigrants were spared the necessity of ferrying that dangerous stream, which had taken a steady toll of animals and men ever since the Bartleson Party had lost a mule in '41. There was also "a substantial bridge" across Laramie River.

The Sonora Road was chiefly used during this year, and no fewer than thirty-four trains were listed as passing over it. Emigrants were noted, also, as arriving at Yreka. To reach that far-northern town, they followed the Applegate Trail to the boundary of Oregon, and then went to the southwest.

On the whole, '53 seems to have been a moderate, prosperous, and uneventful year. . . .

The emigrants of '54 totaled about 12,000. In this year John Hockaday, described as "an experienced mountaineer," opened what we may call a cutoff on a cutoff, by taking wagons through on a new route toward the western end of Sublette's Cutoff. But his route itself was difficult, and was not greatly traveled.

The emigrants who started early went through prosperously. In August a California newspaper noted the arrival of Mrs. Malinda Thompson, aged eighty-one, who had arrived in more robust health than when she started, "having often walked one to two miles at a time." The same newspaper commented upon the arrival of the Gorham Party, by Kinney's and Hudspeth's cutoffs and the south-side road along the Humboldt, with a herd of four hundred cattle. They had come through with "extraordinary speed" in seventy-seven days.

Those who came later were unfortunate in encountering early snows. Among these was that veteran of veterans, Joseph Chiles. He left Independence on May 1, and went by Salt Lake City. He took the Carson Route, which he had helped to open in '41 and '48. Unfortunately, as his custom seems to have been, he had taken his time. Caught by a snowstorm on the pass, he was forced to abandon several loaded wagons, and lost about a hundred cattle. Finally, as he had done so often before, he won through. He arrived with 115 head of fine cattle, including a thoroughbred Durham bull.

Another old-timer of this year was William Finlay. Although he had made no notable contribution to the history of the trail, he had first crossed it, on horseback and from west to east, in '47. The crossing in '54 was reported to be his ninth. If this figure is correct, he must sometimes have made round trips in a single season. He had doubtless been acting as a guide, and to the services of such men, though their identity is often unknown, we must attribute much of the success of the great later migration.

Finlay described the trip in '54 as the worst of all. His party of a hundred included women and children, and there was a large herd of cattle. They were caught in a two-day storm on Carson Pass. Snow piled up to a depth of four feet, and five hundred of the cattle died from want of food. The rest were saved by a purchase of hay from traders at extortionary prices. Such a commercial operation is only another indication of a new era. You were not likely to suffer the fate of the Donner Party in these later years—not if you had money in your pocket.

Even the Indians, it may be argued, were getting to be commercially minded. In these years the tribes at the eastern end of the trail were likely to harass emigrants, not by shooting arrows from ambush, but by charging tolls for a bridge, or by insisting that people pay for pasturing their cattle on Indian land. Yet the Indians were not changing entirely, and there were some ugly stories told by those of the rear guard. Along the Platte, a party driving four thousand sheep had a man murdered and mutilated, and a thousand of their sheep were wantonly driven off and killed. One estimate was that in the season at least three thousand horses had been stolen or killed. A sinister and repeated story was that the depredations, though committed by Indians, were instigated by white renegades.

Anyone taking the larger view of history will maintain that the Indians were becoming restless because the whites were encroaching upon their lands, killing the buffalo, and in many ways disturbing their way of life. But, at the same time, the Indians along the trail were being so debauched by whisky and so reduced

311

by disease that they had rather little will to preserve their way of life. The incident that finally broke the peace was so petty as to be almost sordid.

The *casus belli* was a lame cow! This miserable animal straggled from a Mormon company at the tail end of the migration, got into a camp of Sioux eight miles east of Fort Laramie, and was killed for beef. This detail in itself shows how much the Sioux had lapsed; in the earlier years cattle were considered safe from them, since they preferred buffalo-meat to beef. The Mormons, whose cow had thus been taken, complained at Fort Laramie, and a rash young officer, Lieutenant John Grattan, rode out with twenty-eight men and a small cannon.

The soldiers fired the cannon and wounded two warriors. This was too much for a proud people, even though they had fallen to the point of scavenging on emigrants. The Sioux charged, and in a few minutes, Lieutenant Grattan had twenty-four arrows in him, and his men had been wiped out.

The fat was in the fire, but the Sioux were not yet capable of waging a real war. (They would learn. Before the story was over, Fetterman, Custer, and others would discover how well the Sioux had learned!) Through the rest of '54, and most of the next year halfhearted hostilities dragged on. . . .

Naturally, then, '55 was no time for emigrant trains to be moving across the plains. The numbers of the migration approached the vanishing point, so low that one scarcely cares to try estimating. There might have been a few hundred people.

The remarkable thing is that there were any at all. And another remarkable thing is that we should have from '55 one of the most readable of the records. For, we might say, this is the year of Lydia Waters.

She was English born, a young wife and mother in '55. She had an eye to see, and there was a touch of poetry sometimes in what she wrote, and a stroke of humor too.

Everyone knew that there was war on the plains that summer, and the emigrants waited at Council Bluffs until they could form a strong party. The Waters family set out in a company of thirty wagons, prepared to fight their way through. They never had to do any fighting, but they sometimes saw what seemed to be war-parties, and they heard of one girl speared to death when she was drawing water.

So Lydia wrote of other things than Indian wars. She told of what was already called "the old trail" along the Platte, where the great migrations had beaten it out a hundred feet wide. In the sand hills, where the wheels had cut through the sod, the wind had blown the sand away, and the trail formed a great chasm, as she remembered, eighty feet deep. Along it, where the grass had been killed, the wild flowers were blooming—portulaca, four feet high.

She drove the oxen, when need was. She herded the loose cattle. She shook her apron at a charging buffalo bull to turn him and keep him from running into the wagon. She described a wattled Digger wickiup as being made "like a champagne basket," though, indeed, there could have been little champagne in her life. When a baby was to be born, she was the one to write, "I had to boss the job."

So they went on, from the Humboldt, and across the Forty-mile Desert. In the desert she did not mention hell, but when they came to the Truckee, she wrote, "If ever I saw heaven, I saw it there."

Then they went across Beckwith Pass, and she could write, "For six months and three days we had lived in our wagons." Years later, as she thought back over those many weeks of heat and dust, and threat of Indian attack, she did not remember the hardship and the tension, and her spirits flared up, and the last words that she wrote were "There were many things to laugh about."

Those are not words with which to end the story of the California Trail. And yet, by that summer of '55, the story of the trail, like the trail itself, seems to be splitting into many different branches, and to be changing into something different. On September 2 General William Harney, that swashbuckling dragoon, chastised the Sioux in a battle fought close to where the trail went down into Ash Hollow. There was peace again, but the Sioux remained grumpy, and things were never quite the same. . . .

In '56, with the country thus pacified, some eight thousand men, women, and children went over the trail, and they drove along with them many thousands of cattle and sheep. By this time, people were beginning to complain that things were getting *too* civilized! For instance, around Salt Lake City, you could not pasture your cattle wherever there happened to be grass, but you had to buy pasturage from whoever owned the land.

In this year there was some trouble with mounted Indians along the Humboldt, and in this year, also, the businessmen of Stockton subscribed $5,000 to open the Big Trees Route, which diverted traffic just east of Carson Pass and brought it to Stockton, instead of Sacramento. This route had eight bridges, one of them seventy-five feet long and fourteen feet wide! As usual, agents were sent out to lure traffic to the new road—for it would certainly have to be called a road and not a trail. Many emigrants followed it that year, because what the newspaper described as "the old Johnson road" had been badly washed out in the preceding winter. "The old Johnson road" was aged by this time all of four years, but that indicates how fast things were changing. . . .

In '57 numbers were down again, to about four thousand. This was a bad year along the Humboldt. Since some of the Paiute bands now had both horses and firearms, they had grown correspondingly bolder.

Early on August 13 a small party of seven men, two women, and a baby, having camped by themselves, were just beginning to stir about, and one man was building up the campfire. Suddenly a volley of shots and a flight of arrows came from some near-by willows. Several men and one woman quickly went down. One man fired back but was soon wounded. He managed to reach the river and to find shelter under the bank.

The Indians advanced upon the wagons, and killed a man who lay sick. The remaining woman, who was hiding under the shelter of a tent in her nightgown, started to run with her baby but fell wounded. The Indians first pulled the arrows from her flesh, and thrust them into her again. She restrained any sign of pain. Thinking her dead, they scalped her. They took the baby girl and dashed her brains out against a wheel. They looted the wagons and started to round up the stock, but the approach of another emigrant train caused them to retreat hastily.

The wounded man recovered and so did the scalped woman, whose husband and baby were among the dead. The Indians, in

314

the excitement of their flight, had dropped her scalp. It was recovered, and she had a wig of her own hair made from it. She never fully recovered from the frightful experience, and eventually her mind failed. A photograph of her, apparently wearing the wig, has survived.

Though no one can escape a feeling of horror at such savagery, we should remember that some whites treated the Indians with equal callousness and sometimes even with equal ferocity. From the Indian point of view such an attack as that described was probably nothing more than a retaliation.

Another story of '57 illustrates a new condition that was arising. . . . One hot morning in late August, along the Humboldt, a mule-drawn family wagon of an Englishman named Wood had lagged behind its company. A band of some twenty mounted men, apparently hostile Indians, came galloping down from the hills. The husband quickly cut two mules out of the harness. He mounted his wife and child on one, himself on the other, and they made a dash for it. Wife and child were shot down. The husband, wounded, managed to overtake the wagons ahead. The abandoned wagon was plundered.

Men returned from the wagon train, buried the bodies, and salvaged what they could. English gold coins to the equivalent of $1,500 had been concealed in the bottom of the wagon. This money had been discovered and taken. Either the Diggers were growing remarkably sophisticated, or it was something else!

The wagon train proceeded, its men suspicious and keeping good watch. A day or two later, they were joined by three men with a small wagon. These three were picturesquely dressed in deerskin and were heavily armed. They said that they were accustomed to living in this country, but now considered it unsafe, because the outrages committed by emigrants had enraged the Indians. They asked leave to travel with the company until they should reach safer country. The emigrants granted this seemingly reasonable request, but remained suspicious.

They became more suspicious when the leader of the three, a handsome big fellow called Tooly, inquired with an air of solicitude, "Are you prepared to defend yourself, in case of attack?" As it happened, like many companies in the later years, this one was not well armed or well organized for fighting. But the men to whom the question was addressed, bluffed quickly, giving the impression that they were well prepared and even eager to fight.

Next morning the three men attached a small white flag to their wagon. The emigrants, suspecting that this might be a signal to confederates in the hills, ordered the flag to come down. Later that same day, the wounded Wood, who was being carried inside a wagon, got a glimpse of the strangers, and excitedly declared of Tooly: "I believe that man was with the Indians who killed my wife and child."

Since Wood was in bad condition and suffering from shock, the emigrants did not care to act on his uncertain identification. Tooly and the others, however, must by this time have sensed that they were under suspicion. Later that day, saying that the country was now safe, they withdrew to camp by themselves and thus to go ahead in the morning.

But the next evening the three rode into camp again. Their attitude was bullying. Saying that he would shoot anyone who said that he had acted with the Indians, Tooly flourished a pistol. But a young man of the company got the drop on him, and Tooly was left with his own pistol pointed upward, and with the other's aimed at his breast. The emigrants were peaceable people, not wishing to kill anybody or become engaged in a brawl with three heavily armed ruffians. The matter was patched up; Tooly, with brutal threats against the wounded man, warned Wood to say nothing more; the three rode out of camp.

During the next few days, approaching the sink, the emigrants did a good deal of talking and thinking. Wood continued in his identification of Tooly. Though the men of this company were slow to anger, anger began to burn within them. But now there seemed to be no possibility of taking action against the three ruffians.

At the sink stood a crudely built shack, known as Black's Trading Post, dealing chiefly in whisky. Some of the men visited it and found Tooly there, drinking heavily. He was boasting that he had recently "done up" some emigrants. The men listened a while, then returned to their company, and reported.

Uniting with some others who were camped nearby, the emigrants organized a court, with judge, sheriff, and deputies. At gun point, the sheriff arrested Tooly, and took from him two large revolvers.

The court was convened and a jury was selected—for fairness, largely from the emigrants who had not previously been involved. Wood, with bandaged arm, confronted Tooly, and reaffirmed his belief that Tooly had been with the Indians who had killed Mrs. Wood and the child. Tooly denied everything. The jury refused to convict.

The judge then ordered Tooly to be searched, and for the first time he seemed about to offer resistance. He was searched, and in a money belt he was found to be carrying some English gold coins. When counted, these came to the equivalent of $500, one man's share of the coins stolen from Wood's wagon.

The jury immediately voted a conviction, and the judge proceeded to give Tooly his choice of being shot or of being hanged from the uplifted tongue of a wagon.

At this moment, Tooly made a break for it. A fusillade of shots rang out, and he fell, riddled with bullets. . . .

Less melodramatic, but equally significant of the way in which things were changing, were the explorations conducted in '57 under Federal auspices. After so many years of neglect, the government was at last really doing something about the emigrant road.

One expedition took off eastward from California. More important work was accomplished by an expedition that set out from Missouri, under the command of the energetic and efficient Frederick W. Lander, a civilian engineer. Lander systematically explored the area between South Pass and Cathedral Rocks, investigating sixteen passes. Now, for the first time, someone had an idea of what would be the best over-all route and of where money could be best expended. The route preferred by Lander did not even go through South Pass, but followed still farther up the Sweetwater. It kept in general to the line of an old trappers' trail—according to the encyclopedic Bruff, the route that should by rights have been called Sublette's.

As the result of Lander's recommendations, funds were appropriated, and in '58 gangs of laborers were hard at work. A way was cleared through forty-four miles of heavily forested country, and 62,000 cubic yards of earth were removed. The new road was opened to travel in the summer of '59, and at once became the main route. Thus hewn and excavated across country which would otherwise have been impassable for wagons, the Lander Cutoff cannot be called a trail in the traditional sense of the word.

In '59, then, we may bring the story to a kind of conventional ending. A trail is a fragile and delicate thing—like some kinds of plants and animals, unable to withstand the advances of civilization. Do enough work on a trail and send enough traffic over it, and it necessarily becomes a road.

END OF THE TRAIL

THE COVERED-WAGON MIGRATION is a folk movement of considerable size and of definite historical significance. Down to '57 (the last year for which statistics are at present available) the summation of annual figures indicates that more than 165,000 people crossed to California. The number of animals must have approached a million.

One might argue that even without this migration California could have been conquered and integrated to the United States by sea. Certain it is, the cheapest transporation for freight was always by Cape Horn, and from '49 onward the fastest transportation for people was by sea, with a short crossing by way of Panama or Nicaragua. But thus connected only by long ocean routes, California would have remained an island with respect to the rest of the country. Separatist tendencies might well have developed. Symbolically the overland journey continued the long tradition of the American westward advance, and demonstrated that the republic and the breadth of the continent were one. . . .

Even in the sixties the emigrants were crossing in wagons. There was much droving. The stagecoaches went through, and the pony-express riders galloped, and against the desert sunsets the telegraph poles stood starkly. Along with all this development came ranches and trading posts and stage stations. Also came the Indian wars—with the Paiutes beginning in '60; with the Bannocks, in '62; with the Plains Indians, in '64. At last, in '69 the railroad was finished.

Even after that, the trail was used locally. Sheepherders' wagons followed it, and it gave access to isolated ranches. People even traveled long distances over it. In 1938 I talked to an old man at Fort Bridger who had driven a wagon, about 1890, from Oregon to Fort Bridger. He had used the old trail; there was, as he said, no other road. . . .

The railroad dominated for a generation, and then came the highways, which we still sentimentally call trails. Superimpose a map of the California Trail upon a map of modern highways and you will see that they coincide in many places—evidence that the pioneers often discovered the best routes. Over distances of many hundreds of miles the general lines of the trail are now followed by U.S. 26, 30, 40, 50, and other important roads.

When you drive such a highway, you get a good idea of the type of country through which the emigrants passed. You see the same mountains, and you pass through the same defiles. You rarely, however, see traces of the trail, since the highway itself obliterates them. Because of so much blasting and bulldozing, no one will probably ever be able to rediscover the sites of all the crossings of the Truckee or be certain just where Elisha Stevens brought his wagons up the face of Donner Pass.

In many places, however, the trail and the highway do not coincide. The emigrants frequently did not have enough information to find the best way. Besides, they were tied down by the requirements of water and grass, and were in some places blocked by a single impassable stretch. In such still-undeveloped areas the traces of the trail can often be discerned for many miles.

South Pass itself remains an almost complete wilderness, though a paved highway goes through a little to the north. In 1938 and again in 1960 I drove through between the famous Twin Mounds—those "knolls of decripitating [sic] white stone" that Bruff noted in his journal. The road, if it could be called such, was worn down beneath the general level of the ground, showed several splits, and was essentially nothing more than the old trail itself. Except for my companions, I saw no human beings.

Most of Sublette's and Hudspeth's cutoffs and all the country from the City of Rocks across the Goose Creek Divide and on to the Humboldt is almost deserted. The road that exists to serve a few ranches seems, for the most part, to be simply what is left of the trail. Many stretches that I drove in 1952 and in 1960 (not to be recommended for a modern automobile) still showed the characteristic slight twistings and bendings which result when oxen or mules break their own way across country. One need not be indulging in an impossible flight of fancy to consider that these little meanderings might go clear back to '43.

Trail hunting is a fascinating hobby, and one that I have enjoyed for more than twenty-five years. In a few places, the traces are clear and striking, as at Deep Rut Hill near Guernsey, Wyoming. At Register Cliff, Independence Rock, Names Hill, and other places, the names and years of emigrants can still be read. At the City of Rocks, I once located where Bruff sat to make one of his sketches—beneath the shade of an old juniper tree, where that sensible man would have taken refuge against the sun on that 80-degree August day.

Though local use has maintained the trail in many sections, it has become impassable in some places. In a jeep I once followed the Lassen Route north from Black Rock, until in High Rock Canyon the trackway ended in a V-shaped gully that even a jeep could not take. In many other places the very location of the trail has become uncertain. On the west slope of the Sierra Nevada, where trees and bushes grow rapidly, one must often depend upon finding the chocolate-brown marks on the convex surfaces of granite boulders—showing where wagon wheels once scraped and left a film of iron. On one broad flat rock-surface I have seen, in proper light, long parallel lines of rust, marking where now and then some driver slid a wheel in crossing.

Mementos are hard to find, although the local people can generally show you a few wagon chains. At Black Rock Spring I once collected some forty fragments of pottery, and from them reconstructed most of an old-fashioned water pitcher. It stands on a shelf in the room where I now am. As I lift it down and feel it between my hands, the story of the trail comes close. . . .

Few people can have such tangible evidence. But to many millions of Americans that story is vivid and immediate from its iteration in the mass media, and they may wish to ask about two omissions. Why have we not had The Prairie Fire and The Beleagured Wagon Train?

The answer is simple. We have not had them because I have found neither of them in the documents.

The emigrants could scarcely have experienced a prairie fire because they regularly passed through the prairies while the grass was still green. Farther west, in the dry country, vegetation was too scanty to feed conflagrations. Even the forest on the western slope of the Sierra Nevada then consisted of large well-spaced trees, and was not subject to forest fires as the second-growth forest now is.

There are occasional mentions of what seem to have been small fires, like that which destroyed the powder-laden wagon in '45. The Donner Party, camped at Emigrant Springs in Nevada, almost lost three wagons when a fire escaped and started burning across the campground. But the diaries mention no great "holocausts" which threated to destroy the whole train and thus give the hero his chance to save the situation by quick thinking and decisive action.

As for The Beleagured Wagon Train, we all know what it should be, having read about it, and having seen it presented innumerable times. . . . The wagons are drawn into a circle. Around them gallop the Indians on their ponies, shooting arrows. From the shelter of the wagons, the men fire their rifles. Children cower in the wagon boxes, and women crouch with them or load rifles for the men. Indian after Indian tumbles from his pony. It is one of the great American archetypes.

I have told no such story in this book, because I have never found it so recorded in the authentic sources. Perhaps somewhere it may have occurred, and perhaps someone more fortunate than I will uncover the record. I realize that the proving of a universal negative is generally impossible. But I can at least say that I have found no such record, and I am therefore skeptical.

But I am skeptical, also, because of general improbability. The Indian was a sensible fellow, not wishing more than anyone else to get himself killed. Why should he go galloping around in that silly and hopeless fashion, exposing himself and his pony to rifle fire from men in a sheltered position? A few young braves might have made a dash to show their courage, and have ridden once around the wagons, shooting arrows and galloping off again. But to launch a serious attack in that manner would have been the height of absurdity—the equivalent of light cavalry attacking entrenched infantry. As Mark Twain would have put it, only a Fenimore-Cooper Indian would be as stupid as that!

Besides, what would have been the use? If you wanted to attack a wagon train, you would try to surprise it on the march, when it was spread out along the trail. An incident of '61 may serve for illustration, even though it lies just outside the time limits here assigned. If the record is anywhere nearly accurate, the Massacre of Almo Creek was the greatest disaster of the California Trail and one of the greatest disasters ever to befall the Americans in their more than three centuries of wars with the Indian tribes. This particular train is reported to have included sixty wagons with more than three hundred men, women, and children.

The emigrants made camp one night a few miles east of the City of Rocks. In the morning they set out again, the wagons slowly unrolling from the circle and straggling out in single file. This country was open and moderately well watered, but the trail passed through a sagebrush stretch for several miles.

Unknown to the emigrants, there was encamped a few miles off a large band of hostile Indians, presumably Bannocks. According to an account later told by one of the warriors, this was the largest war band even brought together in that region. The Indians had provisioned their camp so that they could continue operations for some time, if necessary. Their leader—Chief Pocatello, according to one account—had worked out both strategy and tactics.

The Indians suddenly appeared from ambush. The emigrants, quickly and smartly, formed the wagon circle again, with the stock inside. The Indians did not press the attack home. Instead, they kept the train under siege. A stream was not far away, probably less than a mile, but the Indians prevented anyone from reaching water, and by skirmishing kept their opponents constantly disturbed.

The emigrants entrenched themselves, and were safe against assault, but after a day and night without water their situation grew critical. On the third day the thirsty animals became so dangerously restive that they were released and were captured by the Indians. The emigrants dug wells, but no water seeped in. Lacking either numbers or resolution to attack, and in a bad position, they could hope only for the approach of another train to rescue them, but none appeared. As twilight came on the fourth day, the end was close.

After darkness fell, the guide and a young woman crawled through the sagebrush and escaped. Later, a man and two women, one of them with a small baby, also stole out of camp. The mother, crawling on hands and knees, carried the baby by holding its clothes between her teeth. These people managed to reach Raft River and hide in the bushes along its bank, eating rose hips and roots. The guide made for the nearest town—Brigham City, a hundred miles east.

At this settlement an expedition was hastily organized. These rescuers found the people who were hiding near Raft River. At the camp there were no survivors. The bodies lay scattered among the burned wagons.

This story differs greatly from the traditional one. These Indians were obviously much too intelligent to go galloping around, offering themselves as targets. From such evidence and from the lack of actual examples, we must conclude that the conventional beleaguered wagon train is a fictional and fanciful story, though developing early. The idea is now so firmly fixed in the American mind that it is scarcely to be called a fiction, but might better be dignified by the term "myth." In opposing it, one feels vaguely subversive, as if promulgating the idea that George Washington was an egregious liar. . . .

No individual dominates the story of the trail. Yet we may pay a brief tribute to Joseph Chiles. That redheaded Kentucky-born Missourian was already past thirty when he crossed in '41. In '42 and '43 he was the dominating figure. He went east over the trail in '47, and in '48 successfully led the wagons which established part of the Carson Route. In '54 he captained still another party.

Chiles was energetic and resourceful. In the breadth and scope of his geographical insights he was outstanding, as his attempts and achievements in '43 and '48 give evidence. On the other hand, he was not especially successful in '43 and got into

324

trouble in '54. He had a tendency to underestimate difficulties, and to take chances, though he can scarcely be called rash by the standards of the time. We know unfortunately little about him. If we knew more, we might have to rate him even higher. Still, he has necessarily appeared more often than anyone else in the story as here told.

After '54 Chiles was of the poet's persuasion, and went no more a-roving. "The Colonel" then lived for many years on his ranch in Napa County, where Chiles Valley commemorates him. There were other old-timers around such as Charlie Hopper of '41 and '47, and William Trubody, who had been young Bill in '47. You could swap yarns of the trail or go hunting with them. There were grizzlies, then, on the thick-forested slopes of Mount Saint Helena. Charlie Hopper died in '80, a year older than the century. "The Colonel" was only seventy then, and a good man even yet. Bill Trubody, as he told Charlie Camp many years later, remembered him taking a nip, and saying, "Nothing like a little whiskey to warm a man up." As of '86 the historian Bancroft described him briefly: "a famous hunter notwithstanding his years, and a good citizen." Who among us, at the age of seventy-six, would hope for a better notation on his discharge? . . .

Not even Joseph Chiles can be considered a central hero to the epic of the trail. Still, the epic is there, and it tells—as do those older aristocratic ones—of heroism and achievement, and also of labor and suffering and death. Let us recall what price was paid.

Sometimes the diarists even devoted a few words to the memory of the faithful animals. In '50 James Mason wrote, "Here we lost old Sock. He died rather sudden. He was much lamented by the boys, as he was our main standby at the start."

More elaborately, that same year, Leander Loomis wrote, setting the passage off with asterisks:

* * * * * * * * * * * * * * * * * * *

*   This morning old Charlie being so weak, we thought,   *
*   best to shoot him,—he has been a good horse,   *
*   and served us well,—peace be to his ashes.   *

* * * * * * * * * * * * * * * * * * *

In the earlier years, when someone died, they milled the herd on the grave, or drove the wagons across it, so that the Indians could not find it and dig the body up. In the later years they made little headboards or crosses of wood, and wrote upon them. Often the diarists copied the inscriptions, so that we still may read them.

M. De Morst,
of Col: Ohio,
died Sep. 16th. 1849
Aged 50 years,
Of Camp Fever

Jno. A. Dawson,
St. Louis, Mo.
Died Oct. 1st, 1849
from eating a poisonous
root at the spring.

In Memory of Samuel Oliver
of Waukesha, Wisconsin,
who was killed by an arrow shot
from a party of Indians, July 5th, 1850
while standing guard at night.

Died: "Of cholera . . . of cholera . . . of cholera." (That, most often!)

Died: "Of accident discharge of his gun." *Died:* (There was a doctor in this company.) "Disease, Gastro Enterites Typhoid." *Died:* "Of drowning." Often, simply: *"Died."*

Died: "From Southport, Wisconsin . . . Late of Galena, Ill. . . . Of Selma, Alabama . . . From Yorkshire, England . . . Of Buffalo, N.Y." *Died:* sometimes with only the name for identification.

Died: "John Hensley, Aged 73." *Died:* "Mary Jane McClelland, aged 3 yrs. 4 mos." *Died:* "Adison Laughlin, Aged 17 years." *Died:* "Margaret Campbell, Aged 36 years: 4 mon. 23 days."

Died: "Mrs. Mildred Moss, wife of D. H. T. Moss." *Died:* (as if registering in some last hotel) "Robert Gilmore and wife." *Died:* "Frederic Richard, son of James M. and Mary Fulkerson,

326

July 1, 1847. Aged 18 years." *Died:* (two weeks later) "Mary, consort of **J. M. Fulkerson.**" *Died:* "Mrs. Emmaline Barnes, Amanda and Mahela Robbins, three sisters in one grave, Indiana."

To the memory of Columbus, who was found
with his throat cut, and in his hand a
pocket knife with a death grip. June 19, 1850
May he rest in peace.

Some were laid in their graves succinctly, perhaps as time pressed; some were granted a few more words.

Our only child
Little Mary

Samuel McFarlin,
of Wright Co Mo. died
27th Sep. 1849, of fever
Aged 44 years.—
*May he rest peaceably
In this savage unknown
country.*

Jno. Hoover, died, June 18. 49
Aged 12 yrs. Rest in peace,
sweet boy, for thy travels are over.

As Vergil wrote: "*Tantae molis erat Romanam condere gentem.*" Yes, it was of such great labor to establish the Roman people. So also it was to pass the flaming barriers of the deserts and the snowy gates of the mountains, thus to round out the shape of a republic. The trail and the covered wagon stand as the symbols, and we should not forget their dead. "All this too was part of the price of the taking-over of the land."

327

AUTHOR'S NOTE

As a FOOTNOTE in Chapter III indicates, my interest in the California Trail may be traced from 1919 onward. Since 1932, when I began work on the Donner Party, I have written or edited several works dealing with the trail (see below), and its influence may be found even in my novels *Storm* and *Sheep Rock*. I have, therefore, been happy to attempt, in the present work, a synthesis.

No previous work has dealt exclusively with the history of the California Trail, though various volumes on the West have treated the subject briefly. Some information may be gathered also from writings on the Oregon Trail and from Jay Monaghan, *The Overland Trail* (1947). Julia Cooley Altrocchi in *The Old California Trail* (1945) records interesting material without presenting a history. Irene D. Paden in *The Wake of the Prairie Schooner* (1945) and *Prairie Schooner Detours* (1949) offers much valuable information in the form of narratives of personal investigations. H. H. Bancroft's *History of California* (1886–1890, 7 vols.) still cannot be neglected, antique though it is, and it is particularly valuable for its listing of obscure minor sources.

The materials upon which I have based the present work are in general sufficiently well described in the text to be identified by the scholar who wishes to carry his study further. Good bibliographies are to be found in some of the volumes listed below.

Irene D. Paden's bibliography of the diaries of the trail, which I have been kindly allowed to use in manuscript, is soon to be published by the California Historical Society. The bibliography of the subject here may therefore be passed over briefly.

The present work is directly based upon primary sources, i.e., diaries and reminiscences of people who made the journey. In practice, the two cannot always be sharply distinguished. Some "diaries" were obviously written up "once in a while," and so resemble reminiscences. Most printed diaries have suffered more or less reminiscential rewriting. On the other hand, many "reminiscences" are based upon diaries or other contemporary records.

Other source materials are newspaper articles, personal letters, and some government reports.

The country through which the emigrants passed, with its traces of the trail, is in itself an important document, and I have traveled over most of the principal branches of the trail. In a comprehensive work of this kind, however, it has been impossible and would even have been disadvantageous, to map the trail in great detail or to attempt to describe its precise course and record the histories of all its minor deviations—interesting as I personally find such details to be.

In addition to works already listed, the following books are of outstanding value. J. Goldsborough Bruff, *Gold Rush* (1944, 2 vols.), edited by Georgia Willis Read and Ruth P. Gaines; *James Clyman, Frontiersman* (Definitive edition, 1960), edited by Charles L. Camp; Bernard DeVoto, *The Year of Decision* (1943); J. S. Holliday, *The California Gold Rush in Myth and Reality* (typescript, University of California Library, in preparation for publication); W. Turrentine Jackson, *Wagon Roads West* (1952); Roderic J. Korns, "West from Fort Bridger" (1951, *Utah Historical Quarterly*, vol. 19); Heinrich Lienhard, *From St. Louis to Sutter's Fort, 1846*, edited by Erwin G. and Elisabeth K. Gudde (1961); Dale L. Morgan, *The Great Salt Lake* (1947); "Ferries of the Forty-niners" (*Annals of Wyoming*, July, 1949 et seq.); *The Overland Diary of James A. Pritchard* (1959).

The most-read book on the gold rush is probably A. B. Hulbert's *Forty-niners* (1931). It is a strange combination of fact and fiction, mingling post-'49 with genuine '49 material. I have

330

not found it useful. On the other hand, his *Crown Collection* of maps is valuable.

A good set of maps compiled by Dr. William G. Paden is in the Bancroft Library of the University of California. Paul C. Henderson in *Landmarks on the Oregon Trail* (1953) has accurately mapped much of the route in Wyoming. Leslie L. Sudweeks in "The Raft River in Idaho History" (*Pacific Northwest Quarterly*, July, 1941) maps the little-known Hudspeth's Cutoff. In general, however, I have drawn my own maps from study of the original documents, topographical maps, and the country itself.

My own previous writings which I have used as an aid in preparing this one are: *Ordeal by Hunger* (1936, 1960); *Map of the Emigrant Road ... by T. H. Jefferson* (1945); *The Diary of Patrick Breen* (1946); *The Opening of the California Trail* (1953); *Donner Pass* (1960).

I did most of the research in the Bancroft Library, and I wish to thank, as so often before, its director Dr. George P. Hammond and all the members of the staff. I am also endebted to the California State Library (especially for the use of its newspaper index), and to the library of the California Historical Society.

I take the opportunity to express my particularly warm thanks to several comrades who have shared with me the joys and the discomforts of exploring the trail—though one or two whom I might mention have already gone to explore an even longer cutoff than Lassen's. My wife, Theodosia B. Stewart, has several times thus traveled with me. My son, Dr. John H. Stewart, helped me with investigations in the Black Rock Desert in '47, and has also given aid in geological matters. I should commemorate some high points—working over some of the Truckee Route with Wendell Robie in '36, getting to Rabbithole and Black Rock with Charlie Camp in '41, being flown low over the Forty-mile Desert by Lowell Sumner in '50; exploring Goose Creek and the City of Rocks with Jim Hart in '52; going again to Black Rock with John Edwards and Jim Holliday in '53; passing over many sections of the trail, including parts of Hastings's and Hudspeth's cutoffs, with Joe Backus and Dave Lavender in '60.

In connection with the preparation of the present work a

number of people have rendered me aid of various kinds and in different degrees but with equal kindness. I wish to mention with thanks Donald C. Biggs, Charles L. Camp, Helen S. Giffen, Erwin G. Gudde, James D. Hart, J. S. Holliday, David Lavender, Stewart Mitchell, Dale L. Morgan, Irene D. Paden, and Wallace Stegner.

George R. Stewart

Berkeley, California
October 24, 1961

INDEX

References "in passing" are not listed. Many place-names (e.g., names of states, Sierra Nevada, South Pass) appear in the text so frequently that they are either omitted entirely from the index or only their more important occurrences are included.

Trubody, W. A., 188f, 325
Truckee, Chief, 67–69, 81, 164, 275
Truckee (town), 70
Truckee Canyon, 180, 198, 200
Truckee Meadows, 69, 180, 302
Truckee River, 69, 138f, 174, 189, 200
Truckee Route, 206f, 267f, 282, 292, 297, 306
Turnbull, Thomas, 305f
Turner, Capt. ——, 260
Twain, Mark, 302, 323
Twin Sisters, 204

University of North Carolina, 37
Upper California Crossing, 155

Vásquez, Louis, 43, 165, 167, 244–246
Vines, Mrs. Bartlett, 37, 47
Volcano, 305

wagon, covered, see covered wagon
Walker, J. R., 5f, 21, 33, 41f, 44–52, 66f, 90, 165, 205
Walker Lake, 50
Walker Pass, 34, 42, 51
Walker River, 27, 50, 306
"Walker's Train," 258f
Walton, Major, 47, 49

Ware, J. E., 222, 247
Wasatch Mountains, 166, 168, 184, 245
Washington City Company, 277–279, 284
Waters, Lydia, 6, 312f
Weber, Charles, 19, 28
Weber River, 166f
Western Emigration Society, 7
Wiggins, William, 190–192, 194, 208
William Creek, 256
Williams, Joseph, 14f, 17
Williams, ——, 242
Wind River Mountains, 133
Winter, W. H., 146
Wisconsin Hist. Soc. Proceedings, 306
Wistar, I. J., 236, 250, 268, 295
Wolfinger, ——, 180
Wolverine Rangers, 282f
Wood, ——, 315–317

Young, Brigham, 188, 198
Young, Samuel, 147, 176
Young Mrs. Samuel, 176f
Young Party, 155
Yount, George, 31, 33, 37
Yreka, 310

Zins, George, 149, 153